# PRAISE FOR
# YOU ARE NOT SO SMART

"Simply wonderful. An engaging and useful guide to how our brilliant brains can go badly wrong."

**Professor Richard Wiseman** – author of *59 Seconds*

"Fascinating! You'll never trust your brain again."

**Alex Boese** – author of *Elephants on Acid* and *Electric Sheep*

"A much-needed field guide to the limits of our so-called consciousness."

**William Poundstone** – author of
*Are You Smart Enough to Work at Google?*

"Want to get smarter? Read this book."

**David Eagleman** – neuroscientist and author of *Incognito*

"Every chapter is a welcome reminder that you are not so smart – yet you're never made to feel dumb. *You Are Not So Smart* is a dose of psychology research served in tasty anecdotes that will make you better understand both yourself and the rest of us. Give yourself every advantage you can and read this book."

**Alexis Ohanian** – co-founder of Reddit.com

D0270420

# ABOUT THE AUTHOR

David McRaney is a journalist, new media guru, and self-described psychology nerd. Twice-recipient of the William Randolph Hearst Award, his first book, *You Are Not So Smart*, was an international bestseller. He lives in Mississippi and blogs at youarenotsosmart. com.

# YOU CAN BEAT YOUR BRAIN

How to Turn your Enemies into Friends,
How to Make Better Decisions, and
Other Ways to Be Less Dumb

## DAVID McRANEY

ONEWORLD

A Oneworld Book

First published in Great Britain and the Commonwealth by
Oneworld Publications 2013

First published in the USA by Gotham Books, a member of Penguin Group (USA)
Inc., 2013

ISBN 978-1-78074-374-5
eISBN 978-1-78074-316-5

Set in Granjon
Designed by Elke Sigal
Printed and bound by Norhaven A/S, Denmark

Oneworld Publications
10 Bloomsbury Street
London WC1B 3SR

Stay up to date with the latest books,
special offers, and exclusive content from
Oneworld with our monthly newsletter

Sign up on our website
**www.oneworld-publications.com**

*For Maggie.*
*Thanks for helping me get out of that swamp.*

# CONTENTS

# YOU CAN BEAT YOUR BRAIN

# INTRODUCTION

## *Self-Delusion*

---

**THE MISCONCEPTION:** *You are a being of logic and reason.*

**THE TRUTH:** *You are a being capable of logic and reason who falls short of that ideal in predictable ways.*

This is a book about self-delusion, but also a celebration of it. You see, self-delusion is as much a part of the human condition as fingers and toes, and that is what we are going to explore here. Delusions, that is, not phalanges.

You assume you are intelligent, capable, rational, and full of the same glorious reason that invented calculus and ginger snaps. You were born with a chip on your shoulder, and you've grown into a sort of undeserved confidence over the years. It's a human foible that comes in many flavors, and I'm assuming you are human. If you are a hyperintelligent dog, a member of an alien race, or a robot historian from our future, I apologize; please move on to the first chapter. If not, proceed toward your epiphany.

The human mind is obviously vaster and more powerful than any other animal mind, and that's something people throughout all human history couldn't help but notice. You probably considered this the last time you visited the zoo or watched a dog battle its own hind legs. Your kind seems the absolute pinnacle of what evolution can produce, maybe even the apex and final beautiful result of the universe unfolding itself. It is a delectable idea to entertain. Even before we had roller skates and Salvador Dalí, it was a conviction in which great thinkers liked to wallow. Of course, as soon as you settle into that thought, you'll accidentally send an e-mail to your boss meant for your proctologist, or you'll read a news story about how a man got trapped in a public bin in Aberdeen. It's always true that whenever you look at the human condition and get a case of the smugs, a nice heaping helping of ridiculousness plops in your lap and remedies the matter.

The truth is that the human brain generates a mind that is deeply flawed. There are some things you just aren't very good at and never will be. Evidence of your dumbness is everywhere. Calculators, notepads, to-do lists, checkbooks, alarm clocks—there are hundreds of inventions and applications for sale in every marketplace to make up for your shortcomings. Entire fields of expertise exist to make up for a gulf in your abilities.

Our discussion of the scientific study of self-delusion is probably best led off with the concept of preconceived notions, so let's begin with a brief story about the thirty-first time Dartmouth College and Princeton University faced off in American football. That game helped launch an endless fleet of expeditions into the human mind, many of which you will read about after this paragraph concludes.

Both founded in the mid-1700s, Dartmouth and Princeton are part of the Ivy League of universities in the northeastern United States. You may have heard of the other six universities: Brown, Columbia, Cornell, Harvard, Penn, and Yale. *Ivy League* has become synonymous with the sort of people who wear "fancy pants." The names are among the most desired bullet points on a CV, but *Ivy League* began as a term sportswriters used for the eight universities in New England that tended to compete against one another exclusively in athletics and, well, almost everything else.

In 1951, Dartmouth and Princeton squared off in the last game of the season for both universities. Princeton had won every game up to that point. Its star player, Dick Kazmaier, had been featured on the cover of *Time* that same year and would go on to become the last Ivy League player to receive the Heisman Trophy. It was a big game for both teams, which is why Princeton went bonkers in the second quarter, after a Dartmouth player broke Kazmaier's nose. In the next quarter, a Princeton player snapped a Dartmouth player's leg. The whole event was brutal, and both sides racked up plenty of penalties before Princeton finally won by a final score of 13–0.

Psychologists Albert Hastorf at Dartmouth and Hadley Cantril at Princeton noticed soon after the game the student newspapers of each university began printing stories that seemed to suggest two versions of the truth were in open competition to become the official version of reality. A year later, the two published a study that is now considered by many to be the best starting point for talking about self-delusion.

Hastorf and Cantril noticed that Princeton's newspaper and alumni newsletter published accounts of the game that painted the Dartmouth team as bullies who played dirty. At the same time, Dartmouth's newspaper published editorials explaining away the injuries caused by its team while also noting the awfulness of Princeton's tactics. Both sides, the researchers said, remembered seeing different games. What if these students could watch the game again? thought the scientists. Sure, they remembered the game differently, but what if we showed them a film of it? Would they see the game differently in real time as well? To answer this, the scientists acquired a recording of the entire matchup, showed it to undergraduates from both universities, and had those students check when they saw infractions, in addition to marking how severe each infraction seemed. The students also filled out questionnaires.

The results? During the film, Princeton students believed they were watching a violent, uncivilized game and Dartmouth was to blame. Ninety percent wrote they felt Dartmouth had started the unsportsmanlike conduct. They also reported seeing twice as many infractions coming from Dartmouth than they saw coming from Princeton, and they found those infractions committed by their own university's team to be much milder than those committed by their university's opponents. Dartmouth students, however, saw something else. They didn't see the game as unnecessarily barbarous, but as justifiably "rough and fair." The majority of Dartmouth subjects reported both teams were to blame for the aggressive play and Princeton students were just angry because their superstar had gotten hurt. Boo hoo. They recorded an equal number of infractions by both teams but, overall, marked down half as many for their own side than did the Princeton students.

The scientists explained that each person saw a different game despite the fact that all had watched the same film. Each person experienced a different version of reality, of the truth, each in some way adulterated by his allegiance.

The great lesson of Princeton versus Dartmouth concerns how tiny and arbitrary variations can change everything. The students who watched the film, regardless of whether they had attended the real event, experienced two different versions of reality, even though on paper they all seemed like nearly identical people. As students of male-only Ivy League universities three hundred miles apart in the 1950s, they were the same ethnically and socioeconomically. As undergraduates, they were all about the same age. As northeastern U.S. citizens, they had similar cultural and religious beliefs. The only difference between them was which university they had chosen to attend. The research suggests that if you could have turned back time and had those students enroll at different universities, switching the campuses they would later stroll, their realities would also have switched.

This is where preconceived notions lead you, into naive realism—a very old concept in philosophy that was long ago murdered, burned, and buried by science. Naive realism asks this question: Do I see the world as it actually is? The answer, according to a naive realist, is yes. Up until recently, on the grand scale of human history, this what-you-see-is-what-you-get theory of the mind has had its defenders, so, in case the Princeton-Dartmouth example wasn't enough for you, let's go ahead and squash it before we move on.

As a modern person you should know that a motion picture is just individual photographs whizzing by faster than your brain can process. When you look at a flower, you should know that you don't see the same thing a butterfly sees and that if you switched your eyes for insect eyes the floral world would become a psychedelic explosion of madness. Your unnavigable nighttime living room is a completely visible playground to a cat, and if you've ever shined a laser pointer near a feline pal, then surely you've realized something is going on in its tiny cat head that isn't happening in yours. You know the world is not what it seems, and all it takes is one great optical illusion to prove it. Naive realism is, well, naive. The stars are always in the sky, but the light of the sun filtered through the atmosphere makes them difficult to see in the day. If you throw a rock into a pond, and that *sploosh* turns the heads of a frog and a fox, what they see is not what you see. Each creature's version of reality is unique to its nervous system. The frog, the fox, and the person all experience the same real thing but react to differing internal representations. Your perception isn't the only perception out there, and if the inputs can be fooled, then the image is not to be trusted.

Okay, so that's a simple concept, and you've likely pondered it before, but as the football game study shows, there is another level of naive realism that is a lot harder to accept. Like most people, you tend not to question this, and it persists in just about every head on Earth.

Look away and around for a second and come back to this sentence. The things out there that you just saw in your mind aren't generated by those objects. What you see isn't the simple result of light bouncing into your eyeholes. What you see, recall, and feel emotionally is 100 percent created by chemical reactions in your braincase, and that means those things are susceptible to influence, editing, redacting, and all sorts of other ingredients that get added to consciousness when you construct reality out of inputs both external and internal. To paraphrase psychologist Daniel Gilbert, memory, perception, and imagination are representations not replicas.

A memory is least accurate when most reflected upon, and most accurate when least pondered. Together, those two facts make eyewitness testimony basically worthless. This isn't what most people believe. Psychologists Dan Simons and Christopher Chabris published a study in 2011 revealing that 63 percent of those surveyed in the United States believe memory works like a video camera, and another 48 percent believe memories are permanent. An additional 37 percent said that eyewitness testimony was reliable enough to be the only evidence necessary to convict someone accused of a crime. Those are seriously shocking facts to a psychologist or a neuroscientist, because none of those things is true. You don't record everything you see, nor do you notice everything that comes into your mind. The only things that make it past the ears and eyes are those things to which you attend. Memories are not recordings. The moment your first kiss was over, the memory of it began to decay. Each time you recall it, the event is reformed in your mind anew and differently, influenced by your current condition and by all the wisdom you've acquired since and all the erroneous details you've added.

Psychology now knows you make forecasts and decisions based on internal mental models and memories, and you assume those models and memories are accurate and perfect. Over time, with each new study, it has become increasingly clear that those models and memories are flawed, imperfect, and skewed. So it follows that your forecasts and decisions are just as mistaken.

You greatly underestimate how easily and how often you delude yourself, and how your perception can be dramatically altered from within. Throughout this book you will see that you do not passively receive reality. You actively participate in the creation of your personal universe.

The last one hundred years of research suggest that you, and everyone else, still believe in a form of naive realism. You still believe that although your inputs may not be perfect, once you get to thinking and feeling, those thoughts and feelings are reliable and predictable. We now know that there is no way you can ever know an "objective" reality, and we know that you can never know how much of subjective reality is a fabrication, because you never experience anything other than the output of your mind. Everything that's ever happened to you has happened inside your skull. Even the sensation of having an arm is projected by the brain. It feels and looks like your arm is out there in space, but even that can be a misconception. Your arm is actually in your head. Each brain creates its own version of the truth, broadly similar but infinitely different and flawed in its details.

Hastorf and Cantril, the scientists who studied the students at Dartmouth and Princeton, said in their research that the game didn't even exist, when you got right down to it. In the same way that a salad is just a pile of chopped-up vegetables and leaves, the game in question was just the events taking place in one space between two presses of a stopwatch. Sure, people performed actions in front of other people, and the people watching noticed some of what happened, but the game itself is just an idea, a social construct. Out of the billions of things that occurred that day in 1951, fans of both teams placed significance on a particular set of things happening in one location and agreed to call that thing a football game. That culturally defined significance helped observers define their experiences. According to the scientists, unlike most things in life, sports offer up a nice lattice of rules and boundaries, a demarcated space and assigned roles that produce routine actions. In sports, thanks to those parameters, it becomes much easier to agree on what happens during the time allotted. Yet people routinely disagree, even when the whole thing is recorded and can be played back exactly as it occurred. What is real is not just what comes into your eyes and bounces around in your mind. You change your reality as it happens. You alter your own perception unconsciously. The implications are monumental when you apply this knowledge to wars, politics, social movements, economics, and all the other titans of influence in your life that don't happen in an arena with agreed-upon rules and aren't recorded perfectly by history.

You see, being smart is a much more complicated and misunderstood state than you believe. Most of the time, you are terrible at making sense of things. If it were your job, you would long since have been fired. You think you are a rational agent, slowly contemplating your life before making decisions and choices, and though you may sometimes falter, for the most part you keep it together, but that's not the case at all. You are always under the influence of irrational reasoning. You persist in a state of deluded deliberation. You are terrible at explaining yourself to yourself, and you are unaware of the depth and breadth of your faults in this regard. You feel quite the opposite, actually. You maintain an unrealistic confidence in your own perceptions even after your limitations are revealed. It is at this intersection of presumption and weakness, the beautiful combination of assurance and imperfection, where we will be spending most of our time together. This is an exploration of some of the most compelling self-deceptions that have been identified and quantified by science. This is the stuff that should be in the instruction manual for operating a human body—just like the entries science recently added about trans fats and glutens.

Herein lies a catalogue of some of the things science has learned about the flaws of the human mind and how your brain lies to you, how it cheats and edits and alters reality, and how you fall for it over and over again. So, what sorts of things will we be exploring?

Well, when it comes to your mind, you are often unaware of the source of your own feelings and thoughts, your own behaviors and memories, but instead of bumbling about confused and frightened, you possess a giant toolkit of tricks and techniques by which you invent scenarios that make life easier to comprehend, and then you believe in those scenarios. Over years and years, that jumble becomes the story of your life.

One such tool is the heuristic. In order to survive, your ancestors needed to think and act quickly. Heuristics make big, complex, daunting ideas tiny and easier to manage. Simple heuristics explain the world to you in ways that allow you to keep moving without putting too much thought into a situation. When it comes to problem solving and decision making, you have heuristics that render complicated things very simple. You use the affect heuristic, for example, to make decisions based on whether a person, problem, or situation makes you feel positive or negative emotions. Does the guy running for mayor creep you out? Let's not vote for him. Did that doctor paint her offices puke green? Let's not go there again. Heuristics appear in the strangest places, such as when you ponder if you should donate money to those people who make commercials about dogs and cats that get tortured and abandoned. When you wonder if you should write a cheque, you don't ask whether that organization is legitimate, or what the chances are an abused animal can be rehabilitated, or if the organization has a strong track record in resource allocation. You instead ask yourself if the images of abused animals make you sad. The answer to that question is much easier to solve, and you then assume that you've solved the more complicated questions. This mental alchemy is applied to everything in your life, from whether you should quit your job to who should get your vote for president. Complicated and confusing questions morph into gut checks, and gut checks are often unreliable. When you use heuristics, you tend to believe you've been rationally contemplating your existence, when in reality you just took a shortcut and never looked back.

Another giant stumbling block in your mental life is a collection of predictable patterns of thought called cognitive biases. A bias is a tendency to think in one way when other options are just as good, if not better. For instance, if you tend to take a right turn every time you walk into a supermarket when turning to the left would be no better, you have a right-turn bias in your own behavior. Most people are biased in this way, and most large chain stores develop displays and lay out their interiors with this in mind. Most cognitive biases are completely natural and unlearned. They can be teased out of every person with a functioning brain. So, no matter if you were born in Egypt or Aberdeen, in 1902 or 2002, you still have the same collection of inherited cognitive biases every other human must deal with. Scientists speculate that most biases are adaptive, which just means that over millions of years they served as dependable fallback positions when you were unsure how to act or feel. For instance, you have a hindsight bias that makes you believe your predictions about the future are usually accurate because you falsely assume you've been able to predict the outcome of events all your life. The truth, however, is that you are terrible at making predictions but great at rewriting your memories to make it seem as if you were right all along. You also suffer from a confirmation bias that causes you to seek out information that confirms your worldview while avoiding and ignoring threatening information. Over time, this creates a bubble in which it seems there is a monumental amount of consensus for your beliefs.

Heuristics allow you to think and act faster, and biases influence you to behave in ways that typically keep primates alive and active. In modern life, though, your heuristics and biases get challenged all the time, and that's when you pull out logical fallacies. Logical fallacies appear during arguments with yourself and others. You often begin with a conclusion already in mind and then work toward proving that you were not stupid to have drawn that conclusion in the first place. This sort of motivated reasoning often depends on warping logic to make things work out in your head. For instance, you might say hot dogs are a disgusting manufactured food product, and you can't believe your cousin is serving them to his children, because no child should be forced to eat gross food. You've just committed a fallacy because your assumption was in your original statement: hot dogs are nasty. You've proved nothing. Your argument didn't make the case about the nastiness of digestible casings filled with beef trimmings and fat. You've only stated what you believe and then said that what you believe informs your opinions. You can untangle this fallacy by rewording it like so: *Kids shouldn't be forced to eat food I believe is gross*. You get confused in your own logic all the time and end up twisting language to make the world line up with your preconceived notions.

Logical fallacies, fuzzy heuristics, and incorrect cognitive biases are joined by an array of other odd truths about your dull approach to making sense of things. You are only able to pay attention to a very few things at once, but you feel as if you are paying attention to everything that appears before your eyes and emits sound near your ears. When you do pay attention, those senses are themselves very limited and imperfect. You then use what comes into your brain through those senses to construct an internal reality that both introduces into consciousness things that aren't real and subtracts from reality things you would rather not accept. Add to this the complicated and vast system of emotions and intuitions, and you can see how tilted your view of reality can be from moment to moment. That tilted view is translated into incomplete, inaccurate memories that degrade with each recall. The glue of narrative—the innate human skill for storytelling—holds the whole misinformed hodge-podge together. Your ability to tell stories keeps you sane and stable, even if those stories can be pretty far from the truth.

Despite how fallible you are, how gullible and biased and horn-swoggled you tend to be day to day, or how much the image you have of yourself doesn't really match the real you, you get by, most of the time. It's a real problem, though, when politicians, CEOs, and other people with the power to change the way the world works start bungling their arguments for or against things based on self-delusion generated by imperfect minds and senses. In the fields of neuroscience, psychology, and economics, the major faults of your mind have been known for about fifty years now. Work continues in those and other fields, unraveling the nuances, but most of what science has learned on this topic has remained under academic hats. You are lucky to live at a time when that knowledge is just now starting to trickle into the conversations of laypeople. That's the aim here: to get some of these insights into your short-comings out there where they can be put to good use.

Some of what we will discuss has to do with the wiring of the brain, some with cultural influences, and some with ancient behav-ioral routines. The brain in your head was built by evolution, and the world in which your ancestors lived was full of situations you no longer face. Still, you err on the side of caution just in case. If someone throws a rope on you while you are napping, there is really no harm in freaking out, screaming, and flailing around while you try to hold in your pee. If a poisonous snake had fallen on you, such a response would have been an excellent course of action. It would be much more costly if every time you woke up to a snakelike impact you just yawned and calmly brushed it aside. Over the course of millions of years, the creatures who didn't freak out at snake-shaped objects didn't make as many babies as the people who did, and now that same fear is in you, along with fears of skittering creepy crawlies, heights, dark places, and strangers. This sets you up to be more afraid of terrorists than home furniture, even though falling couches and televisions take more lives each year. When you consider the world that shaped your mind is the world you are most equipped to handle, it makes sense that things such as car engines and weight loss and soufflé recipes are so hard to understand, much less laparoscopic medicine and quantum physics.

This is not a book about abnormal psychology. It is about normal psychology, the common, default, baked-into-every-brain sort of thinking you can expect to find in rocket scientists, heads of state, and the lady at the office who has a kitten calendar for personal use and a fireman calendar for business meetings. You think seeing is believing, that your thoughts are always based on reasonable intuitions and rational analysis, and that though you may falter and err from time to time, for the most part you stand as a focused, intelligent operator of the most complicated nervous system on Earth. You believe that your abilities are sound, your memories perfect, your thoughts rational and wholly conscious, the story of your life true and accurate, and your personality stable and stellar. The truth is that your brain lies to you. Inside your skull is a vast and far-reaching personal conspiracy to keep you from uncovering the facts about who you actually are, how capable you tend to be, and how confident you deserve to feel. That undeserved confidence alters your behavior and creates a giant, easily opened back door through which waltz con artists, magicians, public relations employees, advertising executives, pseudoscientists, peddlers of magical charms, and others. You can learn about yourself when you take on the perspective of those who see through your act and know how to manipulate your gullibility. A great deal can be learned and gained by focusing on your failings.

Thanks to a new way of approaching psychology, science is now beginning to paint a picture of your flaws and shortcomings, and this book is a collection of some of the most interesting delusions discovered so far. I hope when you read them you have the same epiphanies I did when I first came across them. Consider this a humility shock-and-awe campaign designed to help you feel more connected with the community of humanity. We're all in this together, and these are our shared mental stumbling blocks. Use what you learn here to be kinder to others and more honest with yourself. There are some concrete, counterintuitive, and fascinating ways to beat your brain.

Let's get started.

# 1.

## *Narrative Bias*

---

**THE MISCONCEPTION:** *You make sense of life through rational contemplation.*
**THE TRUTH:** *You make sense of life through narrative.*

At the Ypsilanti State Hospital in Ypsilanti, Michigan, right around the time the Hula-Hoop was invented, three men began a conversation that would drag each into the depths of madness. Real madness, the kind that earns prescriptions.

This trialogue lasted two years, and at times it soared, with each man literally singing in harmony with the others. At other times it languished, descending into physical violence. Still, each morning, the men met and each tried at length to get the other two to see things his way.

Clyde Benson, Joseph Cassel, and Leon Gabor had lived very different lives leading up to their meeting. Benson was a widowed and remarried heavy-drinking farmer in his seventies. Cassel was a clerk in his fifties with a desire to be a writer, yet was too hobbled and passive, haunted by a terrible childhood, to realize his dream. Gabor was a man nearing forty, wandering from job to job after being transformed by the war. What tied them together was the conviction that they were the living reincarnation of the Messiah. That is to say, each man thought he was Jesus Christ.

The psychologist Milton Rokeach brought the three institutionalized men together in a psychiatric ward where he could observe them. In his book *The Three Christs of Ypsilanti,* Rokeach writes that he had the men assigned adjacent beds, had them eat together, and gave them jobs in which they interacted regularly. In addition, he had them meet daily in a visitation room with a wooden table at its center, across from windows that allowed in light from the world of the sane. Making them constant companions, Rokeach thought, might cause their delusions to cancel one another out. In his opinion, it was a rare and thrilling opportunity to have three individuals claiming the same identity, and not just any identity but one that didn't allow for any wiggle room. The Bible said there was one Son of God, and now three people who asserted that status as their own sat at the same table with science looking on. Surely, Rokeach believed, something would be revealed about the nature of delusion, belief, and the self. Indeed, something was.

When first asked to introduce themselves, Cassel didn't disappoint. He said, "My name is Joseph Cassel," and when asked if he had anything else to add, he said, "Yes. I'm God." Benson was a bit more ambiguous, saying that he "made God five and Jesus six." Gabor followed, saying his birth certificate stated he was the reincarnation of Jesus Christ of Nazareth. Soon after, an argument began, with each man revealing how insulted he was by the others' claims.

Through the lens of hindsight it seems not only unethical but also cruel to toss mentally unstable people in a room just to see what happens, but Rokeach was seeking a cure. He wanted the men to awaken to the epiphany of their true identities because, as he wrote, "it seems a terrible thing for a person not to know who he really is." After that first meeting, Rokeach was crestfallen. As he put it, the "confrontation was less stormy than I had expected." When their meeting adjourned, the three men just sort of walked away feeling confident in their own views of reality. Rokeach wrote, "Perhaps they did not fully grasp the extraordinary nature of this confrontation—at least not in the way we did."

As the men met again and again, their individual delusions unfurled, showing their complex and byzantine structures. Each man's explanation of how it came to be that Jesus Christ was trapped in a psychiatric ward in Michigan manifested as a unique maze of stories and logic that would make sense internally for a moment only to collapse as Rokeach prodded. As the constructs fell apart, the men swiftly rebuilt them, and the conversations took on the appearance of people exchanging lines from different plays. Still, each man often remembered the intricate details of the other two men's explanations, and picked them apart as if he were a political candidate debating the finer points of an opponent's tax plan.

Rokeach wrote that he would attempt in each session to bring the conversation back to the impossibility of three Christs and asked the men to address the problem. When forced to explain, they didn't come to a sudden realization that they were being delusional; they didn't reel in awe after being struck by the insight that their identities were showing cracks. No, they just dismissed the other two men's claims. Benson said the other two were some form of cyborg and not actually alive. Inside them, he said, machines controlled their movements and provided their voices. Gabor believed the other two men were lesser gods who came after him and then were reincarnated. Cassel's explanation was the most accurate and prosaic. He said the other two men were insane patients in a mental hospital.

When asked to explain themselves, the men usually dismissed the fact that they were in an institution. They weren't patients, they said. They were Jesuses who just happened to be in that room at the moment. The poseurs ought to wise up and worship the true Christ, who was, according to each man, he.

Within three weeks, the arguments led to punches, but the violence didn't last. Over the twenty-five months, most of the conversations were quite civil, albeit filled with nonsense. The one thing that stayed constant was that each man refused to budge when it came to his belief. Instead, he desperately defended his delusion, but the methods differed. Benson was stoic but inarticulate, so he lashed out with rage and threats. Cassel was more eccentric, tossing bread into toilets and books out windows. He walked away from the arguments and tried to steer the conversations in a different direction when they threatened his identity. Gabor, though, was the intellectual member of the trio, and his delusions were dazzling to the point of being reasonable at times. He spoke at length at the meetings, delivering impassioned, eloquent soliloquies and often led the discussions and asked his own questions of the other men. Their talks ranged from hunting to whale bones to cookies and England. Still, Gabor's speeches dove right to the bottom of the grandly nonsensical. When quiet, he told Rokeach, he was actually grinding negative engrams in the squelch chamber inside his skull. As time went on, talk of Jesus and God faded.

Rokeach wrote, "The three Christs were, if not rational men, at least men of a type we had all encountered before; they were rationalizing men."

Rationalizing men. The sort of people who find a way to spin everything around them into a tale that makes sense in the context of who they believe themselves to be. The three Christs never changed their beliefs. Over two years of psychiatric care and psychological examination, questioned and challenged, sitting across from people claiming their very identity to be a sham and claiming that identity to be their own, they never gave in. The other two guys had problems; I'm the one who has it all figured out. The fact that the men at Ypsilanti believed themselves to be the same man, Jesus, was the only thing that really stood out about their stories. Everything else they did fell in line with what a psychologist would expect from a human being.

You seem to be able to see through the lies and rationalizations of other people, as Rokeach said. You've encountered enough instances of that sort of thinking that you let it go in person and gossip about it over tea. It's part of life—watching other people lie to themselves to get by. Yet, when you do it, it gets swept under the mental carpet. You probably don't wake up and assume you are brushing the teeth of Jesus, but as you saw with the men in Ypsilanti, even at that level, you would probably still see through your own flaws only when they were copied and pasted onto another person.

Like these three men, all your assumptions about reality come together in a sort of cohesion engine that runs while you are awake and reassures you that things are going as expected, no need to panic. You come along and take the output of the cohesion engine and use it to make sense of reality, and your preferred method (everyone's preferred method) is to couch everything in the form of a story with you as the hero or heroine. It's sort of weird, but it keeps you alive.

The simpler creatures of earth, the worms and amoeba and water-droplet-dwelling protozoa, stay alive with very simple rules. Basically, they go toward things that nourish them and avoid things that harm them. The spectrum of their reality is narrow and uncomplicated. They don't fret about the future or wax poetic about the past; they may not even have a concept of time at all. Their system works, and it has kept them alive for a few billion bookless, mythless, historianless years. Their nervous systems are so simple that their minds, if you can even call them that, don't need much more than the ability to sense things that are usually good and usually bad, and the ability to move in the appropriate direction while avoiding obstacles.

Your nervous system is a bit more complicated, so you have more tools than just stimulus and response. A roundworm has about three hundred neurons. A cat has about a billion, and you have about eighty-five billion. Wire those neurons together and get them processing on multiple levels, and you can navigate the muddy mosaic of the incomprehensible complexity of the cosmos much better than the average kitty. Of course, you still have those old stimulus-and-response routines inherited from way back when—birthday cake and grizzly bears illicit two very different reactions in a normal human brain—but there is so much more at your disposal than just seeking good and avoiding bad. To match the complexity of your conscious experience and your unconscious processing, to deal with the constant confusion bombarding your senses and the noisy chatter of the agencies within your mind, you've developed the ability to knit everything together into something simpler and less accurate, something less informative but more entertaining, and most times more useful. You have a very complex and astonishingly powerful mass of nervous tissue bobbing around on top of your neck, so you search for something other animals do not: meaning. The day-to-day reality of your waking mental life makes sense because you turn events into stories and stories into memories and memories into chapters in the tale of your life. When you gather with others, they tell you about their reality in the same story format, and the better the story, the more likely you are to accept their explanation.

Jokes and movies, comic books and professional wrestling, television shows and news programs—they all present dramatic interpretations of facts and fiction in the format of a narrative for the same reason we put chairs in cars. The shape of a human body fits nicely into a seat. The shape led to the form. The form now belongs wherever butts reside. Babies prefer classical music played forward rather than in reverse. The same motivations that drove Vivaldi to write in one way and not in another drive infants who listen to his music for the first time to enjoy it when played properly, and reject it when played backward. Art is the pursuit of that which symbols represent absent those symbols. The things you find beautiful and ugly arrive in your mind along ancient, predetermined paths toward smiles and frowns, and although those feelings get filtered through cultural attitudes, societal norms, and mores shifting from one era to the next, the bedrock of what you seek and what you avoid begins with primal motivations to expose yourself to that which your knee-jerk responses suggest are positive or negative. Your mind makes sense of its inputs and memories in the form of stories both coming and going, and so that format appears wherever information is presented. The shape of your mind led to the format. That format now appears wherever information migrates between brains.

This is your narrative bias—a bias in that when given the option, you prefer to give and receive information in narrative format. You prefer tales with the structure you've come to understand as the backbone of good storytelling. Three to five acts, an opening with the main character forced to face adversity, a turning point where that character chooses to embark on an adventure in an unfamiliar world, and a journey in which the character grows as a person and eventually wins against great odds thanks to that growth. According to mythologist Joseph Campbell, that is pretty much every story ever written, except for the tragedies. Those are cautionary tales in which the protagonist fails to grow, chooses poorly, submits to weakness, and as a result loses. You enjoy both versions of the story because that's how you make sense of your own life. That is how you boil down and simplify who you are, why you are here, what you've accomplished, and where you are heading. Books, movies, games, lectures—every form of information transfer seems better when couched in the language of storytelling.

Framed within a story, an unbelievable account becomes plausible. Which of these two statements is most likely to be true? A Buddhist monk stripped naked and yelled at a group of children because he lost his temper. A Buddhist monk stripped naked and yelled at a group of children because he lost his temper after learning his village had been burned to the ground during a political uprising. The second one seems more conceivable, right? It seems crazy to imagine a peaceful pacifistic holy man would do something so rash, but when you learn the whole story it seems possible, not necessarily because you have more information but because you can see that information strung up as a narrative. You often move on without skepticism if the question of why gets resolved in a pleasing way. Consider this: Elizabeth burst into flame while trying on a new bra. Elizabeth burst into flame while trying on a new bra after being cursed by an angry gypsy whose foot Elizabeth accidentally ran over with a shopping trolley on the way to the dressing room. Even though the second account seems more likely, the gypsy curse stuff might not work for you, but for some people that would be a fine explanation. This is partially explained by the conjunction fallacy. Your narrative bias is bolstered when you are presented with an abundance of information. The more info you get about a statement, the more likely you are to believe that statement.

The classic example of the conjunction fallacy comes from the work of psychologists Amos Tversky and Daniel Kahneman, the great pioneers of cognitive bias research, who in 1982 presented a puzzle I will showcase here in story form: Linda grew up in San Francisco, and while other girls played with dolls, she read philosophy books. She was always the kind of child who would stomp and snort when she didn't get her way, and her parents had a hard time teaching her not to talk back. She graduated from high school a year early and was accepted to Harvard, where she received a degree in philosophy. Before entering the workforce, Linda spent some time in the Peace Corps helping women gain access to health care in and around the Congo region of the continent of Africa. Unmarried, with no children, she is now back in the United States working on a Ph.D. in political science. Which is more likely? Linda works at a bank, or Linda works at a bank and writes for a feminism blog? This might blow your mind, but the answer is that it is much more likely Linda just works at a bank. All that extra information frames the character of Linda in a way that makes it seem to many people she is a feminist, but that doesn't change the raw statistical truth that a person is more likely to have only one trait out of a bazillion than they are to have two. If I had asked, "Is it more likely Linda is a feminist or Linda is a rally driver?" you would be correct to assume that, based on what you know, Linda prefers studying equality more than she does gear ratios. But that's not what I asked. Simply put, there are many, many more people in this world who work at banks than there are people who work at banks and also write for feminism blogs. In fact, the more possibilities, the more improbable their combination becomes compared with just a single trait. It is very unlikely that Linda works at a bank, runs a feminism blog, votes Democratic, lives in California, donates to the World Wildlife Fund, and enjoys Tori Amos. When you look back on the story of Linda, the chances that any one of these facts is true is pretty high, but the chances that any two of them are true about the same person is much less likely, and any three lesser still, and so on. It sure doesn't seem that way, though, does it? That's your narrative bias at work, supported by the conjunction fallacy and held together with the representativeness heuristic, or your tendency to ignore odds and instead judge the likelihood of something based on how similar an example is to an imagined archetype.

Among the many things the brain does to keep you alive and thriving is to generate a sense that there are causes that lead to the effects you witness and feel, and effects that follow from causes that can be tracked down and highlighted. You believe there are signals amid the noisy weirdness of life, patterns in your chaotic tumbling through time, and predictable rules by which reality can be assumed to operate. You would be surprised to learn how often each of these assumptions is false.

For many years, the U.S. Air Force has trained pilots using a giant contraption called the Holloman centrifuge. The centrifuge is basically a fake cockpit attached to a giant shaft of metal with a tremendously powerful motor at its center. The center spins, rotating the shaft, and propels the cockpit round and round with a pilot inside. Imagine a string tied to a rock, and then imagine spinning that rock around lasso-style, and then imagine you are inside the rock. Pilots do this to feel the effects of g-forces, or gravity. In a high-performance fighter jet, pulling up and away from the Earth or turning hard at insane speeds applies g-forces to the body. When you accelerate in one direction, you feel the pull of Newton's laws in the other. When you hit the accelerator in a car, for example, your head is forced to flop backward. In a jet, that force is much greater, and the blood in your arteries can't get to your brain. The effect is like a chokehold, and pilots often pass out or become incoherent zombies. Either way, pulling too many g's, as they say, can end in disaster.

The air force and agencies such as NASA use centrifuges to create massive g-forces in a controlled environment. This way, they can teach pilots techniques for keeping blood in their brains. Such techniques involve lots of grunting and straining, which would otherwise seem a bit embarrassing if, you know, they weren't fighter pilots. At a certain point, pilots will black out and lose consciousness. As they go in and out of this state, they often report visions, hallucinations of the fantastic and the everyday, like dreams. James Whinnery, a medical doctor for the air force, has studied hundreds of these blackouts over the last thirty years, videotaping them and comparing their nuances, interviewing the pilots and recording their reports. Over time, he has found striking similarities to the same sorts of things reported by patients who lost consciousness on operating tables, in car crashes, and after returning from other nonbreathing states. The tunnel, the white light, friends and family coming to greet you, memories zooming around—the pilots experienced all this. In addition, the centrifuge was pretty good at creating out-of-body experiences. Pilots would float over themselves, or hover nearby, looking on as their heads lurched and waggled about. As Whinnery and other researchers have speculated, the near-death and out-of-body phenomena are both actually the subjective experience of a brain owner watching as his brain tries desperately to figure out what is happening and to orient itself amid its systems going haywire due to oxygen deprivation. Without the ability to map out its borders, the brain often places consciousness outside the head, in a field, swimming in a lake, fighting a dragon—whatever it can connect together as the walls crumble. What the deoxygenated pilots don't experience is a smeared mess of random images and thoughts. Even as the brain is dying, it refuses to stop generating a narrative, the scaffolding upon which it weaves cause and effect, memory and experience, feeling and cognition. Narrative is so important to survival that it is literally the last thing you give up before becoming a sack of meat. It is the framework of your conscious experience. Without it, there would be nothing but noise. Better still, after the pilots regain consciousness they go through the same sort of explanatory routines as patients in emergency rooms who have technically died and returned to life. After the psychedelic wonder of a prolonged loss of oxygen, many people see that light and tunnel as the passage to the afterlife. The stories differ, depending on the belief system, but there is always a story.

One of the most perplexing aspects of the pilots who cross over and come back is that they come back whole. When their brains return to normal, they reassemble back into the person they were before. Neuroscience isn't certain how you reassemble your sense of self each time you wake up in the morning, but your personal narrative certainly has a lot to do with it. In neurologist Oliver Sacks's great book *The Man Who Mistook His Wife for a Hat,* he describes the wild confabulations of his brain-damaged patients and notes that they seemed driven "to replace what was continually being forgotten and lost" because narrative "for each of us is a biography, a story." According to Sacks, to be yourself you must feel as though you own your self. When you feel your story slipping away from you, you "recollect the inner drama" of yourself because your identity depends on feeling as if you have a firm grip on your story so far. That is why studying those whose narratives stray very far from what the people around them are witnessing is intensely revelatory. Let's take a quick stroll through that territory by first returning to the early days of brain science.

After serving as a military surgeon in 1870, Jules Cotard joined a clinic that did what it could with the knowledge of the day. Cotard and others at the clinic treated those with what one lecturer called "madness in all its forms." Cotard was one of the pioneers of neuroscience, connecting behavior to the physical locations in the brain. As he progressed in his career he became particularly interested in patients who exhibited aphasia, or difficulties with language. He would follow those patients past death to the autopsy table in search of the cause of their maladies, and he encouraged other doctors to do the same. In 1880, Cotard introduced a newly identified medical condition to the world. He called it *délire des négations,* or "negation delirium."

He told an audience in Paris that sometimes when a person's brain was injured in just the right way, that person could become convinced he was dead. No amount of reason or cajoling acrobatics could talk the person out of the fantasy. In addition, the condition wasn't purely psychological. It originated from a physiological problem in the brain. That is, this is a state of mind you, too, could suffer should you receive a strong enough blow to the head.

There are about a hundred accounts in the medical literature of people displaying what is now known as Cotard's delusion. It is also sometimes known, unsettlingly, as walking corpse syndrome. If you were to develop Cotard's delusion you might look in the mirror and find your reflection suspicious, or you might cease to feel that the heartbeat in your chest was yours, or you might think parts of your body were rotting away. In the most extreme cases, you might think you'd become a ghost and decide you no longer needed food. One of Cotard's patients died of starvation.

Cotard's syndrome and its delusions are part of a family of symptoms found in other disorders that all share the same central theme: the loss of your ability to connect emotionally with others. It is possible for something to go very wrong inside your skull so that your brain can no longer feel a difference between a stranger and a lover. The emotional flutter of recognition no longer comes, not for your dog, your mother, or your own voice. If you were to see a loved one and not feel the love, you would scramble to make sense of the situation. Sans emotion, loved ones become impostors or robots or doppelgängers. If the connection to your own image is severed, it becomes reasonable to assume that you yourself are an illusion. Faced with such a horrifying perception, you will invent a way to deal with it.

Sufferers of conditions such as Cotard's delusion devise weird, nonsensical explanations for their reality because they are experiencing weird, nonsensical input. The only difference between these patients' explanations and your own explanations is the degree to which they are obviously, verifiably false. Whatever explanations you manufacture at any given moment to explain your state of mind and body could be similarly muddled, but you don't have fact checkers constantly doting over your mental health.

Whether or not your brain is damaged, your mind is always trying to explain itself to itself, and the degree of accuracy varies from moment to moment. Psychologists call these false accounts confabulations—unintentional lies. Confabulations aren't true, but the person making the claims doesn't realize it. Neuroscience now knows that confabulations are common and continuous in both the healthy and the afflicted, but in the case of Cotard's delusion, they are magnified to grotesque proportions. The same narrative bias driving your explanations is what causes confabulation among those with serious physical damage to the brain.

The great neuroscientist V. S. Ramachandran often speaks of confabulation when discussing anosognosia, a medical term for the denial of disease. In his practice he has encountered many people who suffer from a physical disability yet do not explain that disability in a way that corresponds with reality. One of his patients suffered from paralysis in one arm, but denied that she was paralyzed. When asked to explain why she couldn't move her limb, she said it wasn't hers. She said it was her mother's arm, and her mother was hiding under the table playing a prank. He also treats patients with anterograde amnesia, who cannot form new memories. Every ten minutes or so, a person with this problem has her memory rebooted, and to her, it is as if she has suddenly found herself in the hospital, with no recollection of how she arrived there. Instead of freaking out, a patient with this sort of amnesia will often tell caregivers that she works in the hospital or that she is visiting someone. A person with Anton-Babinski syndrome will deny that she is blind, even though a stroke or an accident has rendered her sightless. Doctors are sometimes shocked to learn the patient can no longer see, because patients fail to bring it up during examinations. Often, nurses first learn of the blindness after the patient casually walks into walls or describes his surroundings, pointing out people and objects that don't exist.

A confused mind gets unconfused very quickly. When things seem weird and nonsensical, the brain makes them make sense immediately. Disorientation gets orientated, even if that means temporarily believing in something that is several time zones away from being the truth. A tangled, uncomfortable situation gets straightened out into a narrative so that the organism (you) can get back to the business of making jokes and wondering what's for dinner. The brain turns chaos into order so that you don't bump into walls and pet scorpions, and at the first sign of trouble, the first inkling of befuddlement, your neurons start cranking out false clarity. The three Christs of Ypsilanti, the people who deny their own arms, the people who claim they aren't blind—they are all creating narratives to stay sane. Without that tendency, it would be very difficult to be a person, so it serves you well in most situations, so well you rarely notice it. It's only when things go wrong that confabulation becomes noticeable and problematic, even life-threatening. Still, it is always there in the background. All brains are bards, all selves audiences to the tales of who they are.

Ramachandran told me, "I like to compare it with a military general who is receiving different sources of information while preparing for battle. So he is preparing to launch battle at six in the morning, and at five fifty-five, he's got all the generals lined up and all the scouts have brought him information, and he's going to launch battle at dawn, at six A.M. exactly. Suddenly, one chap comes along and says, 'This is wrong. We've seen the enemy is actually six hundred [soldiers strong], not five hundred. We were misinformed.' What you do is you say, 'Shut up.' You don't revise all your battle plans; it would be too costly. What's the likelihood that

this one guy is right and everybody else is wrong? Let me just ignore what he is saying. This is what we call denial, the tendency to
not accept information that's contrary to your sense of narrative.
But if that chap comes and says, 'They've got nuclear weapons. I've
just looked through the telescope, and they've got nuclear weapons.' Then you would be foolish to launch war. You have to say, no,
let me change my paradigm, let me shift gears."

According to Ramachandran, as an organism, you desire "stability of behavior." The last thing all the various agencies of your
mind want is the whole system going off in random directions, out
of control. When your brain senses trouble, senses that something
out of the ordinary is going down, the first instinct is to create a
narrative as a sort of defense mechanism against chaotic and risky
behavior.

"You can't overdo it," said Ramachandran. "We think all these
denial mechanisms, these Freudian denials—rationalization, confabulation, denial, repression, all of that—mainly occur in the left
hemisphere of the brain. The right hemisphere is your devil's advocate. If the denial becomes excessive, it kicks you in the butt and
says, 'Look, you're overdoing it; you'd better face up to reality.'"

In some people, the right hemisphere can't push back against
seemingly ridiculous narratives produced by the left hemisphere,
Ramachandran explained. Serious damage to the systems on the
right side render it toothless. In those cases, the left hemisphere
gets to make up whatever it wants, and the right hemisphere goes
along with it.

"You see that the arm is paralyzed. The left hemisphere patches
it up and says, 'Don't worry.' The right hemisphere would ordinar-
ily correct it and say, 'Don't be stupid; you are paralyzed.' That
mechanism is messed up, and so the guy denies the paralysis and

denies that the arm belongs to him. But the sort of everyday denial we see all the time is not unique to patients, but it's grotesquely amplified in these patients because of the damage to the right parietal."

If you are free of brain damage, you will experience what Ramachandran calls a "push-pull antagonism" between the hemispheres. The more novel the situation, the more the left brain tries to explain it away and works to generate an "internal sense of narrative," and the more the right brain scrutinizes the dubious nature of that explanation.

Here's a novel situation from my own life: My friend Devon Laird was brushing his teeth one morning when out of the corner of his eye he noticed his living room ceiling give birth to a large adult naked man. The man fell upside down into a wicker papasan chair amid a rain of insulation. The ceiling had ruptured and split apart like a blossoming flower, and in the chaos, Laird stood dumbfounded for a moment while his girlfriend yelled at the crumpled figure, demanding he leave at once. The man stumbled to his feet, politely adjusted the chair upright, opened their front door, and leapt outside. He then spun on his heels and asked Laird and his girlfriend if they would be so kind as to lend him some shorts. What followed was one of the most awkward silences in all of recorded history, promptly broken by more pointing and screaming. Realizing no one was going to fetch him some clothes, the ceiling crasher, naked and silhouetted by the morning sun, snatched a jacket from the coat rack just inside the door and ran away.

My friend and his girlfriend faced each other, bewildered, insulation still wafting to the floor, and waited for an explanation. While they were waiting, their brains started doing what brains do best: making things up. An hour or so later, I was standing with a group of friends listening to Laird tell this story. Later still, I started telling his story to other people, and they started telling it to other people, and at each step, the speculation grew. Eventually the story hit the local media, then bounced around the echo chamber from large market to even larger market, until it made the rounds on national television as one of those News of the Weird segments. By the time the story ran out of gas, there was still no official explanation.

Today we know the solution to the puzzle, and I'll tell you, but take a moment right now to speculate as we did.

Right after it happened, I remember talking to Laird. He said that his initial thoughts while standing there with toothpaste in his mouth, face-to-face with a naked man who had just fallen from his ceiling, were that this guy was trying to burgle his apartment. Later, when they saw police cars outside and learned the crasher was wanted for parole violation, that story seemed even more plausible. We both came up with dozens of other possible scenarios. Maybe this guy was adept at the *Mission: Impossible*–style of burglary and didn't want to risk snagging his clothes on a nail. Maybe he had been living in between the walls for weeks, subsisting on rainwater and whatever he could sneak out of open pantries, and he was naked because maybe it was hot in there. Maybe he was running from the police, had shed his inmate garb, and had slinked into an air vent, and had fallen through only because he trusted what he had learned in action movies. Reading the comment threads and forums right after the story hit the Internet, you could see everyone else was doing the same thing. We were all creating stories, grasping for an explanation. All we had was an aftermath, and it drove us all crazy that we might not know how that man ended up on the floor of a second-story apartment adjusting furniture in a stranger's home sans clothes while covered in insulation. "There has to be more to the story," we all said, but what we meant was that there had to be a story, some story, some explanation, that fit into story form. Otherwise the world would no longer make sense.

Consider the story you have already created concerning the man who appeared nude from the ceiling portal. This is certainly a novel situation, and, as with us, your left hemisphere went right to work trying to come up with an explanation. We didn't presume the guy was a secret agent spying on my friend because our right hemispheres told us that wasn't really a believable story. So what was the real explanation for the man who fell from above? Here you go: He was having sex with his girlfriend (Laird's next-door neighbor) when the cops knocked on the door. His coitus interrupted, and still nude, he scrambled for a way out and saw a hatch in the ceiling of his lady's wardrobe. He lifted the hatch and hoisted himself up into the tiny attic, where he punched through a thin partition that separated her apartment space from the apartment next door. As the wanted man squirmed from one attic to the next along the wooden supports, he slipped, planted his weight in the insulated area between two beams and submitted to the cruel pull of gravity and the maximum load-bearing allowance of drywall.

When this explanation arrived, everyone waiting to understand did what Ramachandran would have expected us to do. We pinged our right hemispheres: Is this within the spectrum of narratives I am willing to accept? Does this account of reality meet our minimum requirements for logic and continuity? Yes, we said. Yes, it does. And then we went on with our lives and ate some pie.

Like all humans, you eventually reduce every confusing element of life down to two questions: Where did we come from, and why are we here? How these questions are answered has formed the nuclei of whole civilizations. Cultures ask these questions of the universe as a whole, of nations and states, of businesses and Girl Guide troops. Existentially speaking, some individuals come up with an answer and stick with it, while some are content to live their lives never satisfied with an explanation.

The emerging field of narrative psychology adds a third fundamental question: Why do you want to know the answer to these questions? Why, asks narrative psychology, do you seek meaning? According to psychologist Dan McAdams, when your attempts at narrative fail you, that's when you free-fall into malaise and ennui, anomie and stagnation. This, he suggests, is why people lose themselves after retirement. Without a narrative binding, their wants, needs, and goals fall apart. McAdams is one of the pioneers of narrative psychology, and across several books he describes the predictable process of personal myth formation and the universal nature of mythology. Storytelling, he writes, appears in every human culture. According to McAdams, meaning is more important than happiness, and "to make meaning is to create dynamic narratives that render sensible and coherent the seeming chaos of human existence."

The central argument of narrative psychology is that you do not use logic and careful analysis to unravel the mysteries of who you are and what you want. You do not hypothesize and test. You don't study, record, and contemplate the variables of life and the people you meet along the way. Objectivity and rationality find it difficult to thrive in your intellectual ecosystem. You perceive time as a path from the past to the present with all the events of your life in between. You imagine life begins in one place and ends in another, and there are obstacles and climaxes along the way. You need a narrator in your head to make sense of the buzz generated by your giant network of neurons. You search for causes and effects that will explain the world in such a way that benefits your self-image. Over your bloodline's long history, the narrative evolved as the best method by which to pass meaning from one person to another, and it remains true inside this sentence.

Narratives are meaning transmitters. They are history-preservation devices. They create and maintain cultures, and they forge identities that emerge out of the malleable, imperfect memories of life events. It makes sense, then, that every aspect of humanity concerned with meaning, with cause and effect, will lean heavily on narratives. For instance, documentaries, books, and films about World War II present it as a story with a definite beginning and an end. In truth, nothing has a beginning and an end. World War II is a vast, blurry labyrinth of causes and effects, a dense morass of confluences with an infinite number of initial conditions and effects that are still reverberating in everything humans are doing across the planet. A good narrative carves a path through that mess, and within the confines of that path, things make sense. This is the basis of your narrative bias. When given the opportunity to make sense of life on your own terms, you prefer to both tell and hear the details in story form. You place yourself at the center of it all as protagonist. You see your life in phases, like chapters, and your past as a series of victories or defeats against antagonists major and minor. Life makes sense when looking in the direction of the past because you can edit it into a story. The past seems so simple, and thanks to narrative, you think it must have also been predictable. This is what psychologists call your hindsight bias. In studies, people who write down their predictions of how major news events will turn out typically recall themselves as being much more accurate than they really were. Since you rarely record your predictions, you rarely notice how wrong they tend to be. As a result, you tend to trust your current predictions far more than you should.

Your narrative bias makes it nearly impossible for you to really absorb the information from the outside world without arranging it into causes and effects. Most animals just do what they do. Sea cucumbers and aardvarks don't think about their actions; they don't feel shame, pride, or regret. You do, even when there is no reason to. If you look back on a behavior, thought, or emotion and feel befuddled, you experience an intense desire to explain it, and that explanation can affect your future behavior, your future thoughts, your future feelings. The most common way you do this is through something termed a post hoc rationalization. A post hoc rationalization is an explanation after the fact that makes enough sense to you that you can move on and not get stalled second-guessing your own motivation. If you want a nice chilled glass of beer after a long day of helping your best friend move into his flat in the middle of the summer the day before his electricity gets turned on, you look back on the situation and find it easy to explain the source of your desire, choice, action, behaviors, and emotions. You were hot. Beer is nice when you are hot and hanging out with friends. Yet, if we could hit Rewind and trace all the millions of influences on your mind leading up to the moment you suggested grabbing a cold one, you might notice that you sat through a particularly silly beer commercial the night before; or that you passed an obnoxious, sudsy billboard; or that the last time you were in the supermarket, you passed a pyramid of beer bottles; or that when you visited your mum last, she forced you to sit through her

*Meerkat Manor* DVD boxed set and somehow the word *Meerkat* made you imagine the as-yet-uninvented Beerbath, which you would love to float in after such a rough day of heaving end tables. Translated from Latin, *post hoc ergo propter hoc* means "after this therefore because of this." Because of your narrative bias, you find it irresistible to connect the dots and invent stories to help explain not only the banal (wanting a cold beer) but also the fantastic (sacrificing a virgin to keep the corn growing). In its purest form, you use post hoc rationalization to explain why one event follows another. If you eat a late-night kebab and get violently ill, the story almost writes itself. Yet that's an inaccurate assumption of reality. You can't know for sure what made you sick, but thanks to post hoc rationalization and the narrative bias, you may never eat a kebab from a kebab van again. Stories are linear, and that linearity helps you make sense of what is happening to you. You prefer a clear cause and effect, but just because the corn grows high after the annual goatball tournament and ritual beheading extravaganza, it doesn't mean the two are connected.

Thanks to your narrative bias, the world doesn't make as much sense unless the players are seen as characters. Great characters by their nature must be infused with human qualities, or they cease to have meaning. So, as you construct your tales, you tend to anthropomorphize the animals or kitchen appliances or landscapes within them.

Narrative bias really shines during moments of reflection in which you ponder the central character in your story: you. You have a real sense that you are you and not that guy next to the cash point who wears Tesco bags for underwear. The idea of personal boundaries—that there is a place where your self ends and the outside world begins, that you are in control of your actions and not being controlled by an alien parasite, that your story is yours—comes together in a gumbo of assumptions you generally refer to as the self.

You might find it alarming, then, to learn that neuroscience and psychology have teamed up over the last twenty years and used their combined powers to reach a strange and unsettling conclusion: The self is not real. It's just a story like all the others, one created by your narrative bias. After all, you are just a pile of atoms. When you eat vanilla pudding, which is also a pile of atoms, you are really just putting those atoms next to your atoms and waiting for some of them to trade places. If things had turned out differently back when your mum had that second glass of wine, the same atoms that glommed together to make your bones and your skin, your tongue and your brain, could have been arranged to make other things. Carbon, oxygen, hydrogen—the whole collection of elements that make up your body right down to the vanadium, molybdenum, and arsenic could be popped off you, collected, and reused to make something else—if such a seemingly impossible technology existed.

Like a cosmic box of Legos, the building blocks of matter can take the shape of every form we know of, from mountains to monkeys. If you think about this long enough, you might stumble into the same odd questions asked by philosopher Derek Parfit. If we had an atom-exchanging machine, and traded one atom at a time from your body with an atom from the body of Edward James Olmos, at what point would you cease to be you and Olmos cease to be Edward James? During that process, would you lose your mind and gain his? Somewhere in the middle, would an Edward James Almost appear? At some point would each person's thoughts and dreams and memories change hands? The weird feeling produced by this thought experiment reveals something about the way you see yourself and others. You have an innate sense that there is something special within people, and most especially yourself. Even if you are a hard-core materialist, you can't prevent the little tug in your gut that makes you feel that something might exist beyond the flesh, something not made of atoms. To you, people have an essence that is more than the sum of their parts. That sense isn't there at birth, though.

As psychologist Bruce Hood writes in his book *The Self Illusion,* you have an origin story and a sense that you've traveled from youth to now along a linear path, with ups and downs that ultimately made you who you are today. Babies don't have that. That sense is built around events that you can recall and place in time. Babies and small children have what Hood calls "unconscious knowledge," which is to say they simply recognize patterns and make associations with stimuli. Without episodic memories, there is no narrative; and without any narrative, there is no self. Somewhere between ages two and three, according to Hood, that sense of self begins to come online, and that awakening corresponds with the ability to tell a story about yourself based on memories. He points to a study by Alison Gopnik and Janet Astington in 1988 in which researchers presented to three-year-olds a box of chocolates, but the children were then surprised to find pencils inside instead of sweets. When they asked each child what the next kid would think was in the box when he or she went through the same experiment, the answer was usually pencils. The children didn't yet know that other people have minds, so they assumed everyone knew what they knew. Once you gain the ability to assume others have their own thoughts, the concept of other minds is so powerful that you project it into everything: plants, glitchy computers, boats with names, anything that makes more sense to you when you can assume, even jokingly, it has a sort of self. That sense of agency is so powerful that people throughout time have assumed a consciousness at the helm of the sun, the moon, the winds, and the seas. Out of that sense of self and other selves come the narratives that have kept whole societies together. The great mythologies of the ancients and moderns are stories made up to make sense of things on a grand scale. So strong is the narrative bias that people live and die for such stories and devote whole lives to them (as well as take lives for them).

The lesson you should take from the deluded men in Michigan, the confabulators, the arm deniers, the children who think everyone knows what they know, is that without your bias for narrative, you would be lost. Remember, your mind is the result of biological processes—chemical and electrical thunderstorms rippling through a cellular custard honeycombed and spiderwebbed with blood vessels and other things you'd rather not get on your hands during a meal. That is who you are, and that is what is producing thought, yet that is not what you perceive when you introspect. Inside, you see a drama. You see romance and tragedy, adventure and twists of fate, with you at the center of it all. At a conference in San Francisco called *Being Human,* the neuroscientist David Eagleman told an audience that after a lifetime of meditation, Buddhist monks are putting only a single toe into the "ocean of the unconscious." To plunge any deeper, as he put it, would be like measuring a transistor to make sense of a joke in a YouTube video. All that gobbledygook of ganglial output became more and more complex as your ancestors changed forms. It had to get tied together somehow, and narrative was a perfect solution. In Eagleman's book, *Incognito,* he speaks of the conscious part of the brain as only a tiny portion of the whole, and when ideas arrive in the mind, the conscious portion tends to take credit for something that was growing without its knowledge in the ocean of the unconscious, maybe for years. You don't have access to the truth of what has happened, but that doesn't stop you from coming up with a story to explain it. In that story, you mistake awareness for creation. In reality, the part of you that is aware is not the sole proprietor of your brain. To paraphrase psychologist George Miller, you don't experience thinking; you experience the result of thinking.

Remember, too, that the narratives that keep you bound together are nearly impervious to direct attack. If three men couldn't see eye to eye on who among them was and was not the real Jesus, your chances of swaying someone on the Internet to trade in his belief system concerning religion, art, wedge issues, politics, or literally anything else at all are pretty grim. Personal narratives and private mythologies don't flip in an instant; they don't trade places in a single argument. If minds change at all, they change slowly. As the author Michael Perry writes in *Off Main Street,* "We accrete truth like silt. It hones us like wind over sandstone."

For all existence, there is an internal narrative upon which you cling, a story you construct minute by minute to assure yourself that you understand what is happening, and you prefer information framed in narrative. You have a tendency to make sense of the world by unconsciously constructing a story and then repeating that story when you need to explain your thoughts, feelings, actions, and everything else that needs an explanation when you stop and wonder who you are and how you came to be where you find yourself. Even now, sitting there, reading this, if put on the spot, you could weave a tale with a beginning, middle, and end. There would be cause and effect, a narrator, a protagonist, and so on. In addition, you have a proclivity for believing and accepting things more readily when they are delivered to you in story form. Raw data may be more accurate, but you'd rather simplify things and move on with your day than pore over charts and data visualizations. An emotional appeal gets into your head better than a statistical analysis. A lecture sprinkled with jokes and unexpected turns will sway you more than one delivered via PowerPoint slides. Truth and accuracy usually lose when pitted against a riveting account—even when that account is coming from inside your noggin. Throughout the rest of this book you will notice that the narrative bias returns in every scenario in which you struggle to beat your brain. Whenever things start to get just a little difficult to understand, you replace that anxiety with false understanding in story form.

You don't just seek food and avoid danger; you don't just react to stimuli. You recall the past and tell better versions of it to new friends; you interpret and arrange, sharpen and dull, reframe and rationalize. When you get right down to it, the self is nothing more than a story. It is the explanation of your own memories to whoever will listen. Who would the three Christs of Ypsilanti be without their narratives? How would they cope with their madness? You may not have convinced yourself you are Jesus returned, but your story serves the same purpose as theirs. It keeps your chapters bound.

You and the three Christs of Ypsilanti are not so different. Their delusions are just much easier to see through. Their mental machinery may have been failing them, but their strategies for making sense of what was happening were identical to your own. They didn't fret and freak out. They defended their identities and their viewpoints. Looking at reality through a shattered lens, they still created narratives, stories that told them and other people who they were. Sure, their stories put them in the lead role as the Son of God, but it's not so much different from the role you've created, just much easier to debunk. Like you, these three souls were unaware that they were deluded, unaware that they were confused and misled by the same brain that had served them well for so many years leading up to their meeting. Just like you, even after seeing the folly of their fallacies, they remained oblivious to their mistaken viewpoints and erroneous beliefs. You share their habit of ignoring foggy perceptions. You, too, are unaware of how unaware you are.

# 2.

## The Common Belief Fallacy

---

THE MISCONCEPTION: *The larger the consensus, the more likely it is correct.*

THE TRUTH: *A belief is not more likely to be accurate just because many people share it.*

Back when Shakespeare said you were the paragon of animals, both noble in reason and infinite in faculties, he did so during a time when physicians believed the body was filled with black bile, yellow bile, phlegm, and blood, and all sickness and health depended on the interaction of those fluids. Lethargic and lazy? Well, that's because you are full of phlegm. Feeling sick? Maybe you've got too much blood and should go see a barber to get drained. The creator of some of the greatest works of the English language believed you could cure a fever with a knife.

In your own time, you may have felt some satisfaction, while sitting in a jet, that your species had mastered flight, but it is important to note that the first powered airplane took off in a country in which women weren't allowed to vote, and a lot of people believed they never should. You might gaze upon distant galaxies and marvel at how in less than sixty years your people went from airplanes to spaceships, but in between that time it also fought two world wars and attended a depressing number of child beauty pageants. A lot of people have believed a lot of things that people don't anymore. Belief is a pretty fragile thing, which is probably why most people guard it so carefully.

Still, compared to your loinclothed cousins from antiquity, you live in an amazing time. You probably carry a supercomputer in your pocket, and unlike most of your ancestors, you'll probably never worry about food or shelter. You don't go to sleep at night wondering if you'll wake up in a lion's mouth. Looking at things in this way, compared to your ancestors, you might count yourself among the modern geniuses of contemporary society. Not so fast. If this afternoon you were zapped back to medieval times and found yourself standing ankle-deep in mud within a bustling village, what would you be able to offer the people of that time from the future? The advances of science and medicine, the technological leaps and bounds—how much of that could you impart to an eager alchemist or inquisitive pyromancer? Even if you were an engineer or a chemist, you couldn't just go out and create an Xbox 360 from scratch. You would probably be digging graves or tending livestock within a week. It's unlikely you would invent the cotton gin or the steam engine. You certainly wouldn't be curing many diseases, either. The best you could probably offer them would be your knowledge of the benefits of sanitation. You see, a lot of what you presume to be evidence of your intelligence is just part of a vast cultural inheritance. If some sort of Reset button were pressed on your slow crawl out of the Stone Age, you would see that you are not much different from people ten thousand years ago. If the planet became a smoldering postnuclear wasteland, what skills and knowledge could you offer the survivors? How much of modern life do you actually understand?

My friend Susannah Gregg was living in South Korea and working there as an English teacher when she first learned about fan death, a common belief among people in that country that oscillating desk fans are among the most deadly inventions known to man. She was stepping out for a beer with a friend when he noticed, to his horror, she had left her fan running with her pet rabbit still inside her house. Her friend, a twenty-eight-year-old university graduate, refused to leave until she turned off the fan. He explained to her that everyone knows you can't leave a fan running inside a room with the windows shut. That would mean certain death. It was shocking to him that she was unaware of something so simple and potentially life-threatening. Susannah thought he was kidding. It took several conversations to convince him it wasn't true and that in her country, in most countries, no one believed such a thing. She successfully avoided the common belief fallacy not because she was smarter than her friend but because she had already done the experiments necessary to disprove the myth. She had slept in a house with a fan running many times and lived to tell about it. Since then, she has asked many friends and coworkers there about fans, and the response has been mixed. Some people think it is silly, and some think fan death is real. Despite the debunking power of a few Google searches, the belief that you shouldn't fall asleep or spend too much time in a room with a running electric fan is so pervasive in South Korea that Susannah told me you can't buy one within their borders without a safety device that turns it off after a set amount of time. The common belief is so deep and strong that fan manufacturers must include a safety switch to soothe the irrational fears of most consumers.

The people who thought the world rested on the back of a great tortoise, or who thought dancing would make it rain—they had the same brain as you; that is to say, they had the same blueprint in their DNA for making brains. So a baby born into their world was the same as one born into yours. Evolution is so slow that not enough has changed in the way brains are made to tell the difference between you and a person from ten thousand years ago. Yet when we look back on the ancients, it's easy to laugh at their silly assumptions. From gods in burning chariots to elves making cookies in trees, your ancestors believed in all sorts of things, thanks to the same faulty reasoning you deal with today. In addition, they, too, were fueled by a desire to make sense of reality and to answer the age-old question: "What, exactly, is happening here?" Instead of letting that question hang in the air, your distant relatives tended to go ahead and answer it, and they kept answering it over and over again, with newer yet equally idiotic ideas.

One of the most profoundly difficult obstacles humans have faced since we started chipping away at flint to make heads for spears is a malfunction of the mind called the common belief fallacy. In Latin, it is *argumentum ad populum,* or "appeal to the people," which should clue you in that this is something your species has worried about for a long time. The fallacy works like this: If most people believe something is true, you are more likely to believe it is true the first time you hear about it. You then pass along that mistaken belief, and on and on it goes. Being a social creature, the first thing you do in a new job, new school, new country, or any other novel situation is ask people who are familiar with the environment to help you get acquainted with the best way to do things, the best places to eat, the hand gestures that might get you beheaded, etc. The problem, of course, is that your info is now based on opinions that are based on things such as conformity and emotions and norms and popularity, and if you've spent any time in a secondary school, on a disco floor, or at a rave, you know that what is popular is not always what is good or true. It isn't exactly something we've overcome, but at least we now have a strategy for dealing with it.

Before we had a method for examining reality, the truth was a slippery fish, which is why your ancestors were so dumb. I'm not just talking about the ones who banged rocks together, but all of them, even the physicians and philosophers. So dumb, in fact, that for a very long time people got smarter in a slow, meandering, and unreliable sort of way until human beings finally invented and adopted a tool with which to dig their way out of the giant hole of stupid into which they kept falling.

The hole here is a metaphor for self-delusion. Your great-great-great-grandparents didn't really keep falling into giant holes, at least not in numbers large enough to justify a chapter on the topic. The tool here is also a metaphor. I'm talking about the scientific method.

Your ancestors invented the scientific method because the common belief fallacy renders your default strategies for making sense of the world generally awful and prone to error. Why do bees like flowers? What causes snow? Where do babies come from? Every explanation in every tribe, city, and nation was as good as the next, even if it was completely made up. Even worse, once an explanation was woven into a culture, it would often become the official explanation for many lifetimes. "What is thunder?" a child might have asked. "Oh, that's the giant snow crab in the sky falling off his bed," a shaman would have explained, and that would have been good enough for everyone until they all had their own kids and eventually died of dysentery. That hamster wheel of limited knowledge kept spinning until the scientific method caught on. Even then, there was a long way to go and lots of cobwebs to be cleared from common sense.

Before formalized science, some very smart people believed in some really weird things. At about the same time Johann Sebastian Bach was composing symphonies, many scientists asserted that "phlogiston" resided within everything you could burn, and once you set it on fire, the phlogiston escaped into the air. If you had some burning wood in a pot and placed a lid over it, the flame would go out because the air could hold only so much phlogiston before it was saturated. Left in the open, a piece of wood eventually turned to ash and was, as they put it, fully dephlogisticated. This idea lasted for about a hundred years before it was debunked by diligent scientific attacks. Eventually, scientists realized there was no such thing as phlogiston, and the real magic element was oxygen. Flames consumed oxygen, and lids starved flames.

Scholars also used to believe that life just sort of happened sometimes. Learned people going all the way back to Aristotle truly believed that if you left meat outside long enough it would spontaneously generate new life in the form of maggots and flies. The same people thought that if you piled up dirty rags and left them alone for a while they would magically turn into mice. Seriously. The idea started to fade in 1668 when a physician named Francesco Redi tested the hypothesis by placing meat and eggs in both sealed and unsealed containers and then checked back to see which ones contained life. The sealed containers didn't spontaneously generate life, and thus the concept began to die. Other thinkers contested his discoveries at first, and it took Louis Pasteur's great fame and his own experiments to put the idea away forever some two centuries later. Many look to Redi's experiment and others during that time in human history as a turning point. An upside-down way of looking at the world was making life better. Some say this meat-in-a-bottle business was the real birth of the scientific method. This was proof that looking for disconfirming evidence was a better way to conduct research than proceeding from common belief.

Your natural tendency is to start from a conclusion and work backward to confirm your assumptions, but the scientific method drives down the wrong side of the road and tries to disconfirm your assumptions. If you eliminate your suspicions the outline of the truth begins to emerge. Once your forefathers and foremothers realized that this approach generated results, in a few generations your species went from burning witches and drinking mercury to mapping the human genome and playing golf on the moon.

Even after your relatives had the scientific method, people still pursued and believed in really weird things, and many old ideas died hard deaths. It's hard to believe, but even simple things such as washing your hands to prevent infection weren't fully accepted by the medical community until relatively recently on the human timeline. Even after it was discovered and documented that washing hands drastically reduced deadly fevers, the idea took a while to catch on. It was just too revolutionary, too weird. The idea of germs and microscopic organisms challenged a variety of other ideas, including that the source of disease was probably linked to things that stank, which was sort of true when you thought about it. In a world that had already invented the telephone and the lightbulb, hand washing to prevent sickness met enough resistance that doctors argued about it for decades.

The twisting path to beating our brains has led to many stops and starts, yet humans persist. You may have noticed something wonderful about all these examples—science no longer believes in any of them, and neither do you. In battling the common belief fallacy, new common beliefs themselves are born. That's because science does something for you that you don't do very well on your own. Science continuously tears apart its models of reality looking for weakness. Sure, scientists are just people, prone to the same silliness as anyone else, but the enterprise, the process, slowly but surely grinds away human weakness. It is a self-correcting system that is always closer to the truth today than it was yesterday.

When it comes to the common belief fallacy in your own life, remember that scientists are always trying to reach better conclusions, and that is something you don't do as an individual, at least not by default, and by extension it is something your institutions are not so great at either. You don't seek out what science calls the null hypothesis. That is, when you believe in something, you rarely seek out evidence to the contrary to see how it matches up with your assumptions. That's the source of urban legends, folklore, superstitions, and all the rest. Skepticism is not your strong suit. Corporations and other institutions rarely set aside a division tasked with paying attention to the faults of the agency. Unlike in science, most human endeavors leave out a special department devoted to looking for the worst in the operation—not just a complaint department, but a department that asks if the organization is on the right path. Every human effort should systematically pause and ask if it is currently mistaken. To beat your brain, you need that department constantly operating in your cranium. You would do well to borrow from the lessons of the scientific method and apply them in your personal life. In the background, while you crochet and golf and browse cat videos, science is fighting against your stupidity. No other human enterprise is fighting as hard, or at least not fighting and winning.

The people who came before you invented science because your natural way of understanding and explaining what you experience is terrible. When you have zero evidence, every assumption is basically equal. You prefer to see causes rather than effects, signals in the noise, patterns in the randomness. You prefer easy-to-understand stories, and thus turn everything in life into a narrative so that complicated problems become easy. Scientists work to remove the narrative, to boil it away, leaving behind only the raw facts. Those data sit there naked and exposed so they can be reflected upon and rearranged by each new visitor. Scientists and laypeople will conjure up new stories using the data, and they will argue, but the data will not budge. They may not even make sense for a hundred years or more, but thanks to the scientific method, the stories, full of biases and fallacies, will crash against the facts and recede into history.

# 3.

# The Benjamin Franklin Effect

---

**THE MISCONCEPTION:** *You do nice things for the people you like and bad things to the people you hate.*
**THE TRUTH:** *You grow to like people for whom you do nice things and hate people you harm.*

Benjamin Franklin knew how to deal with haters.

Born in 1706 as the eighth of seventeen children to a Massachusetts soap and candlestick maker, the chances Benjamin would go on to become a gentleman, scholar, scientist, statesman, musician, author, publisher, and all-around general badass were astronomically low, yet he did just that and more because he was a master of the game of personal politics.

Like many people full of drive and intelligence born into a low station, Franklin developed strong people skills and social powers. All else denied, the analytical mind will pick apart behavior, and Franklin became adroit at human relations. From an early age, he was a talker and a schemer, a man capable of guile, cunning, and persuasive charm. He stockpiled a cache of secret weapons, one of which was the Benjamin Franklin effect, a tool as useful today as it was in the 1730s and still just as counterintuitive. To understand it, let's first rewind back to 1706.

Franklin's prospects were dim. With seventeen children, Josiah and Abiah Franklin could afford only two years of schooling for Benjamin. Instead, they made him work, and when he was twelve he became an apprentice to his brother James, who was a printer in Boston. The printing business gave Benjamin the opportunity to read books and pamphlets. It was as if Ben Franklin was the one kid in the neighborhood who had access to the Internet. He read everything, and taught himself every skill and discipline one could absorb from text.

At age seventeen, Franklin left Boston and started his own printing business, in Philadelphia. At age twenty-one, he formed a "club of mutual improvement" called the Junto. It was a grand scheme to gobble up knowledge. He invited working-class polymaths like him to have the chance to pool together their books and trade thoughts and knowledge of the world on a regular basis. They wrote and recited essays, held debates, and devised ways to acquire currency. Franklin used the Junto as a private consulting firm, a think tank, and he bounced ideas off the other members so he could write and print better pamphlets. Franklin eventually founded the first subscription library in America, writing that it would make "the common tradesman and farmers as intelligent as most gentlemen from other countries," not to mention give him access to whatever books he wanted to buy. Genius.

By the 1730s, Franklin was riding down an information superhighway of his own construction, and the constant stream of information made him a savvy politician in Philadelphia. A celebrity and an entrepreneur who printed both a newspaper and an almanac, Franklin had collected a few enemies by the time he ran for the position of clerk of the general assembly, but he knew how to deal with them. As clerk, he could step into a waterfall of data coming out of the nascent government. He would record and print public records, bills, vote totals, and other official documents. He would also make a fortune literally printing the state's paper money. He won the race, but the next election wasn't going to be as easy. Franklin's autobiography never mentions the guy's name, but when Franklin ran for his second term as clerk, one of his colleagues delivered a long speech to the legislature lambasting him. Franklin still won his second term, but his critic truly pissed him off. In addition, this man was "a gentleman of fortune and education" who Franklin believed would one day become a person of great influence in the government. So Franklin knew he had to be dealt with.

Franklin set out to turn his hater into a fan, but he wanted to do it without "paying any servile respect to him." Franklin's reputation as a book collector and library founder gave him a standing as a man of discerning literary tastes, so Franklin sent a letter to the hater asking if he could borrow a specific selection from his library, one that was a "very scarce and curious book." The rival, flattered, sent it right away. Franklin sent it back a week later with a thank-you note. Mission accomplished. The next time the legislature met, the man approached Franklin and spoke to him in person for the first time. Franklin said the man "ever after manifested a readiness to serve me on all occasions, so that we became great friends, and our friendship continued to his death."

What exactly happened here? How can asking for a favor turn a hater into a fan? How can requesting kindness cause a person to change his opinion about you? The answer to what generates the Benjamin Franklin effect is the answer to much more about why you do what you do.

Let's start with your attitudes. *Attitude* is the psychological term for the bundle of beliefs and feelings you experience toward a person, topic, idea, etc., without having to form concrete thoughts. Let's try it out. Justin Bieber. Feel that? That's your attitude toward him—a cascade of associations and feelings zipping along your neural net. Let's try some more. Read this and then close your eyes: blueberry cheesecake. Nice, huh? One more: nuclear bomb. There you go again, a thunderhead of brain activity is telling you how you feel about that topic. Ask yourself this: How did you form that attitude? It is well known in psychology the cart of behavior often gets before the horse of attitude.

For many things, your attitudes came from actions that led to observations that led to explanations that led to beliefs. Your actions tend to chisel away at the raw marble of your persona, carving into being the self you experience from day to day. It doesn't feel that way, though. To conscious experience, it feels as if you were the one holding the chisel, motivated by existing thoughts and beliefs. It feels as though the person wearing your shoes performed actions consistent with your established character, yet there is plenty of research suggesting otherwise. The things you do often create the things you believe.

At the lowest level, behavior-into-attitude conversion begins with impression management theory, which says you present to your peers the person you wish to be. You engage in something economists call signaling by buying and displaying to your peers the sorts of things that give you social capital. If you live in Essex, you might buy a white Range Rover with a booming sound system. If you live in Shoreditch, you might buy a fixie bicycle. Whatever are the easiest-to-obtain, loudest forms of the ideals you aspire to portray become the things you own, such as bumper stickers signaling to the world you are in one group and not another. These things then influence you to become the sort of person who owns them.

As a primate, you are keen to social cues that portend your possible ostracism from an in-group. In the wild, banishment equals death. So it follows that you work to feel included because the feeling of being left out, being the last to know, being the only one not invited to the party, is a deep and severe wound to your emotional core. Anxiety over being ostracized, over being an outsider, has driven the behavior of billions for millions of years. Impression management theory says you are always thinking about how you appear to others, even when there are no others around. In the absence of onlookers, deep in your mind a mirror reflects back that which you have done, and when you see a person who has behaved in a way that could get you booted from your in-group, the anxiety drives you to seek a realignment. But which came first? Your display or your belief? As a professional, do you feel compelled to wear a suit, or after donning a suit do you conduct yourself in a professional manner? Are you a Labour voter because you champion the welfare state, or do you champion the welfare state because you're a Labour voter? The research says the latter in both cases. As Kurt Vonnegut said, "We are what we pretend to be, so we must be careful about what we pretend to be." When you become a member of a group, or the fan of a genre, or the user of a product—those things have more influence on your attitudes than your attitudes have on them, but why?

Self-perception theory says your attitudes are shaped by observing your own behavior, being unable to pinpoint the cause, and trying to make sense of it. You look back on a situation as if part of an audience, trying to understand your own motivations. You act as observer of your actions, a witness to your thoughts, and you form beliefs about your self based on those observations. Psychologists John Cacioppo, Joseph R. Priester, and Gary Berntson demonstrated this in 1993. They showed Chinese characters to people unfamiliar with Chinese ideographs and asked them to say whether they thought each character was positive or negative. Some people did this while lifting upward on the bottom of a table while others pushed downward against the surface.

On average, the characters rated highest across all subjects were the ones they saw while pulling upward, and the ones they rated as being most negative were the ones they saw while pushing down. Why? Because you unconsciously associate flexing with positive experiences and extension with negative. Pushing and pulling affects your perception because from the time you were an infant you have pulled toward you that which you desired and shoved into the distance that which repulsed you. The very word *repulse* means "to drive away." The neural connections are deep and dense. Self-perception theory divides memories into declarative, or accessible to the conscious mind, and nondeclarative, that which you store unconsciously. You intuitively understand how declarative memories shape, direct, and inform you. If you think about triple-layer chocolate cake you feel warm and fuzzy. Self-perception theory posits that nondeclarative memories are just as powerful. You can't access them, but they pulsate through your nervous system. Your posture, the temperature of the room, the way the muscles of your face tense—these things inform your perception of who you are and what you think. Drawing near is positive; pushing away is negative. Self-perception theory shows that you unconsciously observe your own actions and then explain them in a pleasing way without ever realizing it. Benjamin Franklin's enemy observed himself performing a generous and positive act by offering the treasured tome to his rival, and then he unconsciously explained his own behavior to himself. He must not have hated Franklin after all, he thought; why else would he have done something like that?

Many psychologists would explain the Benjamin Franklin effect through the lens of cognitive dissonance, a giant theory made up of thousands of studies that have pinned down a menagerie of mental stumbling blocks—including the ones discussed in this book, such as confirmation bias, hindsight bias, the backfire effect, and the sunk cost fallacy—but as a general theory it describes something you experience every day.

Sometimes you can't find a logical, moral, or socially acceptable explanation for your actions. Sometimes your behavior runs counter to the expectations of your culture, your social group, your family, or even the person you believe yourself to be. In those moments, you ask, "Why did I do that?" and if the answer damages your self-esteem, a justification is required. You feel as if a bag of sand has ruptured in your head, filling all the nooks and crannies of your brain, and you want relief. You can see the proof in an MRI scan of someone presented with political opinions that conflict with her own. The brain scans of a person shown statements that oppose her political stance show that the highest areas of the cortex, the portions responsible for providing rational thought, get less blood until another statement is presented that confirms her beliefs. Your brain literally begins to shut down when you feel your ideology is threatened. Try it yourself. Watch a pundit you hate for fifteen minutes. Resist the urge to change the channel. Don't complain to the person next to you. Don't get online and rant. Try to let it go. You will find this is excruciatingly difficult.

In their fantastic book about cognitive dissonance, *Mistakes Were Made (But Not by Me),* Carol Tavris and Elliot Aronson write about the great psychologist Leon Festinger, who in 1957 infiltrated a doomsday cult. Dorothy Martin, who called herself Sister Thedra, led the cult. She convinced her followers in Chicago that an alien spacecraft would suck them up and fly away right as a massive flood ended the human race on December 21, 1954. Many of her followers gave away everything they owned, including their homes, as the day approached. Festinger wanted to see what would happen when the spaceship and the flood failed to appear. He hypothesized the cult members faced the choice of either seeing themselves as foolish rubes or assuming their faith had spared them. Would the cult members keep their weird beliefs beyond the date the world was supposed to end and become even more passionate, as had so many groups before them under similar circumstances? Of course they did. Once enough time had passed that they could be pretty sure no spaceships were coming, they began to contact the media with the good news: Their positive energy had convinced God to spare the Earth. They had freaked out and then found a way to calm down. Festinger saw their heightened state of arousal as a special form of anxiety: cognitive dissonance. When you experience this arousal it is as if two competing beliefs are struggling in a mental bar fight, knocking over chairs and smashing bottles over each other's heads. It feels awful, and the feeling persists until one belief knocks the other out cold.

Festinger went on to study cognitive dissonance in a controlled environment. He and his colleague Judson Mills set up an experiment at Stanford in which they invited students to join an exclusive club studying the psychology of sex. They told students that to get in the group they would have to pass an initiation. They secretly divided the applicants into two groups, not one: One read sexual terms out loud from a dictionary to a scientist, and the other read aloud entire passages from *Lady Chatterley's Lover* by D. H. Lawrence. As Tavris and Aronson point out, this was 1950s America, so either task was massively embarrassing, but reading aloud sex scenes filled with *F*- and *C*-bombs evoked a megadose of awkwardness. After the initiation, both groups listened to an audio recording of the sort of group discussion they had just earned the ability to join. The scientists made sure the discussion they heard was as dry and boring and unsexy as they could make it, going so far as to focus the sex talk on the mating habits of birds. They then had the students rate the talk. The people who read from the dictionary told Festinger the sex group was a drag and probably not something they'd like to continue attending. The D. H. Lawrence group who had endured a more painful initiation said the group was exciting and interesting and something they could not wait to begin. Same tape, two realities.

Festinger and another colleague, J. Merrill Carlsmith, pushed ahead with this research in 1959 in what is now considered the landmark study that launched the next forty years of investigation into the phenomenon, an investigation that continues right up until today.

Students at Stanford University signed up for a two-hour experiment called "Measures of Performance" as a requirement to pass a course. Researchers divided them into two groups. One was told they would receive $1 (about $8 in today's money). The other group was told they would receive $20 (about $150 in today's money). The scientists then explained that the students would be helping improve the research department by evaluating a new experiment. They were then led into a room where they had to use one hand to place wooden spools into a tray and remove them over and over again. A half hour later, the task changed to turning square pegs clockwise on a flat board one-quarter spin at a time for half an hour. All the while, an experimenter watched and scribbled. It was one hour of torturous tedium, with a guy watching and taking notes. After the hour was up, the researcher asked the student if he could do the department a favor on his way out by telling the next student scheduled to perform the tasks, who was waiting outside, that the experiment was fun and interesting. Finally, after lying, people in both groups—one with one dollar in their pocket and one with twenty dollars—filled out a survey in which they were asked their true feelings about the study. What do you think they said? Here's a hint: One group not only lied to the person waiting outside but went on to report that they loved repeatedly turning little wooden knobs. Which one do you think internalized the lie? On average, the people paid one dollar reported that the study was stimulating. The people paid twenty dollars reported what they'd just gone through was some astoundingly boring-ass shit. Why the difference?

According to Festinger, both groups lied about the hour, but only one felt cognitive dissonance. It was as if the group paid twenty dollars thought, Well, that was awful, and I just lied about it, but they paid me a lot of money, so . . . no worries. Their mental discomfort was quickly and easily dealt with by a nice external justification. The group paid one dollar had no outside justification, so they turned inward. They altered their beliefs to salve their cerebral sunburn. This is why volunteering feels good and unpaid interns work so hard. Without an obvious outside reward you create an internal one.

That's the cycle of cognitive dissonance; a painful confusion about who you are gets resolved by seeing the world in a more satisfying way. As Festinger said, you make "your view of the world fit with how you feel or what you've done." When you feel anxiety over your actions, you will seek to lower the anxiety by creating a fantasy world in which your anxiety can't exist, and then you come to believe the fantasy is reality, just as Benjamin Franklin's rival did. He couldn't possibly have lent a rare book to a guy he didn't like, so he must actually like him. Problem solved.

So has the Benjamin Franklin effect itself ever been tested? Yes. Jim Jecker and David Landy, building on the work of Festinger, conducted an experiment in 1969 that had actors pretend to be a scientist and a research secretary conducting a study. Subjects came into the lab believing they were going to perform psychological tests in which they could win money. The actor pretending to be the scientist attempted to make the subjects hate him by being rude and demanding as he administered a rigged series of tests. Each subject succeeded twelve times no matter what and received some spending money. After the experiment, the obnoxious actor told the subjects to walk up the stairs and fill out a questionnaire. At this point the actor stopped one-third of all the subjects right as they were leaving. He asked this group for the money back. He told them he was paying for the experiment out of his own pocket and could really use the favor because the study was in danger of running out of funds. Everyone agreed. Another third left the room and filled out the questionnaire in front of an actor pretending to be a secretary. As they were about to answer the questions, the secretary asked people in this group if they would please donate their winnings back into the research department fund, as the department was strapped for cash. Again, everyone agreed. The final third got to leave with their winnings without any hassle.

The real study was to see what the subjects thought of the asshole researcher after doing him a favor. The questionnaire asked how much they liked him on a scale of 1 to 12. On average, those who got to leave with their money rated him as a 5.8. The ones who did the secretary a favor instead gave him a 4.4. The ones who did the researcher a favor gave him a 7.2, suggesting the possibility that the Benjamin Franklin effect made them like him far more than the other two groups.

Benjamin Franklin's hater came to like Franklin after doing him a favor, but what if he had done him harm instead? In 1971, psychologists John Schopler and John Compere asked students to help with an experiment. They had their subjects administer learning tests to accomplices pretending to be other students. The subjects were told the learners would watch as the teachers used sticks to tap out long patterns on a series of wooden cubes. The learners would then be asked to repeat the patterns. Each teacher was to try out two different methods on two different people, one at a time. In one run, the teachers would offer encouragement when the learner got the patterns correct. In the other run of the experiment, the teacher would insult and criticize the learner when he messed up. Afterward, the teachers filled out a debriefing questionnaire that included questions about how charming and likable the learners were. Across the board, teachers rated learners who received insults as having less attractive personalities than the ones who got encouragement. The teachers' behavior created their perception. You tend to like the people to whom you are kind and to dislike the people to whom you are rude. From the Stanford Prison Experiment to Abu Ghraib, to concentration camps and the attitudes of soldiers spilling blood, mountains of evidence suggest that behaviors create attitudes when harming just as they do when helping. Jailers come to look down on inmates; camp guards come to dehumanize their captives; soldiers create derogatory terms for their enemies. It's difficult to hurt someone you admire. It's even more difficult to kill a fellow human being. Seeing the casualties you create as something less than you, something deserving of damage, makes it possible to continue seeing yourself as a good and honest person, to continue being sane.

The Benjamin Franklin effect is the result of your concept of self coming under attack. Every person develops a persona, and that persona persists because inconsistencies in your personal narrative get rewritten, redacted, and misinterpreted. If you are like most people, you have high self-esteem and tend to believe you are above average in just about every way. It keeps you going, keeps your head above water, so when the source of your own behavior is mysterious you will confabulate a story that paints you in a positive light. If you are on the other end of the self-esteem spectrum and tend to see yourself as undeserving and unworthy, Tavris and Aronson say you will rewrite nebulous behavior as the result of attitudes consistent with the persona of an incompetent person, deviant, or whatever flavor of loser you believe yourself to be. Successes will make you uncomfortable, so you will dismiss them as flukes. If people are nice to you, you will assume they have ulterior motives or are mistaken. Whether you love or hate your persona, you protect the self with which you've become comfortable. When you observe your own behavior, or feel the gaze of an outsider, you manipulate the facts so they match your expectations.

Pay attention to when the cart is getting before the horse. Notice when a painful initiation leads to irrational devotion, or when unsatisfying jobs start to seem worthwhile. Remind yourself pledges and promises have power, as do uniforms and parades. Remember in the absence of extrinsic rewards you will seek out or create intrinsic ones. Take into account the higher the price you pay for your decisions the more you value them. See that ambivalence becomes certainty with time. Realize that lukewarm feelings become stronger once you commit to a group, club, or product. Be wary of the roles you play and the acts you put on, because you tend to fulfill the labels you accept. Above all, remember the more harm you cause, the more hate you feel. The more kindness you express, the more you come to love those you help.

Franklin summed it up like so in his autobiography: "This is another instance of the truth of an old maxim I had learned, which says, 'He that has once done you a kindness will be more ready to do you another, than he whom you yourself have obliged.' And it shows how much more profitable it is prudently to remove, than to resent, return, and continue inimical proceedings."

# 4.

## *The Post Hoc Fallacy*

---

**THE MISCONCEPTION:** *You notice when effect doesn't follow cause.*

**THE TRUTH:** *You find it especially difficult to believe a sequence of events means nothing.*

For a while, you could spot the bracelets on the wrists of famous professionals in just about every popular sport. From David Beckham to cricketer Ian Bell, from the Super Bowl to Formula One, the black silicone wristbands with holograms glued to the side were everywhere. Despite their product's incredible popularity, the company responsible for manufacturing the Power Balance brand of performance wristbands filed for bankruptcy in November of 2011.

The Power Balance company made a lot of claims. Their website said that the silicone rings imbued the wearer with a faster brain, faster muscles, more powerful lungs, increased flexibility, and, as the name suggests, improved balance. It also made lots of money. The magic straps were once available in more than thirty countries, and in 2011 a company spokesperson told the Associated

Press that he estimated $34 million in sales that year. In March, they used their earnings to rename the ARCO Arena in California to the Power Balance Pavilion. Later, they would strike a deal with the National Basketball Association (NBA) to place each team's logo on its own version of the band. So the company wasn't experiencing any financial problems when it went bankrupt. In fact, the popularity of the bracelets was peaking. Former U.S. president Bill Clinton was photographed wearing one, as was Robert De Niro, and Gerard Butler, and probably all the uncles in your family who spend more time talking about golf than playing it. The Associated Press reported in 2011 that trainers for the Phoenix Suns basketball team swore by the trinkets, and that a spokesperson for St. Vincent Sports Performance in Indianapolis, where hundreds of professional athletes go to train, estimated that a third of all of its clients wore the bracelet while working out. From 2007 to 2012, from all walks of life, from actors to footballers to politicians, millions of people paid thirty dollars for a magical amulet and wore it proudly in public to, as the company promised, enhance their natural energy fields, resonate with holograms, and increase sporting ability—whatever that means.

Chances are the company would still be going strong had it not been smacked with a $67 million settlement for consumer fraud after an Australian court found it guilty of knowingly deceiving the public. The problem with all the claims, said meddling scientists, was that every single one was completely, absolutely, and obviously false—the bands had no more power than a novelty plastic bracelet. Soon after the court's ruling, Power Balance LLC issued a statement that read in part, "We admit that there is no credible scientific evidence that supports our claims and therefore we engaged in misleading conduct." Then they filed for Chapter 11 bankruptcy. You still see the bracelets from time to time, especially the petrol-station-checkout knockoffs, but the original is dwindling from sight in the countries where they made a name for themselves and enjoyed dozens of celebrity endorsements.

Of course, this isn't the end of the product. The website is still alive, and you can see a variety of new offerings there, ranging from sweatbands to mouth guards. You can still buy the official NBA versions from the association's online shop. There are still plenty of celebrity endorsers as well, if the website is to be believed. A Chinese distributor bought the company in 2012, and according to *The Wall Street Journal,* consumer protection officials believe it will make a big comeback. One official, Filippo Marchino, told the *Journal* the company would likely expand into markets "more vulnerable to alternative health philosophies," especially those lacking consumer watchdogs.

It really doesn't matter. Even if the company eventually tanks, someone else will come along and begin selling magical jewelry and other mystical junk soon enough. There have always been such products—magnetic charms, homeopathic extracts, religious relics, voodoo dolls, weight-loss ear clips, trainers with tiny catapults inside them. The potential for profit will always be there, waiting for a clever marketer to crack into the modern mind's version of ancient gullibility. So why does this work on you? Why do rabbit's feet and four-leaf clovers find their way so easily into your pockets and why does your hard-earned cash so easily find its way into the pockets of their peddlers? At the root of this is a form of magical thinking called the post hoc fallacy. The way it misdirects you while you bathe in the afterglow of the placebo effect has made con artists rich for centuries.

Athletes seem particularly prone to magical thinking. Pelle

Lindbergh, the Swedish National Hockey League goaltender, wore the same orange shirt under his pads for every game. He never washed it, and had it sewn back together multiple times as it rotted away over the years. After a win, tennis star Goran Ivanisevic attempted to repeat every action from that day on the day of his next match, right down to the table settings and the contents of his meals. He wrote on his blog that he looked forward to the end of tournaments because it meant he "could finally eat something else." The Chicken Man, Wade Boggs, widely considered one of the best ever to grace a baseball diamond, was so named because he insisted on eating chicken before every event. He was also obsessed with the number seventeen, and began practice in the batting cage at exactly 5:17, and then ran sprints at exactly 7:17. Once, while in a slump, the announcer forgot to mention Boggs's number when he called out his name to the crowd. Boggs's slump ended with that game, and from then on he asked the announcer not to mention his number before play. One biographer wrote that Boggs's entire life consisted of these routines. He was a clockwork man, a person who ritualized everything in order to keep track of his output. By remaining consistent and mechanical, Boggs saw his performance become measurable, comparable. Sports can do that to people, make players and fans into statistical neurotics more compulsive than any *Dungeons and Dragons* master could hope to be. It is this devotion to a quantified lifestyle that causes so many athletes to adopt magical beliefs. If they look at the numbers and see an improvement, everything that preceded that bump is suspect. Everything that comes before a positive outcome is lumped into the mixture of rituals and behaviors worth repeating. This is the post hoc fallacy. It's been an uncontrollable tick in every human head going back farther than the oldest-known lucky charms buried with cave dwellers and pharaohs alike.

The words *post hoc* come, again, from that Latin phrase *post hoc ergo propter hoc*: "after this therefore because of this." It is the natural assumption that appears in your head when one event follows another event. You may not realize how fundamental this line of thought is to your daily operation of human consciousness. Button-operated devices make intuitive sense because of your natural tendency to think in a linear, post hoc sort of way. You press the doorbell button; you hear the doorbell ring. You press the lift button; the button lights up. You touch the screen, and the app comes alive. You press the button on the vending machine, and a soft drink comes rattling down the chute. You've pressed buttons and been rewarded your whole life. It's conditioning at its simplest—just like a rat pressing a lever to get a pellet of food. There might be some invisible magic taking place between the moment you press a button and when you get the expected result. You can never really be sure you caused the soft drink to appear without opening up the vending machine to see how it works. Maybe there's a man inside who pulls out the can of soda and puts it in the chute. Maybe there's a camera watching the machine, and someone in a distant control room who tells the machine to dispense your pop. You just don't know. As long as you get the result you were looking for after you press the button, it doesn't matter. You will be more likely to press the button in the future or less likely to stop depending on how the events unfold. Children automatically avoid power outlets after one bad experience with a penny. A child doesn't need a complex lesson on the discovery of electricity and the long, perilous journey toward harnessing its power. Once zapped, he does not need an explanation of the economic and industrial processes required to complete a functioning power grid. To get something out of that experience, it doesn't matter if you understand electromagnetism or even believe it exists. The truth about what is happening in between the action and the result is something most animals never consider and never need to worry about. If your toddler is blown back by a wall socket and forever must explain why Lincoln's profile is burnt into her thumb, you can rest assured the experiment won't be repeated, because evolution favors the sort of brain that says, "After this, because of this," and "I'm never doing that again."

Because you are so eager to commit the post hoc fallacy, you have a habit of thinking that when one event follows another, the two events must be related, and that the second event was caused or at least influenced by the first. Because of this, the post hoc fallacy is the kingpin of irrational thought. Post hoc rationalization is the fairy godmother of all things inaccurate, nonscientific, mystical, mythological, and superstitious. It makes sense that this sort of thinking would lead you into dark waters because recognizing patterns, especially "if this, then that" situations, is crucially important for navigating life. It's just that you aren't very good at noticing when that way of thinking is dumb, and it often is. For instance, most colds last only seven days, so whatever you take often treats only the symptoms. Still, a slew of home remedies and over-the-counter medications are probably close to your heart because you believe that getting better depends on those things even though you would have gotten better just as quickly without them. Your civilization may dance at the same time every year to bring the rains so that your harvest grows tall and bountiful, but that doesn't mean your dancing has anything to do with growth of crops. Your team may gather and pray super hard before every game, but that doesn't mean you won the championship because you persuaded an all-knowing deity to provide your team with strength against your pagan kickball rivals. Despite the usefulness of automatically coming to such conclusions, that way of thinking is still fallacious. Erring on the side of caution is still the best bet in most situations, so that's the factory setting for your whole species.

Post hoc thinking, unlike other fallacies, gets a special biological boost from a weird physiological quirk called the placebo effect. You have probably heard of placebos. The term once used to encompass all folk remedies, such as eating cobwebs to cure a headache or downing warm whiskey mixed with sugar to fight the body aches of the flu. The term later came to mean any treatment that was more likely to make the patient happy than well. In 1955, doctor and activist Henry K. Beecher gave us the modern definition of a placebo in his paper "The Powerful Placebo." Beecher argued that medical trials should include double-blind methods for research and the inclusion of placebos so that new drugs and treatments could be measured against dummy versions. In a double-blind study, neither the researcher nor the subject knows which treatment is the placebo and which is the real thing. It worked. Science and medicine took notice, and since his paper's publication, placebos have been studied on their own and have become an integral part of drug research. Many treatments have turned out over the years to be no better than placebos, and placebos, we have learned, are now known to be one of the strongest anomalies of the mind.

The placebo effect is disturbingly easy to produce, and chances are you experience it every day. Whenever you want something to work in the way you believe it will, sometimes your faith alone can alter your perception. In 2009, German researchers told subjects they were going to apply to their arms an anesthetic cream, but the cream was fake. They then applied painful heat to the subjects' arms where the cream had been applied. Thanks to the placebo effect, the subjects reported feeling less pain around the spot where the relief was expected, even though the cream did not really have the power to kill pain. Crazier still, in brain scans the scientists could clearly see that the people in the study were reacting as if they truly were getting pain relief. Somehow, just believing the signals would be blocked caused the bodies of the subjects to block them. In 2010, researchers at Harvard gave patients placebo pills to alleviate irritable bowel syndrome. There was a twist in this study, however: The researchers told the subjects beforehand that they were taking fake medicine. Oddly enough, the people who received the fake pills and who knew full well those pills weren't real were twice as likely to report relief of their symptoms than a group that received no pills at all. The researchers concluded that the ritual of going to a doctor and trusting your health to his training can by itself illicit the placebo effect.

The post hoc fallacy and the placebo effect often turn up together. In combination, they create all sorts of interesting phenomena. Some of my favorites are nonfunctioning mechanisms that people continue to use. These are called placebo buttons, and they're everywhere. They work on the "after pressing this, therefore because I pressed this" principle. The Close button doesn't close the doors in many lifts built in the United States since the Americans with Disabilities Act. The button is there for workers and emergency personnel to use, and it works only with a key. Whether or not you press the button, the doors will eventually close. But if you do press the button, and later the doors come together, a little spurt of happiness will cascade through your brain.

Your behavior was just reinforced. You will keep pressing the button in the future. According to a 2004 investigation by *The New York Times,* the city of New York deactivated the pedestrian-powered manual operation of traffic signals long ago, and "more than 2,500 of the 3,250 walk buttons that still exist function essentially as mechanical placebos." Computers and timers now control the lights at most intersections, but at one time the little buttons at crosswalks allowed people to trigger the signal change. The task of replacing or removing all those buttons is usually so great most cities just leave them there. You still press them, though, because the light eventually changes. You don't have the time to do a double-blind study of traffic signals, so a version of the placebo effect takes over following a faulty post hoc analysis. In an investigation by ABC News in 2010, only one functioning crosswalk button could be found in the cities of Austin, Texas; Gainesville, Florida; and Syracuse, New York.

The effect is everywhere. In many offices and cubicle farms, the thermostats on the wall are not connected to anything. For decades, landlords, engineers, and HVAC specialists have installed dummy thermostats to keep people from costing companies money by constantly adjusting the temperature. According to a 2003 article in *The Wall Street Journal,* one HVAC specialist surmised that 90 percent of all office thermostats were fake. Some companies even install noise generators to complete the illusion after you turn the knob. In a survey conducted in 2003 by *Air-Conditioning, Heating, and Refrigeration News,* 72 percent of respondents admitted to installing dummy thermostats.

To be sure, the placebo effect has its limits. No doctor would advise positive thinking over actual treatment, but the effect of the former is real and measurable. Expectation and belief can and do change your perception of reality so powerfully that your body can unconsciously change its response to match. So it should be no surprise that the placebo effect will appear whenever you expect an effect from an agent you trust. From gingko biloba to wheatgrass, from chiropractic adjustment to acupuncture, there is little scientific evidence for the efficacy of most dietary supplements and alternative treatments. Debunking, though, rarely puts much of a dent in the practice and sales of these sundries and mystical medical claims. A cornucopia of alternative medicines and mystical objects continue to be available both online and in major department stores, and part of the reason it is so hard to eradicate nonsense treatments is that they often do make people feel better in some small way. As far as science is concerned, there is no way a magnetic bracelet could psychically ease the pain of arthritis or improve the flow of blood, but in clinical trials people often do feel better when they think the bracelets work. The key phrase here is "feel better." The important thing to remember when you don one of these enchanted baubles or visit one of these pseudoscientific or mystical alternative medicine practitioners is that your belief is doing all the work. The objects and treatments are just placeholders designed to produce a post hoc rationalization—after wearing this bracelet, therefore because I wore the bracelet.

In some ways, you can see the scientific method as a necessary invention to combat the post hoc fallacy. Without it, it's hard to say what causes are truly connected to the effects you want to see repeated or hope to avoid forever. It's too bad that major events in history can never be analyzed in that way. You can never know if any decision was the right one, whether your own or that of Alexander the Great or Harry Truman. All we get are the results, and we know that after this is not necessarily because of this. Thankfully, some events and effects can be studied. Science had its say in the matter of placebo jewelry thanks to the insane popularity of Power Balance. In 2010, researchers at the University of Wales had subjects run through a series of physical challenges while wearing a blindfold and either a dummy bracelet or a Power Balance bracelet. They found no differences between the two. Additionally, in 2011, researchers at RMIT University in Australia had subjects wear Power Balance bracelets with the holograms intact or replaced with tiny metal discs and ran those subjects through a battery of tests of physical prowess, including balance. They, too, found no significant difference.

It is unlikely we'll ever be rid of these objects. When psychologist Lysann Damischin in 2010 handed half her subjects a golf ball that she explained was lucky and handed the other half a golf ball that was presented as normal, the half with the lucky ball sank 35 percent more putts. The lucky ball wasn't actually lucky, of course. She randomly assigned the description. A coin toss decided who would be told the ball was or was not magical. The belief, though, had an effect. She speculated the lucky ball made the players believe they were more in control and caused them to be more persistent, it lowered their anxiety, and all this boosted their confidence and therefore their performance. So it went with the bracelets. When racecar drivers and weight lifters and public speakers noticed improvements in performance while wearing Power Balance bracelets, the likely culprit was the placebo effect. The wearers could have replaced the bracelet with a bit of string and gotten the same real-world results, if they maintained the same level of belief. Thanks to the post hoc fallacy, when they noticed some sort of difference, they didn't assume it was their own mind causing the changes. Instead, they looked for a cause to the effect that was more obvious: the holographic armband.

Ask yourself if it is the medication or treatment or your expectation making you feel better, especially if it is something that didn't come from a medical doctor. Just because your family has been using frozen lettuce to cure aching nipples for centuries doesn't mean that lettuce is the important ingredient in that cure. Just because Gwyneth Paltrow is a fan of cupping (a practice from ancient Chinese medicine) doesn't mean that it will help cure your whiplash. As comedian Tim Minchin says in his song "Storm," "Do you know what they call alternative medicine that's been proved to work? Medicine." Ask yourself if you count on certain objects or rituals in the same way someone might count on a luck-bearing rock. Be prepared to accept that thinking about a person and then receiving his or her phone call is not magical in any way whatsoever. To beat your brain, remember your propensity for post hoc postulation and the power positive permutations of the placebo effect have to pollute your perspicacity. The fact that one thing follows another proves nothing. Magical amulets do not exist, and even if they did, think about how expensive it would be to hire a factory full of wizards to enchant enough of them for worldwide distribution.

# 5.

## *The Halo Effect*

---

**THE MISCONCEPTION:** *You objectively appraise the individual attributes of other people.*

**THE TRUTH:** *You judge specific qualities of others based on your global evaluation of their character and appearance.*

You might think height would be a casting consideration when a Hollywood studio puts $200 million or so behind a movie, but the people working in the movie business are not troubled when they learn their lead actor is a bit shorter than most men, shorter even than the actress cast as his love interest. After decades of dealing with the issue, a director can choose from an assortment of well-known solutions.

The simplest answer is to use an apple box, a little wooden crate that was originally used for storage. Over time these became an essential part of filmmaking thanks to their excellent utility as a gravity-resistance device. Some even have supports installed inside to make them sturdier. Production crews use them to hold up just about everything that needs to be higher while cameras are rolling, and they are so ubiquitous on a film set that there is a production shorthand to explain what side of the box should be facing down—"L.A." or "full apple" for normal placement; "New York" for standing it on its end. When your actor is too short for the shot you want, you can just put a couple of these boxes under him and avoid revealing his feet. That's why, in the movie business, they sometimes call apple boxes "man makers."

To make short actors such as Tom Cruise, Al Pacino, Humphrey Bogart, and James Cagney seem taller, film crews have also used special shoes, low camera angles, and specially constructed out-of-proportion door frames. They have even dug long trenches in which the other people in a scene walked alongside the leading man while the camera was running. But why do we want a leading man to be tall? The answer to this reveals the power of a psychological phenomenon that taints just about every bit of information that gets into your head.

The psychologist Edward L. Thorndike was one of the founders of educational and occupational psychology. In the early twentieth century he helped create tests for the U.S. Army for use in evaluating the intelligence and aptitude of soldiers, and he went on to develop learning tools for teachers. He was particularly interested in what happens when you are asked to turn the qualitative into the quantitative, something businesses and universities still do all the time in the pursuit of efficiency and excellence. In their efforts to get a bit better each semester and quarter, institutions have long adored reports, exams, tests, and reviews. Turning people into numbers makes it a lot easier to present charts and graphs to your CEO or university board. So it made sense that such an environment would be a great place to observe the effect of quantification on behavior and perception.

Over time, as Thorndike was exposed to more and more reports, he began to notice a strange phenomenon. When a corpora-

tion put a person on paper, all that person's traits seemed to corre-
late. That is, people seemed a lot less nuanced when described one
aspect at a time. If a person were rated high on one measure (reli-
ability, for example), he would be rated highly on all the other unrelated measures as well (such as intelligence and specific technical
skills). The pattern was so pervasive that, in 1915, Thorndike published a study in which he gathered up U.S. Army officer reviews.
He showed that when superior-ranking officers evaluated their
subordinates with specific instructions to judge each category separately and independently, the commanding officers couldn't do it.
If they highly rated their soldiers' neatness or endurance or loyalty,
they would also highly rate their ability to make decisions in a crisis
or say they had above-average administrative skills. If they found
their subordinate to be a bit lacking in tact or initiative, the officers
tended to rate him as wanting in his ability to inspire his men or
issue and execute commands. Across the board, each measure
tended to match in magnitude its neighbor.

Thorndike was particularly concerned with how pilots who
got great ratings on their ability to handle an airplane tended to get
stellar marks from their superiors on their ability to lead. He wrote
that, considering how young most pilots were, it was unlikely a
dashing aerial hero could have developed equally impressive leadership skills. Yet, in the reviews, superior officers tended to see flying aces as prime officer material, rating them highly on unrelated
skills and attributes. He called it a "halo of general merit." Thorndike noted that when a person was considered great at something
specific and desirable, that trait influenced all other measures. The
point, Thorndike wrote, was that this was an error. The other
measures were made inaccurate by what would later become
known in psychology as the halo effect.

So, considering that the halo effect turns you into an unwitting liar to yourself and others, why would such an anomalous filter endure in your mind?

To speed up processing, your brain tends first to apply very simple labels to the things you encounter minute by minute. You can thank your ancestors for paying attention to these labels for millions of years, because some of the things you are most likely to encounter in life are now hardwired into your mind as being good or bad, desirable or undesirable. This is good, you think, when you eat a strawberry dipped in chocolate. This is bad, you think, when you see your ex-boyfriend approaching you in a bar with a stranger on his arm. Fanged, spindly, crawling things, for example, are undesirable and should be avoided, and when you see anything resembling a spider skittering across the floor, you instinctively recoil. Thick red, yellow, or green liquids trigger feelings of disgust, while thick blue liquids do not. The sight of a juicy steak makes your mouth water. Fill it with maggots, and your stomach turns. Open fields with water nearby universally make people happy, while dark, tangled swamps universally make you wary.

When you make decisions and kindle beliefs based on innate sensations, psychologists say you are using the affect heuristic. An affect, in psychological terms, is a feeling that needs no further analysis. It isn't a coherent thought with words and symbols attached, but rather, a raw emotional state, a twinge or a jolt or just a general sensation that sets a tone or a mood. You can glide through an affect, or slowly submerge into one, and sometimes an affect slaps you like a fish to the forehead. When it comes to keeping you alive over the long run, the affect heuristic serves you well. It keeps you out of unfamiliar and seemingly dangerous situations and it tells you to avoid weirdos and creeps. It's a blunt tool, though, and very inaccurate from one specific situation to the next. Over the course of human history much harm has arrived behind twinkling eyes and glimmering smiles, and those who seem the least among you often deliver the most good. This tendency greatly pollutes your judgment of risk. You are much more likely to die in a car wreck on the way to the airport than you are once inside the airplane. You are actually more likely to win an Academy Award over the course of your lifetime than get mauled by a shark. Your instinctive, automatic feelings of love and fear are strongly influenced by an inexact devotion to the affect heuristic.

So why is height so important for a leading man? Why do moviemakers go out of their way to make the protagonists tall? It is because the human form has qualities that elicit your gut response from the affect heuristic. Symmetry is one. Babies as young as two days old will stare at symmetrical faces for much longer than asymmetric ones. Muscle tone, vocal pitch, walking gait—you have heuristic responses to each, but height gets the royal treatment by the affect heuristic. When a director wants to generate a positive emotion in relation to a character, it really helps to make that person tall.

Every inch of height above six feet earns a person an extra $789 a year on average, according to a study published in 2004 in the *Journal of Applied Psychology.* The scientists, Timothy Judge and Daniel Cable, followed 8,500 British and American citizens from youth through adulthood and found that height was strongly correlated with business success. Judge speculated that the very act of looking down on others made people more confident. Likewise, literally looking up at people who are tall leads to the sort of feelings that come from figuratively looking up to them for other reasons. The strongest correlation, Judge and Cable found, was in jobs where social interaction is most common—sales and management—

followed by other careers where confidence is important. It should come as no shock, then, that the shorter candidate for U.S. president has lost about 80 percent of the time going back to 1904, when historians started keeping up with that sort of thing. A study in 2009 by psychologist Gayle Brewer showed that the taller a man is, the less jealousy he tends to experience in romantic relationships. Likewise, tall men are less likely to engage in mate retention behaviors such as constantly making sure he knows where his partner is and provoking fights with flirtatious men, according to Brewer. Then again, the tall men in her study were also less likely to spend time worrying about their appearance or making romantic gestures.

Why is being tall so important to people outside the movie industry? After all, we are talking about only a few inches here, and being tall doesn't really make you a better leader or a better salesperson. The researchers in the salary study speculate that it is just a heuristic at work. You have a height bias that tells you taller is better because it was adaptive to think such things for some unknown reason over the last few million years. We can't know for sure; maybe it had to do with extra physical strength in taller people and the prowess it offered in other tasks. Maybe taller people seemed better nourished and healthier than shorter peers. Whatever the source, today studies show taller people are more intimidating, more commanding, and that the halo effect makes you believe taller people are more desirable for things in which height doesn't necessarily matter.

The halo effect causes one trait about a person to color your attitude and perceptions of all her other traits. Even stranger, the more noticeable the aspect is when you form your first impression, the more difficult it becomes to change your attitude about that aspect. So, for example, if you are bowled over by the warmth and kindness of a coworker in your first week at a new job, you'll let him get away with a host of obnoxious behaviors later on, maybe even for years. If the first year of a relationship is stellar and life-altering, it can take a long time to notice if things turn sour later. If you like specific aspects of an individual, the halo effect causes the positive appraisal to spread to other measurements and to resist attack. Beautiful people seem more intelligent, strong people seem nobler, friendly people seem more trustworthy, and so on. When they fall short, you forgive and defend them, sometimes unconsciously.

In the last one hundred years of research, beauty seems to be the one thing that most reliably produces the halo effect. *Beauty* is shorthand, a placeholder term for an invisible mental process in which you are privy only to the final output. Like the words *delicious* and *disgusting,* it describes a distinct variation of the affect heuristic. To see and judge a face as beautiful is to experience a tempest of brain activity informed by your culture, your experiences, and the influence of your deep evolutionary inheritance. It all adds up to an awareness that a person is or is not beautiful in a process still waiting to be unraveled. Regardless of why, people living in the same era and culture tend to agree upon standards of beauty, and those standards unconsciously influence other judgments. Psychologists often quote the ancient Greek poet Sappho when beginning this discussion because she once wrote, "What is beautiful is good, and who is good will soon be beautiful." The research suggests that you tend to agree with Sappho without realizing it. Unaware of the contribution of biological, psychological, and socially influenced chemical reactions inside your head, you tend to believe that what is beautiful is better than what is not in measures of worth unrelated to appearance. The affect heuristic unconsciously tells you to seek or avoid that which is considered beautiful in your culture and era, and you then follow that response with a rationalization as to why you've been struck by those feelings, whether or not you truly know the source.

In 1972, Karen Dion, Ellen Berscheid, and Elaine Walster conducted a study into how physical beauty alone can induce the halo effect. They told the subjects in the study the scientists were researching the accuracy of first impressions. Each person received three envelopes, each containing a different photograph researchers had rated beforehand on a scale of attractiveness. Those photographs—one highly attractive, one average, one not so attractive—each came with a scorecard. The subjects looked at the photographs and then judged twenty-seven different personality traits, each on a six-point scale. The subjects also put the three photos side by side and determined who among the three people would most strongly possess each of those traits. The traits ranged all over and included things such as altruism, stability, sophistication, and sexual permissiveness. The scientists also had the people in the study estimate how happy they thought the people in the photographs were in a variety of pursuits such as marriage and parenting. Finally, the psychologists presented one possible profession at a time and asked the subjects to pick the person in the pictures most likely to do that job for a living. The results in each leg of the experiment showed that with nothing else to go on, people tended to say the most attractive people possessed the most desirable traits, and possessed them more strongly than the other people in the photographs. Again, all the subjects saw was the person's face. The more attractive the person, the more the subjects rated the likelihood of her happiness, and the more joy they assumed the person felt in her marriage, job, and experience as a parent. The more beautiful the person in the photo, the more likely the subjects said it was that the person worked in a high-status career.

This tendency of the halo effect to cause physical attractiveness to color assumptions about everything else about a person sets up two scenarios, said Dion, Berscheid, and Walster. One, beautiful people don't just have the advantage of beauty, but you treat them as if they have a host of other presumed advantages that compound that advantage. And two, after years of walking through life receiving treatment as though they possess the personality traits we like to see in others, beautiful people tend to believe and act as though they truly possess those attributes. Pretty people believe they are kind, smart, decent, and whatever else the halo effect produces in the eyes of their audience—whether or not those things are true.

The way the halo effect produces the benefit of doubt you bestow upon the loveliest among us reveals itself just about everywhere. In 1974, psychologists David Landy and Harold Sigall published a study in which they handed out essays to subjects, each with one of two photos of two different women attached. Some subjects received an essay with a photo included of a woman deemed by the scientists to be attractive, and others got essays with a photo of a woman deemed unattractive. They asked the participants to rate the quality of the writing in the essays but made no mention of the photo. The more attractive the woman in the picture, the better the score, and when asked about the overall creativity and the depth of the ideas in the essay, the papers attached to the beautiful photograph were rated as being of higher quality in both areas. The essays, of course, were identical. The only difference was the photo attached. When the scientists ran the study with essays purposely written to be awful, the disparity between the ratings was magnified. As Landy and Sigall wrote, you expect better performances from attractive people, but when they fail, you are also more likely to forgive them.

A similar study, conducted by Margaret Clifford and Elaine Walster in 1973, provided more than five hundred fifth-grade teachers with files on new students that included information on their scholastic aptitude, a report card, and a photograph. The teachers believed they were helping the school determine the thoroughness and utility of their school's record-keeping system. Each file was identical, and the report cards showed scores well above the expected average. The only difference was the photo each teacher received. In a survey beforehand, twenty teachers rated a group of photographs of fifth-grade students on a scale of physical attractiveness. Out of those, researchers selected twelve photos, the three most attractive boys and the three most attractive girls along with the three most unattractive of each. In their survey, the psychologists asked another group of teachers to use the materials provided to come up with an estimate of each child's IQ, his social standing with peers, the child's parents' attitude toward school, and the student's chances of dropping out. Remember, the information was the same for each teacher; only the photo differed. What do you think they said? The results fell right in line with what psychologists expect from the halo effect. The more attractive the student, the higher the teacher estimated his IQ, the higher they rated the likelihood his parents would be involved in his education, the better-liked the student would be with friends, and the lower they estimated the chances the child would drop out. When asked to comment on their ratings, the teachers rarely mentioned the child's appearance.

In 1975, psychologists Harold Sigall and Nancy Ostrove conducted a study that showed strong evidence that criminals get lighter sentences the more physically attractive they seem to judges and jurors. In a mock trial, the researchers had subjects read an account of a burglary after reading the bio of a defendant with a photograph attached either of a highly attractive woman or of an unattractive woman (the researchers made this distinction in appearance). They then told the subjects the woman was guilty and to select an appropriate sentence of between one and fifteen years in jail. The pretty woman got three years on average. The ugly woman got, on average, five years—the same as a control that included no photograph at all.

Studies into how beauty causes you to use the halo effect as a reality-distorting filter could fill the rest of this book. Beauty provides a level of local celebrity even before a person attains widespread fame, no matter your gender or sexual orientation, and no matter the other person's. You tend to see beautiful people as more intelligent, more competent, better at whatever they do for a living, and generally happier than the rest of us. In short, as Landy and Sigall pointed out, you expect more from pretty people well before you know anything else about them, and when they fall short of your expectations, you give them more of a chance to prove themselves than you do people less symmetrical or slender or muscle-bound or bosom-heaving or whatever cultural or era-appropriate norms of attractiveness are woven into your perception.

In psychology, they call the holistic view you form about another person your global evaluation. As you can see, your global evaluation about the height or beauty of another person greatly affects your other estimations, but many other global evaluations can produce the halo effect. When it comes to your favorite bands, directors, brands, or companies, you often lie to yourself about their shortcomings. For example, if you really, truly love a particular musician or band, you will forgive their poorer works much more readily than will a less-devoted fan. You may find yourself defending their latest album, explaining the nuances to the uninitiated, wondering why they can't appreciate it. Or maybe you absolutely love a particular director or author, and believe her to be a genius who can do no wrong. When critics slam her latest movie or book,

how do you react? Like most fanatics, you probably see the dissent-
ers as naysayers and nitpickers drunk on their own haterade. The
halo effect nullifies your objectivity. The things you love and the
people who make those things get graded on a curve shaped by your
existing feelings. Their new offerings benefit from the way their old
offerings made you feel way back when. Once you think someone
is a genius, you see everything she makes as the work of a genius.

In 1977, psychologists Richard Nisbett and Timothy Wilson
showed how a global evaluation could distort one's reality by exposing American students to a Belgian accent.

They told the students that scientists needed their help figuring
out whether the results of teacher evaluations taken right after
meeting a professor were similar to the results of evaluations taken
at the end of a term. The subjects didn't know that they were actually being divided into two groups, and each would see the same
professor answer the same questions in the same Belgian lilt, but
that professor would take on a different attitude for each group.

In a video, the students saw the professor answer questions
about his teaching style. For instance, in one tape, when asked how
he preferred to handle group discussions, he said that he encouraged them. He said he loved the "give-and-take it provided" and
how group discussions generated interest in the topic. In the other
tape, asked the same question, the professor said he believed in
strict roles for students and teachers, and that students should shut
up and listen. After all, he added, he "wouldn't be the professor if
he didn't know more than they did." For one group, the professor
with the Belgian accent was warm and friendly, and for the other
group he was cold and severe. The researchers went so far as to
have the nice version of the professor explain how he was lenient
with his tests and that they allowed for the exploration of free

thoughts. The mean professor said he gave quizzes every week because he didn't trust students to do their readings.

After watching the tapes, the two groups of students then had to fill out the teacher evaluation form they had been tricked into thinking was part of some other experiment. In the evaluation, the students had to answer how much they thought they would enjoy a class with him and to rate different aspects, such as his mannerisms and physical appearance. The most important question on the form, the one that drew a chalk outline around the halo effect in each subject's brain, was the one that asked how annoying or charming they found the professor's accent.

The findings of the study showed that the students who saw the warm and friendly version of the professor thought he was attractive and had appealing mannerisms, and that his accent was no problem. About half actually thought his accent was nice. The majority of the other group, the one that saw a cold, no-nonsense professor, thought he was unpleasant to look at and had peculiar mannerisms. The biggest difference, though, was in the accent. Eighty percent of the group who met the mean version of the professor said his accent was irritating. Both groups listened to the same professor wearing the same clothes talk to them through the same Belgian accent, but for some the way he talked was fun, and for others it was grating. The only things that changed were the words he said through Belgian intonations. For one group, that accent was just another reason to like the laid-back professor given to meandering talk and daydreams. For the other group, that accent was yet another one of his defects they couldn't imagine having to deal with for an entire course. The accent didn't change; the halo did. When asked at the end of the study if they believed the professor's attitude had affected how they felt about his accent, the majority of subjects said it hadn't. They had no idea that the halo effect was changing their view of reality.

When others do this sort of thing, you sometimes notice, especially among the most extreme—for example, doting parents and fanboy fanatics. Your feelings, after all, may differ from theirs, and that is enough to bust the illusion. But as Nisbett and Wilson showed in their study, that just means they sometimes see through you as well. In between, neither party has any clue when their global evaluations prevent rational, unbiased analysis of specific traits as simple as an accent or a smile.

Falling out of love with a person's accent is just a small-scale example of the power of the halo effect to change behavior. Its power can cause much more far-reaching and damaging results. In 1976, psychologists Glen Foster and James Ysseldyke conducted a study in which they gathered primary school teachers, each with about ten years' experience, and randomly assigned each to one of four groups. Each teacher believed the study was concerned with a new form for evaluating students, but each group received a different description of the sort of students they would be describing with that form. The scientists told one group they would be dealing with emotionally disturbed children. They told another group their children were learning disabled, and a third group believed they would be dealing with the mentally retarded. The fourth group served as a control and learned nothing about their students beforehand.

Every teacher in each group then watched the same video of a fourth-grade boy going through a series of activities. The boy was specially selected to be absolutely average according to a battery of tests on everything from intelligence to appearance, and on the tape the boy performed a number of mental and physical challenges before playing for a while. On all the tests, the child scored within the expected range for a normal fourth-grader, but the teachers were not privy to that information. After the tape ended, the teachers filled out another form evaluating the child they had all watched. The scientists also asked the teachers to fill out a personality questionnaire as if they were the child, answering the questions in the manner they believed the child in the tape would. After everything was turned in and tallied, the researchers found what you've probably guessed. The teachers who believed the child was disturbed, disabled, or retarded graded him much more harshly than those who received no initial label and thus had no expectations. The child who was expected to perform poorly did indeed fulfill that expectation even though each teacher saw the same identical child perform the same identical acts in the same identical way on a video that differed in no way whatsoever from observer to observer. To the people who had no expectations going in, the perfectly normal nondeviant child completed the tasks in an acceptable manner and seemed like a typical fourth-grader. The other three groups saw a child struggling to comprehend, fraught with little demons and handicaps. Those who believed he was mentally retarded graded him worst of all.

Why did this happen? The psychologists agreed it was the halo effect in action. The teachers who had nothing to go on watched the tape and made assumptions based mostly on what they saw. The others knew exactly one fact about the child going in, and it colored everything else they added to their knowledge. As the researchers pointed out, the halo effect caused the teachers to resist conflicting evidence and maintain their initial beliefs. Instead of updating the way they saw the fourth-grader, instead of seeing him shatter their expectations, they forced him inside the confines of the box generated by the halo effect. The danger here is clear. Ignorance of the halo effect can easily set in motion a self-fulfilling prophecy in which attitude changes behavior, which then loops back around over and over for the persons both giving and receiving a label.

Politicians and corporations depend on the halo effect to survive. In the modern world any institution, be it a campaign for office or a new product launch, lives and dies by way of its reputation and must devote as much time to how others feel in their gut as they do to the quality of their products, policies, and actions. If a politician can come across as likable—as nice, genuine, and friendly—she's won most of her votes already. That initial appraisal will spread and elevate all other appraisals. Gaffes will be forgiven.

This is why it is so vitally important for a business to control its image and stay vigilant about what the public is saying about it both in private and in the echo chamber of the World Wide Web. The more likable company will usually win the pounds of consumers even when its competitor is superior in other ways. This is why so many stories appear daily in the business world about who is winning, who is in the lead, who is loved and hated. The narrative that forms around a company that is seen as a beloved champion is similar to the one that forms around the beautiful and the tall. You expect great things but readily forgive when it makes a mistake. Another company, one with a negative halo, might make the same sort of mistake and get lambasted.

The affect heuristic reduces your deep, simple, emotional, unconscious response to a person, company, product, or brand to a simple thumbs-up or thumbs-down, and then everything else produced by that source is either graded more or less harshly than if you had never been exposed before. The halo effect is such a predictable and reliable marketing tool that many halos have now become institutions in their own right. Laurels such as the Pulitzer

Prize, a Nobel Laureate, Richard and Judy's Book Club, or a *New York Times* bestseller are powerful halos that literally alter your perceptions of the content granted the accolade. Likewise, a well-written two-star review can return your debit card to your wallet.

The halo effect causes facets of a person that could easily be evaluated objectively on their own merits independent of that person's personality to become instead telling examples that further demonstrate his very nature. Qualities that would be unambiguous if contemplated alone are altered by the way you feel about a person overall. When you fall in love, your loved one's terrible rendition of "Total Eclipse of the Heart" on karaoke night is endearing and sweet. When the relationship is on the rocks, that same performance raises hackles. If your professor is easy and fun, his aloofness and unorganized office are part of his overall appeal. If his tests are pulling down your grade, his absent-mindedness causes your fists to flex whenever he is near. If your sister is fun to be around and makes you laugh, she can show up late to dinner, and you will just chalk it up to another wonderfully silly aspect of her persona. If she is a morose grouch, her lack of punctuality is one more thing you have to put up with. True objectivity, then, is almost impossible when dealing with the subtle nuances of the people in your life. Thinking about people changes your perceptions of their appearance, voice, actions, and everything else. It creates filters that alter the raw sensory experience.

Don't put people, or anything else, on pedestals, not even your children. Avoid global labels such as *genius* or *weirdo*. Realize those closest get the benefit of the doubt and so do the most beautiful and radiant among us. Know the halo effect causes you to see a nice person as temporarily angry and an angry person as temporarily nice. Know that one good quality, or a memory of several, can keep in your life people who may be doing you more harm than good. Pay attention to the fact that when someone seems nice and upbeat, the words coming out of his or her mouth will change in meaning, and if that same person were depressive, arrogant, or foul in some other way, your perceptions of those same exact words would change along with the person's other features.

When evaluating a person's skills, make an effort to keep her attributes separate from her appearance or demeanor or fame. Make sure the person is anonymous during your final evaluation, and then evaluate each attribute separately. If comparing, don't compare people as a whole, but judge them against each other one attribute at a time. Erase the names and faces; quantify and compare. The more you can force an accomplishment, a skill, or a measure of performance to stand on its own, the less likely any one ingredient will taint the whole batch. You can't prevent the halo effect, but you can use your knowledge of its power to limit its effects.

Normally, on average, the halo effect is benign and may even be preferable to cold, objective scrutiny. But it can betray you in situations that are still alien to the way your mind works. If you are in a position of authority or in a position affected by authority, know that the evaluations and assumptions of everyone from teachers to generals is perpetually in error, clouded and tinted by the global and emotionally charged assessments of the overall qualities of others. When making judgments of character, such as choosing who deserves your vote, know that things such as business experience or speaking skills or height or symmetry or seeming capacity to enjoy beer in your presence are not trivial matters. They can powerfully change the way you judge all the person's other qualities. The people in your life possess or lack virtues colored by the radiance or gloom of the halo you create for them early on.

# 6.

## Ego Depletion

**THE MISCONCEPTION:** *Willpower is just a metaphor.*

**THE TRUTH:** *Willpower is a finite resource.*

In 2005 a team of psychologists made a group of students feel like scum.

The researchers invited the undergraduates into their lab and asked them to just hang out for a while and get to know one another. The setting was designed to simulate a casual meet-and-greet atmosphere, like at a reception or an office Christmas party—the sort of thing that never really feels all that casual.

The students, divided into same-sex clusters of about six people each, chatted for twenty minutes using conversation starters provided by the researchers. They asked each other things such as "Where are you from?" and "What are you studying?" and "If you could travel anywhere in the world, where would you go?" Researchers asked the students beforehand to make an effort to learn one another's names during the hangout period, which was important, because the next task was to move into a room, sit alone, and write down the names of two people from the fake party with whom the subjects would most like to be partnered for the next part of the study. The researchers noted the responses and asked the students to wait to be called. Unbeknownst to the subjects, their choices were tossed aside while they waited.

The researchers, Roy F. Baumeister, C. Nathan DeWall, Natalie J. Ciarocco, and Jean M. Twenge, then asked the young men and women to proceed to the next stage of the activity in which the subjects would learn what sort of impression they had made on their new acquaintances at the meet-and-greet. This is where things got funky.

The scientists individually told the members of one group of randomly selected people, "Everyone chose you as someone they'd like to work with." To keep each person in the "wanted" group isolated, the researchers also told each person the groups were already too big and that he or she would have to work alone. Students in the wanted group proceeded to the next task with a spring in their step, their hearts filled with moonbeams and fireworks. The scientists individually told each member of another group of randomly selected people, "I hate to tell you this, but no one chose you as someone they wanted to work with." Believing that absolutely no one wanted to hang out with them, people in this group then learned they would have to work by themselves. Punched in the soul, their self-esteem dripping with inky sludge, the people in the unwanted group proceeded to the main task.

The task, the whole point of going through all this as far as the students knew, was to sit in front of a bowl containing thirty-five mini chocolate chip cookies and judge those cookies on taste, smell, and texture. The subjects learned they could eat as many as they wanted while filling out a form commonly used in corporate taste tests. The researchers left them alone with the cookies for ten minutes.

This was the actual experiment: measuring cookie consumption based on social acceptance. How many cookies would the wanted people eat, and how would their behavior differ from that of the unwanted? Well, if you've had much contact with human beings, and especially if you've ever felt the icy embrace of being left out of the party or getting picked last in dodgeball, your hypothesis is probably the same as the one put forth by the psychologists. They predicted the rejects would gorge themselves, and indeed they did. On average, the rejects ate twice as many cookies as the popular people. It was the same setting, same work, similar students sitting alone in front of scrumptious cookies. In their heads, though, they were on different planets. For those on the sunny planet with the double-rainbow sky, the cookies were easy to resist. Those on the rocky, lifeless world where the forgotten go to fade away found it more difficult to stay their hands when their desire to reach into the cookie bowl surfaced.

Why did the rejected group feel motivated to keep mushing cookies into their sad faces? Why is it, as explained by the scientists in this study, that social exclusion impairs self-regulation? The answer has to do with something psychologists now call ego depletion, and you would be surprised to learn how many things can cause it, how often you feel it, and how much in life depends on it. Before we get into all of that, let's briefly discuss the ego.

So there was this guy named Sigismund Schlomo Freud. He was born in 1856, the oldest of eight children. He grew up and became a doctor. He loved cocaine and cigars. He escaped the Nazis but lost his sisters to concentration camps, and in 1939, an old man in great pain from mouth cancer, he used assisted suicide to shuffle off his mortal coil. He was one of the most important thinkers of the twentieth century. He is why the word *ego* is part of everyday language, and he is probably the first face you imagine when someone says "psychology."

Despite his fame, the late 1800s wasn't a good time to be in need of mental or physical care. Medical school was mostly about anatomy, physiology, and the classics. You drew the insides of things and wondered what they did. You learned where the heart was, how to amputate a leg, and what Plato had to say about his cave. Pretty much everything useful that doctors know today was yet to be discovered or understood. Sore throat? No problem. Tie some peppered bacon around your neck. Hernia? Lie down so you can anally absorb a little tobacco smoke. The Wild West of science and medicine was only just becoming tamed, so in many places there was still debate over things such as washing your hands after dealing with a fetid corpse before inserting them still sticky into the body of a woman giving birth.

Near the end of his studies, Freud set himself to the squishy, messy task of slicing apart eels. He dissected four hundred of them, looking for testicles, a feature of the animal still unknown to science at the time. It was thoroughly disgusting and unfulfilling work, and it went nowhere. If he had found testes, his name might appear in different textbooks today. Instead, he earned his medical degree and went to work in a hospital, where he spent years studying the brain, drawing neurons, and searching in its gelatinous goop much as he had the innards of the eels. But, as it does for so many of us, money became a central concern, and to pay the bills, he abandoned the laboratory to set up his own medical practice. He remained the same intense, obsessive Freud as he searched for the source of nervous disorders by going farther and farther back into the childhoods and histories of his patients. He began to sketch out his theories about the geography and anatomy of the mind. This is how he came to produce his model of the psyche. Freud imagined behavior and thought, neurosis and malady, were all the result of an interplay and communication between mental agencies each with its own functions. He called those agencies *das Es, das Ich,* and *das Über-Ich,* or "the it," "the I," and the "over-I"—what would famously become known to English speakers as the id, the ego, and the superego. In Freud's view, the id was the primal part of the mind, residing in the unconscious and always seeking pleasure while avoiding uncomfortable situations. The ego was the realistic part of the mind, the one that considered the consequences of punching people in the face or stealing their French fries. When the ego lost a battle with the id over control of the mind, the superego would tower over the whole system and shake its metaphorical head in disgust. This, Freud thought, forced the ego to take control or hide behind denial or rationalization or any one of many defense mechanisms, so as to avoid the harsh judgment of the superego, from which morals and cultural norms exerted their influence. Of course, none of this is actually true. It was just the speculation of a well-educated man at about the same time penicillin was being discovered.

Doctors such as Freud could hypothesize whatever they wished, and if they were charismatic enough in person and on paper, they would lead the conversation in science. Once, Freud treated a female patient who complained of menstrual cramps. He sent her to an ear, nose, and throat doctor he knew who had a hypothesis that runny noses and menstruation were connected. During recovery, after her nasal cavity had received a proper chiseling, she complained of a growing pain in her sinuses that not even morphine could abate, and one night she produced two bowls of pus before horking out a piece of bone the size of a water chestnut. Freud concluded the hemorrhage was the result of a hysterical episode fueled by repressed sexual longings. A return trip to the surgeon determined the source was actually a leftover piece of gauze. Freud remained unconvinced, claiming the woman's relief had come from psychoanalysis.

The point here is that psychology has come a long way since then. Literary critic Harold Bloom said Freud's contributions to the human race, considering he was a master of metaphor, were probably best compared to Shakespeare than to Copernicus. Freud's work is still a big part of pop culture and everyday language—*Freudian slips, repression, anal retentiveness*, etc.—but it's mostly bunk, and you know this because psychology became a proper science over the last century, with rigorous lab work published in peer-reviewed journals. Still, at least one of Freud's metaphors may not have been totally mythological, and that brings us back to Roy F. Baumeister and his bowl of cookies.

In the 1990s, Baumeister and his colleagues spent a lot of time researching self-regulation through the careful application of chocolate. Self-regulation is an important part of being a person. Remember from earlier, you are the central character in the story of your life, the unreliable narrator in the epic tale of your past, present, and future. You have a sense there is a boundary between you and all the other atoms around you, a sense of being a separate entity and not just a bag of organs and cells and molecules that flopped out of the sea 530 million years ago. That sense of self cascades into a variety of other notions about your body and your mind called volition, the feeling of free will that provides you with the belief that you are in control of your decisions and choices. Volition makes you feel responsible for your actions both before and after they occur. There are a few thousand years of debate over what this actually means and whether it is an illusion through and through, but Baumeister's research over the last decade or so has pinned down ways that sense of self-control can be manipulated.

In 1998, Baumeister and his colleagues Ellen Bratlavsky, Mark Muraven, and Dianne M. Tice gathered subjects for a study. They told the participants the research was focused on taste perception, and thus each person was to skip a meal before the experiment and arrive with an empty stomach. The scientists led the subjects one at a time into a room with an oven that had just finished baking sweets and had each person sit down in front of a selection of two foods—chocolate chip cookies stacked high and a lone bowl of radishes. The subjects didn't know they had been divided into three groups. The researchers asked members of one group to eat only the radishes and to take note of the sensations for follow-up questions the next day. Another group was to eat only the cookies. A final group wasn't brought into the cookies and radishes room at all. The psychologists left the testing room for five minutes and returned with a questionnaire about mood. According to Baumeister's book on his research, *Willpower,* written with the help of John Tierney, the typical radish eater stared the cookies down like a gunfighter at high noon. Some even went so far as to grab the cookies and put them to their noses. If they couldn't have the taste, they could at least take a long, deep drag on the aroma. Still, the radish group stuck to the rules; not one of them ate a cookie, but not without some anguish. Next the subjects in groups that ate food moved on to a second experiment along with the group that skipped the food completely. The task was to sit and solve puzzles. All each subject had to do was trace a geometric figure without lifting his or her pencil or retracing any lines. They were told they could take as long as they wanted, but they weren't told that the puzzles were impossible to solve. For the next thirty minutes, the scientists watched and recorded the behavior of the participants, eager to see how long it would take each one to give up.

On average, the people left out of the room with the radishes and the cookies worked for about 20 minutes before admitting defeat. The people allowed cookies persevered for about nineteen minutes. The people who got stuck with the radishes, and had to fight off their impulse to gobble up a delicious confection in a room saturated with chocolate fumes, quit after approximately eight minutes. Baumeister said of this, "Resisting temptation seems to have produced a psychic cost." Somehow the evidence suggested that the more you restrain that which Freud would have called your id, the more difficult it becomes to restrain it. Freud would probably have said the more your ego fought the id, the more it held it down, the more tired, exhausted, and weak your ego became. With a nod and wink, Baumeister named this process ego depletion.

Baumeister and his colleagues soon discovered many other ways to get people to give up early. In one study, students were divided into three groups. One group had to give a speech supporting raising tuition costs at their university. A second group chose between a speech for or against tuition hikes. A third group proceeded directly to the second stage: those devious, unsolvable puzzles. This time both the no-speech group and the group that gave the speech with which they likely disagreed lasted about twice as long as the people who got to choose which side to take in their speech. The results suggested it wasn't just restraint in the face of desire that could deplete your ego, but any choice at all. The subjects who didn't have to choose a topic were able to allow their volition to take a break, and their ego energy reserves remained intact for the later puzzle test.

Another study had participants attempt to show and feel no emotion while watching a video of either stand-up comedy or an actor pretending to die from cancer. They then tried to solve word puzzles along with people who had watched the same videos with the freedom to feel whatever they wished. This time the people who exerted emotional restraint subsequently solved fewer puzzles than those who let their feelings flow.

In a study about active and passive choices, subjects had to find all instances of the letter *e* on a piece of paper filled with nonsense text. Another group had to find every *e* that was at least two letters distant from a vowel. Try it yourself in this paragraph and you'll notice that the first group's task was way easier and required little effort. Next, people in each group individually watched a video of a blank wall while holding a remote control. For some people, pressing a button would end the video. For others, pressing down kept the video running. The subjects then had to watch the boring video until they believed they had seen enough to answer a questionnaire about it. Nothing ever happened in the video, but something might have happened at any moment as far as the subjects knew. Each person was also told as soon as he or she ended the video that they would get to watch a clip from the comedy show *Saturday Night Live*. The people who first performed the easy task and then had to press a button to end the boring video did so much sooner than the depleted group. They also held the button down longer when letting it go meant ending the clip. The depleted group just went with whatever was the most passive option. If it was to press a button, they procrastinated. If it was to hold a button down, they gave up sooner. The results suggested that focused concentration made people less eager to make active choices later.

A great deal of your thoughts and behaviors are automatic and unconscious. Blinking and breathing, for example, need no help from the conscious part of you. A good chunk of your behavior, such as driving to work or toweling off after a shower, just happens while your conscious mind drifts off to think about *Game of Thrones* or how you'll approach your boss for a raise. If you touch a hot stove, you recoil without thought. Your desire to avoid dark alleys and approach embraces occurs without your input. When moved by a song or a painting or a kitten, the emotional rush comes without volition. Much of your mental life is simply not under your conscious control, and Baumeister's research suggests that once you take the helm every act of volition diminishes the next.

It is as if the mind were a terribly designed experimental spaceship. As long as the ship travels in a straight line it burns very little fuel, but as soon as the pilot takes over in any way, to dive or bank or climb, this imaginary ship burns fuel at an alarming rate, leaving behind less fuel with which to steer in the future. At some point you must return the craft to autopilot until it can be refueled, or else it crashes. In this analogy, taking control of the human mind includes making choices, avoiding temptation, suppressing emotions and thoughts, and acting in a way deemed appropriate by your culture. Saying no to every naughty impulse, from raiding the refrigerator to skipping class, requires a little bit of willpower fuel, and once you spend that fuel it becomes harder to say no the next time. All Baumeister's research suggests that self-control is a strenuous act. As your ego depletes, your automatic processes get louder, and each successive attempt to take control of your impulses is less successful than the last. Yet ego depletion is not just the effects of fatigue. Being sleepy, drunk, or in the middle of a meth binge will certainly diminish your ability to resist pie, but what makes ego depletion so weird is that the research suggests the system can also get worn out just from regular use. Inhibiting and redirecting your own behavior in any way makes it more difficult to delay gratification and persevere in the face of adversity or boredom in the future.

So why is it, then, that the students hit by the rejection bus, the ones told that no one had picked them after listening to them prattle at the fake party, couldn't keep the cookies out of their mouths? It seems that ego depletion can go both ways. Getting along with others requires effort, and thus much of what we call prosocial behavior involves the sort of things that deplete the ego. The results of the social exclusion study suggest that when you've been rejected by society it's as if somewhere deep inside you ask yourself, "Why keep regulating my behavior if no one cares what I do?"

You may have felt the urge to shut down your computer, shed your clothes, and walk naked into the woods, but you don't do it. With differing motivations, many people have famously exited society to be alone: Ted Kaczynski, Henry David Thoreau, and Christopher McCandless, to name a few. As with these three, most don't go so far as to shed all remnants of the tools and trappings of modern living. You may decide one day to throw middle fingers at the material world and head into the wild, but you'll probably keep your shoes on and take a pocketknife at the very least. It's a compelling idea nonetheless—leaving society with no company. You enjoy watching shows such as *Born Survivor*. You revisit tales such as *Castaway* and *Robinson Crusoe* and *Life of Pi*. It's in our shared experience, a curiosity and a fear, the idea of total expulsion from the rest of your kin.

Ostracism is a potent and painful experience. The word comes from a form of punishment in ancient Athens and other large cities. The Greeks often expelled those who broke the trust of their society. Shards of pottery, *ostracon,* were used as voting tokens when a person's fate was on the ballot. Primates like you survive and thrive because you stick together and form groups, keeping up with those prickly social variables such as status and alliance, temperament and skill, political affiliation and sexual disposition, to prevent ostracism. For a primate, banishment is death. Even among your cousins the chimps, banishment is rare. The only lone chimps are usually ex-alpha males defeated in power takeovers. Chimpanzees will stop hanging out with the ostracized one, stop grooming him, but they rarely banish. A human completely on his own usually doesn't make it very long. Your ancestors probably survived not only by keeping away from spiders, snakes, and lions, but also by making friends and not rocking the boat too much back at the village. It makes sense, then, that you feel an intense, deep pain when rejected socially. You have an innate system for considering that which might get you ostracized. When you get down to it, most of what you know others will consider socially unacceptable are behaviors that would demonstrate selfishness. People who are unreliable, who don't pitch in, or share, or consider the feelings of others, get pushed to the fringe. In the big picture, stealing, raping, murdering, committing fraud, and so on harm others while sating some selfish desire of an individual or a splinter group. Baumeister and his group wrote in the social-exclusion paper that being part of society means accepting a bargain between you and others. If you will self-regulate and not be selfish, then you get to stay and enjoy the rewards of having a circle of friends and society as a whole, but if you break that bargain, society will break its promise and reject you. Your friend groups will stop inviting you to parties and will unfollow you on Twitter. If you are too selfish in your larger social group, it might reject you by sending you to jail or worse.

The researchers in the "no one chose you" study proposed that since self-regulation is required to be prosocial, you expect some sort of reward for regulating your behavior. People in the unwanted group felt the sting of ostracism, and that reframed their self-regulation as being wasteful. It was as if they thought, Why play by the rules if no one cares? It poked a hole in their willpower fuel tanks, and when they sat in front of the cookies, they couldn't control their impulses as well as the others could. Other studies show that when you feel ostracized and unwanted, you can't solve puzzles as well; you become less likely to cooperate, less motivated to work, more likely to drink and smoke and do other self-destructive things. Rejection obliterates self-control, and thus it seems it's one of the many avenues toward a state of ego depletion.

So, looking back on all this, what about the nutty propositions put forth by Freud? All this talk about mental energy, impulses, and cultural judgment sounds as if we are validating the ideas of the id, ego, and superego, right? Well, that's why psychologists have been working so hard to pinpoint what is being depleted when we speak of ego depletion, and according to one hypothesis it may just be the fuel your brain gains from digested food: glucose.

A study published in 2010 conducted by Jonathan Leval, Shai Danziger, and Liora Avniam-Pesso looked at 1,112 judicial rulings concerning prisoner paroles over the course of ten months. They found that right after breakfast and lunch, your chances of getting paroled were at their highest. On average, the judges granted parole to around 60 percent of prisoners right after the judge had eaten a meal. The rate of approval crept down after that. Right before a meal, the judges granted parole to about 20 percent of those appearing before them. The less glucose in judges' bodies— that is, the longer they'd gone since eating—the less willing they were to make the active choice of setting a person free and accepting the consequences and the more likely they were to go with the passive choice to put the fate of the prisoner off until a future date.

The glucose correlation is made stronger by another study by

Baumeister, in 2007, in which he had people watch a silent video of a woman talking while words flashed in the lower right-hand corner. The subjects' task was to try as best they could to ignore the words. The scientists tested blood glucose levels before and after the video and compared them with those of a control group who watched the video without special instructions. Sure enough, the people who avoided the words had lower blood glucose levels after the video than the control group. In subsequent experiments the subjects drank either Kool-Aid with sugar or Kool-Aid with Splenda right after the video and then proceeded to the sorts of tasks that tend to reveal ego depletion in the lab: word puzzles, geometric line tracing puzzles, tests of emotional restraint, tests of suppression of prejudicial attitudes, tests of altruism, etc. The people who thought they'd gotten an energy boost (the Splenda group) tended to perform worse than those who actually got their glucose replenished (the sugar group). Thus it seems you are more able to exert willpower and control, to make decisions and suppress naughtiness, by eating and drinking beforehand (which sucks if the things over which you need willpower are food and drink).

The research into what is called the resource model of self-control is still new and incomplete. Some scientists have challenged the idea that glucose is the resource being depleted because a conscious brain should have plenty of glucose available to exert self-control at any given time. They argue that some other psychological mechanism is governing its release, and speculate that the effects are more likely some sort of evolutionarily molded resource-allocation program. Once you've completed a task requiring significant self-control, your motivation and attention are manipulated by internal forces to seek rewards for a while. But if an even better prospect emerges or a serious threat looms, your motivation will be freed up again so you can press on. For instance, you might chase a deer for an hour, refusing to give in to the pain in your legs, but once you slay the beast, you feel a strong desire to rest and eat. If a hungry predator appears at that moment, you forget the relaxation and go back to running. This is called the process model of ego depletion, and it hypothesizes that although you have the glucose to spend, your brain becomes frugal after mental exertion and dampens your motivation. Reward cues become more salient in the environment, and tasks requiring self-control become less attractive. If at that moment the brain becomes highly motivated, it will happily use its available glucose, say proponents of the process model. In some experiments subjects are able to stave off ego depletion after receiving a gift, a swish of sugar water, or a chance to engage in nonboring tasks, which adds more evidence that the reward system of the brain plays a significant role in ego depletion and that glucose is not the only factor. Research continues, and for now the idea of ego depletion is still a metaphor for something more complex and nuanced that has yet to be fully understood.

The current understanding of this is that all brain functions require fuel, but the executive functions seem to require the most. Or, if you prefer, the executive branch of the mind has the most expensive operating costs. Studies show that when low on glucose, or when the brain becomes frugal toward its reserves, those executive functions suffer. That mental state harkens back to the way Freud and his contemporaries saw the psyche as a battle between brute primal desires and the contemplative self. The early psychologists would have said your id runs amok when your ego is weak. We now know it may just be your prefrontal cortex dealing with a lack of glucose or your internal banker refusing to release funds.

Remember, no matter what the self-help books say, the research suggests that willpower isn't a skill. If it were, there would be some consistency from one task to the next. Instead, every time you exert control over the giant system that is you, that control gets weaker. If you hold back laughter in a church or classroom, every subsequent silly notion is that much funnier, until you run the risk of bursting into snorts.

The only way to avoid this state of mind is to predict what might cause it in your daily life and to avoid those things when you need the most volition. Modern life requires more self-control than ever. Just knowing Reddit.com is out there beckoning your browser, or that your iPad is waiting for your caress, or that your smartphone is bursting with status updates, requires a level of impulse control unique to the human mind. Each abstained vagary strengthens the pull of the next. Remember, too, that you can dampen your executive functions in many ways, such as by staying up all night for a few days, or downing a few alcoholic beverages, or holding your tongue at a family gathering, or resisting the pleas of a child for the umpteenth time. Having an important job can lead to decision fatigue, which may lead to ego depletion simply because big decisions require lots of energy, literally, and when you slump, you go passive. A long day of dealing with bullshit often leads to an evening of no-decision television in which you don't even feel like switching the channel to get Kim Kardashian's face off your screen, or watching a censored *Goodfellas* between commercials even when you own a DVD of the film and it's sitting five feet away. If so, no big deal, but if you find yourself in control of air traffic or a heart bypass, or you need to lose two hundred pounds, that's when it's time to plan ahead. If you want the most control over your own mind so that you can alter your responses to the world instead of giving in and doing what comes naturally, stay fresh. Take breaks. Get some sleep. And until we understand just what ego depletion really is, don't make important decisions on an empty stomach.

# 7.

## The Misattribution of Arousal

---

**THE MISCONCEPTION:** *You always know why you feel the way you feel.*

**THE TRUTH:** *You can experience emotional states without knowing why, even if you believe you can pinpoint the source.*

The bridge is in British Columbia, long and scary, still sagging across the Capilano Canyon, daring people to traverse it.

If you were to place the Statue of Liberty underneath the bridge, base and all, the bridge would lightly drape across her copper shoulders. It is about as wide as a park bench for its entire suspended length, and when you try to cross it, feeling it sway and rock in the wind, hearing it creak and buckle, it is difficult to take your eyes off the rocks and roaring water 230 feet below—far enough for you to feel in your stomach the distance between you and a messy, crumpled death. Not everyone makes it across.

In 1974, psychologists Art Aron and Donald Dutton hired a woman to stand in the middle of this suspension bridge. As men passed her on their way across, she asked them if they would be willing to fill out a questionnaire. At the end of the questions, she asked them to examine an illustration of a woman covering her face and then make up a back story to explain it. She then told each man she would be more than happy to discuss the study further if he wanted to call her that night, then tore off a portion of the paper, wrote down her number, and handed it over.

The scientists knew the fear in the men's bellies would be impossible to ignore, and they wanted to know how a brain soaked in anxiety juices would make sense of what had just happened. To do this, they needed another bridge to serve as a control, one that wouldn't produce terror, so they had their assistant go through the same routine on a wide, sturdy, wooden bridge standing fixed just a few feet off the ground.

After running the experiment at both locations, they compared the results and found that 50 percent of the men who got the digits on the dangerous suspension bridge picked up a phone and called looking for the lady of the canyon. Of the men questioned on the secure bridge, the percentage who came calling dropped to 12.5. That wasn't the only significant difference. When they compared the stories the subjects made up about the illustration, they found that the men on the scary bridge were almost twice as likely to come up with sexually suggestive narratives.

What was going on here? One bridge made men flirty and eager to follow up with a female interviewer, and one did not. To make sense of it, you must understand something psychologists call arousal, mentioned earlier in the form of cognitive dissonance, and how easy it is to falsely identify its source. Mistaken emotional origins can save relationships, create amorous mirages, and lead you into behaviors and attitudes both sublime and hypocritical.

Arousal, in the psychological sense, is not limited to sexual situations. It can envelop you in a number of ways. You've felt it: increased heart rate, focused attention, sweaty palms, dry mouth, big breaths followed by bigger sighs. It is that wide-eyed, electricity-in-your-veins feeling you get when the wind picks up and the rain begins to pour. It is a state of wakefulness, more alert and aware than normal, in which your mind is paying full attention to the moment. This isn't the action-roll-out-of bed-feeling you get when a fire alarm snaps you out of a deep sleep. No, arousal is prolonged and total; it builds and saturates. Arousal comes from deep inside the brain, in those primal regions of the autonomic nervous system where ingoing and outgoing signals are monitored and where the glass over the big Fight-or-Flight button waits to be smashed. You feel it as a soldier waiting to see if the next mortar has his name on it, as a musician walking onstage inside a sold-out stadium, as a crowd member elevated by a powerful speech, in a group circling a fire and singing and drumming, as a member of a congregation swimming in the Gospel and swaying with hands raised, in a couple at the center of a packed dance floor. Your eyes water with ease. You want to weep and laugh simultaneously. You could just explode.

The men on the bridge experienced this heightened state of clarity, fear, anxiety, and dread, and when they met an attractive woman, those feelings continued to flow into their hearts and heads, but the source got scrambled. Was it the bridge or the woman? Was she just being nice, or was she interested in me? Why did she pick me? My heart is pounding; is she making me feel this way? When Aron and Dutton ran the bridge experiment with a male interviewer (and male subjects), the lopsided results disappeared. The men no longer considered the interviewer as a possible cause for their arousal—or, if they did, they suppressed it. The misattribution of arousal also went away when they ran the experiment on a safe bridge. No heightened state, no need to explain it. On a hunch, Aron and Dutton decided to move the experiment away from the real world, with all its uncontrollable variables, and attack the puzzle from another direction, in the lab.

In the lab experiment male students entered a room filled with scientific-looking electrical equipment where a researcher greeted them by asking if they had seen another student wandering around. When the men said they hadn't, the scientists pretended to go looking for the other subject, leaving the men behind to read material concerning learning and painful electric shocks. When the scientists felt that enough time had passed, they brought in an actress who pretended to be a student who had also volunteered for the study. The men, one at a time, would then sit beside the woman and listen as the scientists explained that one of the two would soon be shocked with either a terrible, bowel-loosening megablast or a "mere tingle." After this, the researchers flipped a coin to determine who would be getting which level of shock. They weren't actually going to shock anyone; they just wanted to scare the bejeezus out of the men. The researchers then handed over a questionnaire similar to the one from the bridge experiment, complete with the illustration-interpretation portion, and told the men to work on it while they, the researchers, prepared the electrocution machines.

The questionnaire asked the men to rate their anxiety and their attraction to the female subject. As the scientists suspected, the results matched those from the bridge. The men who expected a terrible, painful shock rated their anxiety and their attraction to the woman as significantly higher than those expecting mild tingles. When it came to the narratives explaining the illustrations, once again the more anxious the men, the more sexual imagery they produced in their descriptions. Afterward, the subjects were de-briefed and told there would be no electrical torture after all.

Aron and Dutton showed that when you feel aroused, you naturally look for context, an explanation as to why you feel so alive. This search for meaning happens automatically and uncon-sciously, and whatever answer you come up with is rarely ques-tioned because you don't realize you are asking. Like the men on the bridge, you sometimes make up a reason for why you feel the way you do, and then you believe your own narrative and move on. It would be easy to pinpoint the source of your contorted face and toothy grin if you took peyote at the Burning Man festival and were twirling glow sticks to the beat of a pulsating lizard-faced bassoon quartet. The source of your coursing blood would be more ambiguous if you had just drunk a Red Bull before heading into a darkened cinema to watch an action movie. You can't know for sure if it is the explosions or the caffeinated taurine water, but, damn, if this movie doesn't rock. In many situations you either can't know or fail to notice what got you physiologically amped, and you mistakenly attribute the source to something in your im-mediate environment. People are your favorite explanations, as studies show that when given the option, you prefer to see other human beings as the source of your heightened state of arousal. The men expecting to get electrocuted misattributed a portion of their pulse's pace to the woman by their side. Aron and Dutton focused on fear and anxiety, but in the years since, research has revealed that just about any emotional state can be misattributed, and this has led to important findings on how to keep a marriage together.

In 2008, psychologist James Graham conducted a study to see what sorts of activities kept partners bonded. He had twenty couples who lived together carry around digital devices while conducting their normal daily activities. Whenever the device went off, they had to use it to text back to the researchers and tell them what they were up to. They then answered a few questions about their mood and how they felt toward their partner. After more than a thousand of these buzz-report-introspect-text moments, Graham looked over the data and found that couples who routinely performed difficult tasks together as partners were also more likely to like each other. Over the course of his experiments, he found that partners tended to feel closer, more attracted to, and more in love with each other when their skills were routinely challenged. He reasoned the buzz you get when you break through a frustrating trial and succeed was directly tied to bonding. Just spending time together is not enough, he said. The sorts of activities you engage in are vital. Graham concluded you are driven to grow, to expand, to add to your abilities and knowledge. When you satisfy this motivation for self-expansion by incorporating aspects of your romantic partner or friend into your own skills, philosophies, and self, it does more to strengthen your bond than any other act of love. This opens the door to one of the best things about misattribution of emotion. If, like those in the study, you persevere through a challenge—be it remodeling a kitchen yourself or learning how to dance the Dougie—that glowing feeling of becoming wiser, that buoyant sense of self-expansion, will be partially misattributed to the presence of the other person. You become conditioned over time to see the relationship itself as a source for those sorts of emotions, and you become less likely to want to sever your bond with the other party. In the beginning, just learning how to relate to the other person and interpret his or her nonverbal cues, emotional mood swings, and strange food aversions is an exercise in self-expansion. The frequency of novelty can diminish as the relationship ages and you settle into routines. The bond can seem to weaken. To build it up again you need adversity, even if simulated. Taking ballroom dancing lessons or teaming up against friends in a game of mini-golf is more likely to keep the flame flickering than wine and Marvin Gaye.

The arousal you are prone to misattributing can also come from within, especially if you find yourself on questionable moral ground. In 1978, Mark Zanna and Joel Cooper gave placebo pills to a group of subjects. They told half the pill takers the drug would make them feel relaxed, and the other half that it would make them feel tense. They then asked the subjects to write an essay explaining why free speech should be banned. Most people were reluctant and felt terrible about expressing an opinion counter to their true beliefs. When the researchers gave all the participants a chance to go back and change their papers, the ones who thought they had taken a downer were far more likely to take them up on the offer. The ones who thought they had taken a speed pill assumed the heat under their collars was from the drug instead of their own cognitive dissonance, so they didn't feel the need to change their positions. The other group had no scapegoat for their emotional state, so they wanted to rewrite the paper because they suspected it would ease their minds and bring their arousal back down to normal. Once again you can see how cognitive dissonance, behaving or thinking in a way that seems to run counter to your beliefs, cranks up arousal in a way that feels awful. The subjects in the Zanna and Cooper experiment wanted to alleviate this, but only those who thought they swallowed downers could pinpoint the source of their mental discomfort. For the other group, the fake upper, instead of their own negative emotions, became the explanation.

Misattribution of arousal is another phenomenon, like the Benjamin Franklin effect, that falls under the self-perception theory. If you recall, the theory posits that your attitudes are shaped by observing your own behavior and trying to make sense of it. One of the founders of psychology, William James, believed you often look back on a situation as if in an audience trying to understand your own motivations. James would say if you saw a cricket on your arm and then flailed about rubbing your body up and down while screaming incoherently, you would later assume you had experienced fear and might then believe you were afraid of crickets. Sometimes you jump to conclusions without all the facts. You often act as an observer of your actions, a witness to your thoughts, and you form beliefs about yourself based on those observations. To explore this, psychologist Fritz Strack devised a simple experiment in 1988 in which he had subjects hold a pen straight out between their incisors and bare their teeth as they read comic strips. The subjects tended to find the cartoons funnier than when they held the pen between their lips. When the pen was between the teeth, some of the muscles used for smiling were contracted; when it was between the lips, the muscles used for frowning were contracted. He concluded that the subjects felt themselves smiling and decided somewhere deep in their minds that they must be enjoying the comic strip. When they felt themselves frowning, they assumed they thought the comics were dull. In a similar experiment done in 1980 by Gary Wells and Richard Petty, subjects were asked to test out headphones by either nodding or shaking their heads while listening to a pundit delivering an editorial. Sure enough, when questioned later, the nodders tended to agree with the opinion of the speaker more than the shakers. In 2003, Jens Förster asked volunteers to rate food items as their names moved across a large screen. Sometimes the food names moved up and down, and sometimes from side to side, thus producing unconscious head nodding or shaking. As in the pundit study, people tended to say they preferred the foods that made them nod, unless they were disgusting. In Förster's and other similar studies, positive and negative opinions became stronger, but if a person hated broccoli, for example, no amount of head nodding would change his mind.

Arousal can fill up the spaces in your brain when you least expect it. It could be a rousing movie trailer or a plea for mercy from a distant person reaching out over YouTube. Like a coterie of prairie dogs standing alert as if living periscopes, your ancestors were built to pay attention when it mattered, but with cognition comes pattern recognition and all the silly ways you misinterpret your inputs. The source of your emotional state is often difficult or impossible to detect. The time to pay attention can pass, or the details become lodged in a place beneath consciousness. In those instances, you feel but you know not why. When you find yourself in this situation you tend to lock onto a target, especially if there is another person who fits with the narrative you are about to spin. It feels good to assume you've discovered what is causing you to feel happy, to feel rejected, to feel angry or lovesick. It helps you move forward. Why question it?

The research into arousal says you are bad at explaining yourself to yourself, but it sheds light on why so many successful dates include roller coasters, horror films, and conversations over coffee. There is a reason that playful wrestling can lead to passionate kissing, that a great friend can turn a heaving cry into a belly laugh. There is a reason great struggle brings you closer to friends, family, and lovers. There is a reason John Lewis commercials show a woman going through life's traditional milestones while Fyfe Dangerfield sings Billy Joel's "She's Always a Woman." When you want to know why you feel the way you do but are denied the correct answer, you don't stop searching. You settle on something—the person beside you, the product in front of you, the drug in your brain. You don't always know the right answer, but when you are flirting over a latte, don't point it out.

# 8.

## *The Illusion of External Agency*

---

**THE MISCONCEPTION:** *You always know when you are making the best of things.*
**THE TRUTH:** *You often incorrectly give credit to outside forces for providing your optimism.*

When you are happy, you rarely take the metacognitive step backward required to realize that your brain is responsible for that emotion.

You think, I am happy because I've just eaten a key lime cupcake, but you rarely think, I am happy because my brain is telling me to be happy because I've just eaten a key lime cupcake. Just parsing out the language is confusing. When you think of the person who is you, are you thinking of your entire brain and body, or only a portion? Probably the whole organism. Although neuroscience asks us more urgently each year to see our conscious self as only a fraction of the total mind produced by the brain, it isn't something you can easily accept.

Sitting there now, reading this, you feel as if you were the self you imagine, the self who is in control of your body and who experiences inputs both corporeal and intangible, tactile and emotional. You are the thinker. You are the feeler. Yet there are situations in which those sensations of ownership and volition can be manipulated and drastically altered. In fact, there are times throughout your life when you have given credit for your emotions to imaginary sources. Take a second if you have to. I realize this idea furrows the brow, but in the lab, it is possible to demonstrate that you sometimes can't tell you are the person responsible for your own thoughts and emotions. Not only that, but it is also possible to redirect ownership of those feelings to someone or something else.

In psychology, the notion that there is a thinking being behind an event is called agency, and an agency-detection system comes preinstalled in every human brain. The most common example is to imagine yourself in a jungle. You hear a rustling in the leaves. Is it the wind or a tiger? Best not dally, so let's assume it is a tiger and choose the fight-or-flight or the stop-breathing-and-hope-it-walks-the-other-way response. That default sense that unknown forces might be caused by conscious, hungry things is your sense of agency. It is why you find it so difficult to ignore suspicious bumps in the night. Some part of you asks the other parts of you to investigate just in case there is an agent behind the noise. The driving force behind investigations into a great deal of spooky, mysterious, weird, and unexplained phenomena is the human instinct to assume there must be agency behind all manner of creepy things, whether or not there is much evidence for it.

You don't just assume agency for outside forces. You also assume there is an agent behind your own actions: you. You naturally assume that you are the agent behind the decision to move your arm, and that you are the agent responsible for the words coming out of your mouth. It seems pretty obvious, but it isn't a perfect system. In fact, it is the source of one of your most common and least detectable cognitive errors. You don't always recognize your own agency, and the entire system can be scrambled with just a little manipulation. To understand how, let's cover a few building blocks of your self-delusion.

*Affect,* as you may recall from before, is the technical term for how you subjectively experience your emotional state. In psychology, the act of predicting the future of your emotions is called affective forecasting. If someone came around the corner right now and handed you a slice of cherry cobbler, complimented you on your facial features, read a poem that related to how your week was going, and then hugged you before disappearing to take care of your laundry for the week, how would that make you feel? Your act of prediction just now was affective forecasting. Over the course of hundreds of studies going back to when it was okay to wear sequined jumpsuits to night clubs, one thing has become clear as crystal: You are really bad at affective forecasting. You are strongly biased to overestimate the impact of both good and bad outcomes on your emotional hereafter. When you imagine a good event such as winning the lottery, or a bad event such as a car crash, your predictions about what you would feel following those events are often way off. That, psychologists say, is your impact bias. You are biased to overestimate the emotional impact of future events. Like a weatherman who tells viewers to expect torrential floods from light showers, your internal mood forecaster is always blowing out of proportion predictions of the future of your heart. Thus, your impact bias contaminates your affective forecasting, making that forecasting much less accurate.

In 1978, psychologist Phillip Brickman and his colleagues questioned major lottery winners and paralyzed accident victims about their overall happiness and found there was little difference, not only between the two groups but also between either group and the general public. A sort of happiness homeostasis prevented the accident victims from becoming depressed yet also kept the lottery winners from floating away in bliss. There was something happening in their minds over time—a regression to the mean. Like a bobber on a fishing line, no matter how deep their moods sank or how high they arose, their moods eventually returned to a previous state just slightly above the midpoint. The time it took for the extreme emotions to fade varied, but two or three months was about all it took for most people. Brickman helped coin a term to describe this phenomenon: *the hedonic treadmill.*

Okay, so that gets us to where we need to be. Affective forecasting and the hedonic treadmill are part of a larger phenomenon called, unimaginatively, your psychological immune system. When you feel damaged by rejection, loss, shame, humiliation, powerlessness, and all the other dark emotional states, or what psychology calls negative affects, your mind has a tremendous capacity for psychological healing. If you move to a new city to start a new career and then get laid off right after your children's first day of school, you will get over it, and soon. Should your house burn down with your entire collection of out-of-production air sickness bags, you will quickly feel just fine about losing both the collection and the home. Should you poop your pants on television while attempting to juggle reproduction Nazca pottery, your shame will rapidly fade. Of course, you don't believe any of that when predicting the future, much less during the awful event itself, because you are terrible at affective forecasting.

One of the components of your psychological immune system with the most potential to cause self-delusion is called subjective optimization. To truly beat your brain, you need to understand how it forces you to refuse credit when credit is due.

You know that friend of yours who got pregnant and moved away to marry the guy she had sex with one time instead of going to nursing college, and who then ended up having another baby and getting a divorce before meeting and marrying that guy who owns a homemade dog treat business that makes their house smell like charred liver? She will never know if moving away instead of heading to college was the right decision, but she seems to think it was. When you talk to her, she says life couldn't be better, but how would she know? That, my friend, is what psychologists call subjective optimization—seeing life as it is as being the best it could be. Like the font Helvetica, once you learn about subjective optimization, you'll see it everywhere. Except, of course, in yourself. When you find yourself in a bad situation that can't be easily escaped, you have the power to transmogrify misfortune into luck. Like everything else that happens within your psychological immune system, it is completely invisible to your conscious mind.

Subjective optimization complements sour grapes, the inclination to see that which you can't have as that which you didn't want in the first place. Subjective optimization makes whatever you get stuck with seem better than that which you can no longer obtain. Metaphorically, it is the process that makes lemons into lemonade. Unconsciously, your automatic systems work to force your attention to the bright side of bad outcomes. You receive the mental lemonade and enjoy it, but you never see the lemons from which it was squeezed.

You can see subjective optimization coming to rescue those in a state of loss in a 1999 study by psychologists Daniel Gilbert and Jane Jenkins. They created a photography course at Harvard, and to the students it seemed like a normal course on how to use a camera and develop film. Each person was tasked with going out and snapping pictures of things she wanted to remember from her time at university. Once the students had twelve photos ready to be developed, the instructors told them to pick two negatives that would be blown up into eight-by-ten portraits. Once they had the photos in front of them, big and beautiful and meaningful, the students were then told to pick only one to keep. The other they would have to leave behind with the instructors as proof that they had finished the assignment, and that photo would not be returned. They were told they had to make their decision right away, but a second group was given time to think and could change their minds as many times as they needed before settling on one photo. When questioned much later, the group who was forced to pick and stick reported loving their choices. The photo they had to give up was long forgotten. The group who had a few days to decide reported feeling as though they had made a mistake. They were left wondering, maybe forever, if the photo they were stuck with was less meaningful to them than the one with which they had parted. They yearned to go back in time and change their choices. The researchers concluded that you are more likely to subjectively optimize, to make lemonade out of lemons, in an unchangeable situation. The people without a choice were later happy. The people with a choice were later sad. Getting locked into a situation with no hope of escape activates subjective optimization.

Some say that because in the modern, industrialized, and affluent world nothing is limited to one or two options anymore, that power to make yourself happy is being hampered. Head over to Amazon and search for paper clips. You'll find over two thousand varieties to choose from. What about peanut butter? A quick search pulls up nearly five thousand products from creamy to chunky to individually wrapped gourmet drops. The bewildering amount of choice you have when it comes to how you spend your money is mirrored in all the ways you can spend your life. As psychologist Barry Schwartz points out in his book *The Paradox of Choice,* just one hundred years ago your options as to career, spouse, and hometown were so limited as to be almost nonexistent in comparison with the options you have today. This lack of choice was true for humans going back all the way to your fishlike ancestors. Most of the history of sapient beings was spent locked up in a life with little opportunity and living through situations they had no choice but to deal with or get kicked out of the gene pool. It makes sense, then, that you evolved a nifty mechanism to deal with the loads of crap your brain predicts will eventually fall into your lap.

That system works well, in part because it happens unconsciously. The downside is that you find it difficult to predict your own unconscious systems. Gilbert and Jenkins asked the subjects at the beginning of the photo study which situation they would rather be in, and most people said they would much rather be in the group with more choice—what psychologists call a changeable outcome. That's what you always think you want, more choice, more outs, more options, but the results suggest that sort of situation saps the power of your psychological immune system. Since it works in the shadows, underneath consciousness, you have a very hard time factoring it into your predictions. The researchers called this tendency to be blind to your psychological immune system and to make predictions based on events instead of on your likely interpretation of those events immune neglect.

Subjective optimization ensures that if you were kidnapped and locked away in a dungeon with a bucket, a book about bowties, and a daily regimen of dirt-seasoned oatmeal, you would find a way to look on the bright side (at least they gave you a book). If your marriage crumbled, or your business went belly-up, somehow, in a covert operation hidden from your conscious mind, you would find a way to say it was the best thing that had ever happened to you. You have a hard time believing this, but that's because immune neglect redacts every shred of evidence that would prove you are actively changing your reality to stay happy and sane.

This brings us to one of the most powerful self-delusions your mind is capable of producing, and back to where we started in this chapter. You'll recognize it immediately now that you understand its foundations.

In a series of studies in 2000, psychologists Daniel Gilbert, Ryan Brown, Elizabeth Pinel, and Timothy Wilson showed that subjective optimization can lead you to believe in invisible forces, forces controlling your happiness and fate. First, though, they had to get people in a controlled environment to subjectively optimize.

It turns out that it is actually rather easy to induce subjective optimization in a test subject. All you have to do is offer a selection of possible outcomes, things that the test subject will or will not receive at some point in the study. Next, make sure one of those outcomes sucks, and then rig the system so your subject gets the crappy outcome. You can now sit back and watch the magic as your subject instinctively changes the way she sees the thing she got stuck with. If you've done your job well, the subject will form a positive viewpoint about a thing she would otherwise have rated as unwanted. If you are an ethical scientist, you will debrief your subject at the end to reveal your manipulation; otherwise your subject, thanks to her immune neglect, will never know she changed her own mind.

Gilbert, Brown, Pinel, and Wilson were counting on that last part when they created their study. They hypothesized that since you are always generating artificial sunshine to brighten up your day, yet you remain unaware of that process, when you reflect on your life and wonder where all the brightness is coming from, you rarely point the finger at your own head. Instead, you point toward whatever invisible forces match up with your beliefs. You see an intangible benevolence that harmonizes with your worldview as the source of your good fortune.

In one study, they placed women in cubicles. To make physical attraction less a factor, everyone in the study was female. The scientists explained to them that each was taking part in research along with four other women who were also in cubicles nearby. This was a lie. The subjects were actually alone. The researchers then told each subject that eventually she was to pick one of the other women as her partner based on a short autobiography and survey. To that end, each subject then had to fill out a bio and a survey, believing that the other people in the study would use those items to make their own choices as well. At this point, the subjects were divided into two groups. Group A received the biographies of the four fake potential partners and rated how well they liked each one. Group B just moved on to the next section.

Next, each participant watched a video puzzle in which letters jumped around the screen. The researchers explained that this video would help them judge the subjects' abilities and asked them to mark down each time a vowel appeared. During the video, flashes of light would occasionally interrupt the action. The researchers told the subjects to ignore the flashes. Those were just technical difficulties, the scientists said.

After all this, each subject from both groups was shown four folders, each with a different symbol printed on the outside. In the interest of fairness, the scientists explained, they had decided to randomly assign partners instead of letting the participants choose, and in each folder was the biography of one of the other subjects. What the subjects didn't know was that each folder contained the bio of the subject most people had said they wanted to be partnered with the least. The subjects made their choices, each picking one of the four folders, and each then believed she had randomly received the crappy outcome.

Next, the women in Group A again rated the same four biographies they received in the beginning, when they thought they would have a choice. Group B also rated all four, but for the first time. After this, the scientists told everyone involved that the study was over, but it wasn't. They were pulling one of the best tricks in psychological research: the fake debriefing.

In the fake debriefing, the experimenters told each subject that the flashes of light in the video were actually subliminal messages designed to influence her choice of folder by implanting a symbol in her mind. The scientists explained that they used the survey materials to decide who would be the best choice for the subject out of the four possible partners and then used the subliminal messages to get her to pick the best one. This is where the true purpose of the study, unbeknownst to the subjects, came into play. The researchers asked each woman, now that she knew the "truth," to rate which of the four fake subjects she felt was truly the best partner and to rate the effectiveness of the subliminal flashes. Remember, the flashes were fake; there had been no subliminal messages. Each folder contained the same partner for each person, and that partner was the least desired choice.

The majority of women in both Group A and Group B said

that, yes, the partner they got stuck with was the best possible partner out of the four. All subjectively optimized, just as the scientists expected them to. But when it came to the subliminal messages, the groups differed. Women in Group B, the group that did not get to rate their possible partners at the beginning, reported significantly more belief in the power of the subliminal messages. As the scientists pointed out in the study, it is well known in psychology that you find it difficult to change your mind about a person after your first impression. They speculated that this meant that people in Group A found it harder to subjectively optimize than people in Group B because they had already picked someone out of the four. Even though they eventually reported liking their random partner best, they reported liking their partner to a lesser degree than did people in Group B. As the scientists wrote in their paper, "it is easier to subjectively optimize in prospect than in retrospect." All the subjects manipulated their personal realities to match the outcome they got stuck with and now believed the worst choice for them was the best choice for them. In hindsight, they made themselves feel that they had lucked out, but people in Group B did so much more quickly and smoothly than did Group A. When presented with a ready-made narrative—we, the benevolent scientists with insight into your mind, have influenced the outcome in your favor—the people in Group B were much more likely to accept that explanation and be happy with it. This, the scientists said, showcased your strange habit of attributing your emotional well-being to someone or something not inside you. Even though everyone in the study was responsible for how they viewed reality and how happy they were with their fates, when given the option to place responsibility for that fate outside themselves, they took it. The psychologists coined a term to describe this: *the illusion of external agency.*

*David McRaney*

In another version of the experiment, the researchers told people that they were testing two new radio programs similar to Pandora, Last.fm, Spotify, and other such services that use the participants' tastes to select new songs for them. Based on the answers the subjects provided in a pre-study questionnaire, the scientists explained, the subjects would hear a selection of music that matched their responses. One group listened to short clips of both a nice song and a song the scientists predicted the subjects would find awful, and then that group was told the computer program believed they had preferred the awful song. They then were asked to listen to the bad song three times in a row. For a second group, the scientists switched the order of the procedure. The researchers forced the second group to first listen to the awful song three times in a row and then said afterward the program had picked that song for them based on their tastes. After that, the second group then listened to clips from both the good and bad songs. So the same information went into the brains of the participants in each group, but the order of how it was presented differed. After the listening sessions, people in both groups rated the music they had just heard. The scientists then asked people in both groups if they would like to listen to more music chosen by the program they had been using so far, or if they would like to switch to a new program. Eighty-one percent of the first group switched, but only 57 percent of the second group opted to try the new service. Whether they chose to keep the original or use a new program, each group heard the same music after that choice. Finally, the scientists asked the subjects how likely it was they would pay to use either computer program if those programs ever made it to market.

The results showed that the people who first heard clips from both the good song and the bad song rated the two appropriately, and then paid attention to the things they disliked about the bad song when they later endured it three times in a row. Because of this, the people in the first group didn't believe the music program demonstrated much insight into their preferences. The people in the second group, who heard the bad song first, were then told it had been selected based on their tastes, and then heard clips of the good song, said at the end that they liked both songs equally. As you may have guessed, the people in Group A said they probably wouldn't pay for the service, but people in Group B said they would.

It was as if Group A thought, Oh, yuck, one of these songs is not very good. Then, when they had to hear that song three times in a row, they were primed to pay attention to the things that confirmed their first impression. When they learned that the program disagreed, they thought, Based on my emotions, I think this program is crap. I would not buy it. Meanwhile, it was as if Group B thought, I am about to hear a song this program says I will like. When they listened to it three times in a row, they gave it the benefit of the doubt and attended more to what they liked about it than what they did not. When they then heard it alongside another song that was obviously good, they thought, I like the first song, so I must like both of these songs about the same. Based on my emotions, I think this program is not crap. I would buy it. The people in the second group, unaware it was happening, used subjective optimization to talk themselves into liking a song they would otherwise have hated, and then made a choice based on an invisible self-delusion: trust in a fallible external agent. Stranger still, there was no program. The scientists set everything up to fool people into giving credit for their self-generated emotional states to a nonexistent machine.

In both groups, the more a person said he liked the awful song, the more likely he was to say he would buy the service that picked it for him. Thanks to immune neglect, when a person in either group liked the bad song, he had no idea he had fooled himself into believing he enjoyed music he would probably have avoided in another setting. With nothing else to go on, he assumed he was pleased because an outside force must have insight into what he preferred. Just as in the other study, the scientists provided a reasonable source for this insight, and the subjects who subjectively optimized accepted it.

When you subjectively optimize an inescapably bad situation, you focus on the positive elements alone and see them as far more desirable and awesome than you would if you were standing on the outside. You will manipulate every outcome to seem as if it were the best possible outcome for you. Since you do this all the time, there will come moments in your life when it will seem that everything is going your way when it actually isn't. Over time, you might become a bit curious as to how so much good fortune could be bestowed upon you on a daily basis. You can't see that it is coming from within, so you assume it must be coming from without, and thus you look for an agent. If you find one, you will disavow your own ability to make the best of a bad situation and put that power in the hands of something else if a reasonable option is presented.

This is a mistake, a delusion that is generating ideas that are not true, yet you believe them, often for the rest of your life. In the end, this is just pattern recognition gone haywire. In your effort to turn chaos into order, noise into signal, and to trace down causes to the effects in your life, you erroneously look outside yourself when sometimes the source is in your own mind. You are making things seem better than they are, but you can't believe it, so you blame something else. This is not necessarily a bad thing. The alternative, after all, is the stark, cold truth of a world without anything in your subjective reality optimized or touched up to seem more beautiful, more delicious, more desirable, more nourishing, more meaningful, than it would be without this lens. To beat your brain is to see the danger in believing in forces that do not exist and trusting them when you would do better to trust yourself. Remember the people who believed they enjoyed a bad song? All it took was presenting the information in just the right order for those people to mistake their own perceptions. Had the situation been real, they would have bought into a program that was terrible at selecting music for them to enjoy. Pretend these last few sentences aren't describing a study, but that they are a metaphor for every moment in your life henceforth. Before you buy into any system, before you place trust in any external agent real or invisible, ask yourself if the positive emotions you are feeling come from within or without.

So much of life is impossible to do over, so many situations are impossible to change without harming people important to you, that you learn to change the way you see the world because it is easier than changing the world itself. As the scientists put it, you have a "healthy capacity for generating satisfaction" within the tribulations of an imperfect life. When you discuss world history, you may argue over whether one course of action or another was the right move, but you will never know if you are right, because history gets one run-through. The nearly infinite alternate courses it could have taken are forever unknowable. Likewise, when you argue whether your friends, family, or acquaintances should have gone down one path or another, you can be disappointed and upset on the outside, but they are not. They always seem pleased—

blessed, even—that things worked out the way they did. That's because they have the same capacity to alter their view of reality that you possess. Your personal historian is usually quite happy with the outcome of your life so far. Sure, it could have gone this way or that, but then you wouldn't have all the nice things you are thankful for, no matter whom you thank when you count your blessings.

# 9.

## *The Backfire Effect*

---

**THE MISCONCEPTION:** *You alter your opinions and incorporate the new information into your thinking after your beliefs are challenged with facts.*

**THE TRUTH:** *When your deepest convictions are challenged by contradictory evidence, your beliefs get stronger.*

*Wired, The Times, Backyard Poultry Magazine*—they all do it. Sometimes they screw up and get the facts wrong. Via ink or in photons, a reputable news source takes the time to say "my bad."

If you are in the news business and want to maintain your reputation for accuracy, you publish corrections. For most topics this works just fine, but what most news organizations don't realize is a correction can further push readers away from the facts if the issue at hand is close to the heart. In fact, those pithy blurbs hidden on a deep page in every newspaper point to one of the most powerful forces shaping the way you think, feel, and decide—a behavior keeping you from accepting the truth.

In 2006, researchers Brendan Nyhan and Jason Reifler created fake newspaper articles about polarizing political issues. The articles were written in a way that would confirm a widespread mis-conception about certain ideas in American politics. As soon as a person read a fake article, experimenters then handed over a true article that corrected the first. For instance, one article suggested that the United States had found weapons of mass destruction in Iraq. The next article corrected the first and said that the United States had never found them, which was the truth. Those opposed to the war or who had strong liberal leanings tended to disagree with the original article and accept the second. Those who sup-ported the war and leaned more toward the conservative camp tended to agree with the first article and strongly disagree with the second. These reactions shouldn't surprise you. What should give you pause, though, is how conservatives felt about the correction. After reading that there were no WMDs, they reported being even more certain than before that there actually were WMDs and that their original beliefs were correct.

The researchers repeated the experiment with other wedge is-sues, such as stem cell research and tax reform, and once again they found that corrections tended to increase the strength of the par-ticipants' misconceptions if those corrections contradicted their ideologies. People on opposing sides of the political spectrum read the same articles and then the same corrections, and when new evidence was interpreted as threatening to their beliefs, they dou-bled down. The corrections backfired.

Researchers Kelly Garrett and Brian Weeks expanded on this work in 2013. In their study, people already suspicious of electronic health records read factually incorrect articles about such technolo-gies that supported those subjects' beliefs. In those articles, the sci-entists had already identified any misinformation and placed it within brackets, highlighted it in red, and italicized the text. After they finished reading the articles, people who said beforehand that they opposed electronic health records reported no change in their opinions and felt even more strongly about the issue than before. The corrections had strengthened their biases instead of weakening them.

Once something is added to your collection of beliefs, you protect it from harm. You do this instinctively and unconsciously when confronted with attitude-inconsistent information. Just as confirmation bias shields you when you actively seek information, the backfire effect defends you when the information seeks you, when it blindsides you. Coming or going, you stick to your beliefs instead of questioning them. When someone tries to correct you, tries to dilute your misconceptions, it backfires and strengthens those misconceptions instead. Over time, the backfire effect makes you less skeptical of those things that allow you to continue seeing your beliefs and attitudes as true and proper.

In 1976, when Ronald Reagan was running for president of the United States, he often told a story about a Chicago woman who was scamming the welfare system to earn her income. Reagan said the woman had eighty names, thirty addresses, and twelve Social Security cards she used to get food stamps, along with more than her fair share of money from Medicaid and other welfare entitlements. He said she drove a Cadillac, didn't work, and didn't pay taxes. He talked about this woman, whom he never named, in just about every small town he visited, and it tended to infuriate his audiences. The story solidified the term *welfare queen* in American political discourse and influenced not only the national conversation for the next thirty years, but public policy as well. It also wasn't true.

Sure, there have always been people who scam the government, but historians say no one who fit Reagan's description ever existed. The woman most historians believe Reagan's anecdote was based on was a con artist with four aliases who moved from place to place wearing disguises, not some stay-at-home mum surrounded by mewling children.

Despite the debunking and the passage of time, the story is still alive. The imaginary lady who Scrooge McDives into a vault of food stamps between naps while hardworking Americans struggle still appears every day on the Internet. The mimetic staying power of the narrative is impressive, and stories like this often provide one of the main foundations for the backfire effect. Psychologists call them narrative scripts, stories that tell you what you want to hear, stories that confirm your beliefs and give you permission to continue feeling as you already do. If believing in welfare queens protects your ideology, you accept it and move on. You might find Reagan's anecdote repugnant or risible, but you've accepted without question a similar anecdote about pharmaceutical companies blocking research, or unwarranted police searches, or the health benefits of chocolate. You've watched a documentary about the evils of . . . something you dislike, and you probably loved it. For every Michael Moore documentary passed around as the truth there is an anti–Michael Moore documentary with its own proponents trying to convince you their version of the truth is the better choice.

A great example of selective skepticism is the website literally unbelievable.org. It collects the Facebook comments of people who believe that articles from the satire newspaper *The Onion* are real. Articles about Justin Bieber ending up in intensive care after being badly booed, Kim Jong-Un coming out in support of gay marriage, and George W. Bush saying he still believes the Iraq war was "the fun thing to do"—all these are commented on with the same sort of "yeah, that figures" outrage. As the psychologist Thomas Gilovich said, "When examining evidence relevant to a given belief, people are inclined to see what they expect to see, and conclude what they expect to conclude . . . for desired conclusions, we ask ourselves, 'Can I believe this?,' but for unpalatable conclusions we ask, 'Must I believe this?'"

This is why hard-core doubters who believe Barack Obama was not born in the United States will never be satisfied with any amount of evidence put forth suggesting otherwise. When the Obama administration released the president's long-form birth certificate in April of 2011, the reaction from so-called birthers was as the backfire effect predicts: They scrutinized the timing, appearance, and format of the certificate and then gathered online and mocked it. They became even more certain than before of their beliefs. The same has been and will forever be true for any conspiracy theory or fringe belief. As famous conspiracy debunker and neurologist Steven Novella says, contradictory evidence strengthens the position of the believer. It is seen as part of the conspiracy, and missing evidence is dismissed as part of the cover-up.

This helps explain how strange, ancient, and kooky beliefs resist science, reason, and reportage. As the Internet becomes simpler to search and more broadly accessed, it becomes easier to retreat to a safe haven of disparaging evidence. Perhaps that's why polls show that, in the United States, belief in evolution has remained at about 39 percent since the 1980s, even as more evidence is added daily to the mountain already available online. It's also a likely culprit behind the sharp drop in the belief in global warming, going from 77 percent acceptance in the United States in 2006 to 67 percent acceptance in 2012. Without a doubt, the backfire effect is also making it difficult to snuff out the thriving antivaccination move-ment, despite millions of dollars in research indicating that vac-cines are safe. The persistent efforts of U.S. antivaccination activ-ists in the face of evidence of vaccines' validity caused the worst outbreak of whooping cough in the U.S. in seventy years in 2012, according to *Forbes*.

On these issues, you probably count yourself among the reason-able. You don't see yourself as a kook. You don't think thunder is a deity going for a 7-10 split. Your beliefs are rational, logical and fact-based, right? Well, consider a topic such as spanking. Is it right or wrong? Is it harmless or harmful? Is it lazy parenting or tough love? Science has an answer, but let's get to that later. For now, savor your emotional reaction to the issue and realize you are willing to be swayed, willing to be edified on a great many things, but you keep a special set of topics separate. The last time you got into, or sat on the sidelines of, an argument online with someone who thought she knew all there was to know about immigration reform, the European Union, gay marriage, climate change, Scot-tish independence, the budget deficit, Dr Who or whether or not 0.9999 repeated to infinity was equal to one—how did it go?

Did you teach the other party a valuable lesson? Did she thank you for edifying her on the intricacies of the issue after cursing her heretofore ignorance, doffing her virtual hat as she parted from the keyboard a better person?

No, probably not. Most online battles follow a similar pattern, with each side launching attacks and pulling evidence from deep inside the Web to back up its position until, out of frustration, one party resorts to an all-out ad hominem nuclear strike. If you are lucky, the comment thread will get derailed in time for you to keep your dignity, or a neighboring commenter will help initiate a text-based dog pile on your opponent.

What should be evident from the studies on the backfire effect is you can never win an argument online. When you start to pull out facts and figures, hyperlinks and quotes, you are actually making the opponent feel even surer of his position than before you started the debate. As he matches your fervor, the same thing happens in your skull. The backfire effect pushes both of you deeper into your original beliefs.

Climate scientist John Cook and psychologist Stephan Lewandowsky write in their pamphlet, *The Debunking Handbook*, "A simple myth is more cognitively attractive than an over-complicated correction." Multiple lines of research back up this advice. The more difficult it becomes to process a series of statements, the less credit you give them overall. During metacognition, the process of thinking about your own thinking, if you take a step back and notice that one way of looking at an argument is much easier than another, you will tend to prefer the easier way to process information and then leap to the conclusion that it is also more likely to be correct. In experiments where two facts were placed side by side, subjects tended to rate statements as more likely to be true when those statements were presented in simple, legible type than when printed in a weird font with a difficult-to-read color pattern. Similarly, a barrage of counterarguments taking up a full page seems to be less persuasive to a naysayer than a single, simple, powerful statement.

Have you ever noticed the peculiar tendency you have to let praise pass through you, but to feel crushed by criticism? A thousand positive remarks can slip by unnoticed, but one "you suck" can linger in your head for days. One hypothesis as to why this and the backfire effect happen is that you spend much more time considering information you disagree with than you do information you accept. Information that lines up with what you already believe passes through the mind like a vapor, but when you come across something that threatens your beliefs, something that conflicts with your preconceived notions of how the world works, you seize up and take notice. Some psychologists speculate there is an evolutionary explanation. Your ancestors paid more attention and spent more time thinking about negative stimuli than positive because bad things required a response. Those who failed to address negative stimuli failed to keep breathing.

In 1992, Peter Ditto and David Lopez conducted a study in which subjects dipped little strips of paper into cups of saliva. The paper wasn't special, but the psychologists told half the subjects the strips would turn green if they had an enzyme deficiency that made it more likely to develop a pancreatic disorder in the future, and told the other half it would turn green if they were free and clear. Both groups were told the reaction would take about twenty seconds, but in reality the paper would never change to green. The people who were told the strip would turn green if they were safe, and then saw the color remain unchanged, tended to wait much longer to see if it would change, far past the time they were told it would take. When it didn't change color, 52 percent retested just to make sure. The other group, the ones for whom a green strip would be very bad news, tended to wait only twenty seconds and move on. Only 18 percent retested.

When you read a negative comment, when someone shits on what you love, when your beliefs are challenged, you pore over the data, picking it apart in search of weaknesses. The cognitive dissonance locks up the gears of your mind until you deal with it. In the process, you form more neural connections, build new memories, and put out effort—once you finally move on, your original convictions are stronger than ever.

The backfire effect constantly shapes your beliefs and memory, keeping you consistently leaning one way or the other through a process that psychologists call biased assimilation. Decades of research into a variety of cognitive biases show you tend to see the world through thick Coke-bottle lenses forged from belief and smudged with attitudes and ideologies. When scientists had people watch Bob Dole debate Bill Clinton in 1996, they found supporters tended to believe their preferred candidate won. In 2000, when psychologists studied Clinton lovers and haters throughout the Monica Lewinsky scandal, they found Clinton lovers tended to see Lewinsky as an untrustworthy home wrecker and found it difficult to believe Clinton had lied under oath. The haters, of course, felt quite the opposite. Flash-forward to 2011, and you have the right-wing Fox News and the liberal MSNBC battling for cable journalism territory, both promising a viewpoint that will never challenge the beliefs of a certain portion of the audience. Biased assimilation guaranteed.

Geoffrey Munro and Peter Ditto concocted a series of fake scientific studies in 1997. One set of studies said homosexuality was probably a mental illness. The other set suggested homosexuality was normal and natural. They then separated subjects into two groups. One group said they believed homosexuality was a mental illness, and the other did not. Each group then read the fake studies full of pretend facts and figures suggesting that their worldview was wrong. On either side of the issue, after reading studies that did not support their beliefs, most people didn't report an epiphany, a realization that they'd been wrong all those years. Instead, they said the issue was something science couldn't understand. When asked about other topics later on, such as spanking or astrology, these same people said they no longer trusted research to determine the truth. Rather than shed their belief and face facts, they rejected science altogether.

Science and fiction once imagined the future in which you now live. Books and films and graphic novels of yore featured cyberpunks surfing data streams and personal communicators joining a chorus of beeps and tones all around you. Short stories and late-night pocket-protected gabfests portended a time when the combined knowledge and artistic output of your entire species would be instantly available at your command, and billions of human lives would be connected and visible to all who wished to be seen.

So, here you are, in the future, surrounded by computers that can deliver to you just about every fact humans know, the instructions for any task, the steps to any skill, the explanation for every single thing your species has figured out so far. This once-imaginary place is now your daily life.

If the future we were promised is now here, why isn't it the ultimate triumph of science and reason? Why don't you live in a social and political technotopia, an empirical nirvana, an Asgard of analytical thought minus the jumpsuits and neon headbands where the truth is known to all?

Among the many biases and delusions in between you and your microprocessor-rich, skinny-jean Arcadia is a great big psychological beast called the backfire effect. It has always been there, meddling in the way you and your ancestors understood the world, but the Internet unchained its potential, elevated its expression, and you've been none the wiser for years.

As social media and advertising progress, confirmation bias and the backfire effect will become more and more difficult to overcome. You will have more opportunities to pick and choose the kind of information that gets into your head, along with the kinds of outlets you trust to give you that information. Services such as Facebook already employ algorithms that edit the posts from your contacts so that what you see from moment to moment inside their walled gardens is most likely to be something with which you agree. In addition, advertisers will continue to adapt, not only generating ads based on what they know about you, but also creating advertising strategies on the fly based on what has and has not worked on you so far. The media of the future may be delivered based on not only your preferences, but also how you vote, where you grew up, your mood, the time of day or year—every element of you that can be quantified. In a world where everything comes to you on demand, your beliefs may never be challenged, and when they are, you can retreat into a bubble of confirmation and denial more easily than ever before.

Three thousand spoilers per second rippled away from Twitter in the hours before Barack Obama walked up to his presidential lectern and told the world that Osama bin Laden was dead. Novelty Facebook pages, get-rich-quick websites, and millions of e-mails, texts, and instant messages related to the event preceded the official announcement. Stories went up, comments poured in, search engines burned white hot. Between 7:30 and 8:30 P.M. on the first day, Google searches for bin Laden saw a 1 million percent increase from the number the day before.

It was a dazzling display of how much the world of information exchange had changed in the years since September 2001, except in one predictable and probably immutable way: Within minutes of learning about Seal Team Six, the headshot tweeted around the world, and bin Laden's swift burial at sea, conspiracy theories began to bubble in the ooze of the Internet sea. Days later, when the world learned they would be denied photographic proof, the conspiracy theories grew legs, left the ocean, and evolved into self-sustaining undebunkable life forms.

It requires real changes in the physiology of your brain to accept new information demanding that you see the world in a new way. Neuroscientist Kevin Dunbar showcased this when he put students in a brain scanner and showed them research debunking their own theories. He established what the students believed about the effectiveness of antidepressants, and then placed the subjects in the machine, where he showed them data that either backed up or disproved what they said they believed. When shown data that agreed with their opinions, Dunbar saw the areas in the students' brains associated with learning light up and take in more blood. When the students were shown information debunking their preconceived notions, the learning areas of their brains didn't come online; instead, the areas associated with effortful thinking and thought suppression showed increased activation. According to Dunbar, you shouldn't expect people to change their minds just because you present them with facts that contradict their misconceptions. If you do, those brains will actively prevent learning from taking place. The good news is that Dunbar's research has also shown this working in the other direction. In studies of students who are close to earning a degree in physics, he saw the same sort of thought suppression and effortful thinking when they watched videos illustrating commonly held misconceptions about gravity and motion. They damped their old, naïve intuitions in the same way the other students had dampened their acceptance of new ideas. Non-physics students didn't have the same reaction. This suggests that people can come around to the truth, but it takes a long time, and you shouldn't expect one argument or one conversation to make much of an impact.

As information technology progresses, the behaviors you are most likely to engage in when it comes to belief, dogma, politics, and ideology seem to remain fixed. In a world blossoming with new knowledge, burgeoning with scientific insights into every element of the human experience, like most people, you still pick and choose what to accept even when it comes out of a lab and is based on a hundred years of research.

So, how about spanking? After reading all this, do you think you are ready to know what science has to say about the issue? Here's the skinny: Psychologists are still studying the matter, but the current thinking says spanking generates compliance in children under seven if done infrequently, in private, and using only the hands. Now, here's a slight correction: Other methods of behavior modification, such as positive reinforcement, token economies, time out, and so on are also quite effective and don't require any violence.

Reading those words, you probably had a strong emotional response. Now that you know the truth, has your opinion changed?

# 10.

*Pluralistic Ignorance*

---

**THE MISCONCEPTION:** *Many of your private beliefs are in disagreement with what most people think.*
**THE TRUTH:** *On certain issues, the majority of the people believe that the majority of the people in a group believe what, in truth, the minority of the members believe.*

Have you ever been befuddled in a classroom, or a business meeting, or an intervention, and when the person running the show asks, "Okay, raise your hand if you don't understand," you pass on the opportunity to clear up your confusion? Why do you do that?

When a person asks a question this way—say, a professor in an algebra course—she is unwittingly conjuring up a psychological phenomenon that has diverted the lives of millions going back to the first humans. You are probably familiar with what follows the moment an instructor asks, "Show of hands, who is confused?" You usually pause for three seconds, frantically dart your eyes around the room, and decide you must be the only person who has no idea what is going on and then decide to keep your hand right where it is. After a few more seconds, the teacher says, "Okay, great. Moving on . . ."

If you could have moved into the minds of your classmates, you would have seen that most of them also had no clue, and that they, too, waited to see if they were alone and then did nothing. In a situation like this, a wave of insecure uncertainty passes through the collective, with all persons wondering if they are alone in their confusion. Each person then refuses to act because she fears the hundred-eye gaze of disrespect that might turn toward her. The result is a totally inaccurate view of reality in which everyone thinks she knows what the majority is thinking, and each person believes she is in the mental minority. In the end, the ignorance is telepathically transferred to the teacher, who moves on to new material thinking her classroom is particularly sharp and her technique brilliant. The topics of the day may have been clarified for you, and your grade might have improved because of it, if not for a nasty little booger called pluralistic ignorance. To understand how it dominates other aspects of your life, we must first explore some basic sociology.

As the philosopher Terence McKenna liked to say, cultures are operating systems for brains. To continue the metaphor—the shared beliefs, values, and norms of your society are the software running on the hardware in your head. Of course, the hardware in your head isn't hard; it's a goopy undercooked flan of neurons and supportive cells, but you get the idea. You come hardwired for all sorts of situations, but that hardware gets modified, enhanced, suppressed, and rerouted by the cultural milieu into which you were born. Beliefs are the things most people believe to be true. Values are the interpretation of what is right and wrong, important and silly, ethical and unethical. Norms, though, have the most influence on your actions and thoughts. Norms are the rules of behavior within a culture that determine what is and is not acceptable from one circumstance to the next. Sometimes they are written down, maybe even codified into law; sometimes they osmote into your sensibilities as you grow up immersed in a society. The fascinating thing about beliefs, values, and norms is that they change over time. As the biologist Richard Dawkins writes in his fantastic book about natural selection, *The Selfish Gene,* units of culture, which he calls memes, mutate and compete just like genes, and over time memes evolve to better fit the environment and to help the organisms they serve survive and thrive. Just as the shape and size of horses has changed dramatically, going from a wolf-size forest creature fifty million years ago to a plains-trampling beast today, so, too, have the norms surrounding ideas such as prostitution, homosexuality, property rights, dining etiquette, and every other intangible aspect of the complex human renditions of primate social behavior. Your culture is a highly evolved system suited for survival, just like your brain.

One of the best things about owning a brain is how you often seem to phase out of normalcy and briefly see your culture with a weirdly objective frame of mind. At some point every child realizes money is made up of slips of paper with no intrinsic value, and wonders why aloud. So, too, will children ask adults what's up with shaking hands, or putting your fork on one side of the plate, or saying "Bless you" after a sneeze. Parents apply the glue that holds a culture together when explaining to a child that his socks must match, or that punctuality is paramount, or that picking his nose in public is a terrible habit. When a parent tells a boy he shouldn't play with dolls, or a girl that she shouldn't dream of being a footballer, they are enforcing norms. When a kid asks, "But, why?" she is rightfully bringing to the attention of the adult world that all this stuff is just made up and mostly arbitrary nonsense often clung to for some long-forgotten reason. That feeling you sometimes get when you snap out of your culture for a moment, when the operating system crashes and slowly reboots, has been the subject of literature and drama for thousands of years. It was so perfectly concentrated and presented in Shirley Jackson's 1948 short story "The Lottery" that many people cancelled their subscriptions to *The New Yorker* for publishing something so subversive. In the story, residents of a small town gather each year to draw names of people in their community and then stone to death the person chosen at random. No one knows why they do it, and no one remembers how it all got started, but everyone seems to enjoy the event, and the old-timers revel in the town's enthusiasm for holding to tradition.

In every new situation, you innately seek out and follow norms like spilled water seeking its level, because doing so is an adaptive response built into the primate brain. A person who faces the entire universe alone rarely prospers for long. Fears of embarrassment and ostracism, and the pleasure of belonging and feeling acceptance, are always pushing and pulling on your behavior. Knowing this deep down, you instinctively work to ingratiate yourself with a group, and groups work off norms. Conforming to those norms and other group expectations keeps social creatures such as you alive. The only problem with this strategy is that you are really, really bad at understanding other people, much less the intricate topography of group dynamics.

You've likely noticed over the years that people often tend to adhere to norms of behavior they internally don't agree with. If you aren't particularly religious, you still say grace before your grandmother cuts into the turkey, and if you are particularly religious, you still hit the casino from time to time. If you've been at your job for a while, you could probably spend an afternoon explaining to your boss all the things you and your coworkers think should change around there, things no one says when the boss is in the room. The norms that hold a culture together escalate by an arrangement of concentric circles of tradition. Your family has its ways of doing things; then your friends, your employer or university, your community, your ethnic subculture, your socioeconomic peer group, your town, nation, and so on. Since norms alter your behavior from one setting to the next, they can build upon one another until they dictate voting, policy making, governance, and giant social movements. Still, in many situations, people stick to norms only when everyone is watching. In Mississippi, the deeply religious culture of the region influenced lawmakers to write legislation that said casinos couldn't operate in the state. But casinos are allowed to operate right off the beaches, moored to the ocean floor, as long as there is the semblance of a separation from the land. But is the water along the border really in the state? In designing this setup, it was as if the religious and political hive mind said, "I mean, really, what is land anyway? If you wade out into the ocean, who is to say when you are and are not in Mississippi?" An interesting side effect of allowing casinos to conduct business in this way was that although devout Baptists denounced the evils of gambling between the pews on Sundays, they often found themselves laughing away their embarrassment on Saturdays when a fellow congregate waved from the other side of the nickel slots.

When you display an attitude that matches the attitude of the majority, even though you disagree with the implications of that attitude, you might be in what psychologists call a state of pluralistic ignorance—a state, by definition, shared by many others. Pluralistic ignorance is the erroneous belief that the majority is acting in a way that matches its internal philosophies, and that you are one of a small number of people who feel differently, when in reality the majority agrees with you on the inside but is afraid to admit it outright or imply such through its behavior. It is as if your beliefs and behaviors get tangled up like a cat in a skein of yarn. The problem is that you play it safe and adhere to the norms, but the norms are just beliefs themselves. You get stuck in a logic spiral in which the thing that everyone calls a norm is actually just what the majority believes is the norm. Confused? Let's proceed to some examples so you can beat your brain.

In the early 1990s, Deborah Prentice and Dale Miller attempted to provide answers to some of the looming questions concerning norms in sociology and psychology. If it is generally accepted that you usually conform publicly to the norms of whatever culture in which you rest your bones, then how did you figure out what those norms were in the first place? What makes you feel like you have accurately identified the norms that will provide you with social acceptance?

In a study published in 1993, Prentice and Miller gathered students at Princeton University and had them fill out surveys about alcohol consumption. Binge drinking and the overall culture of drunken revelry on university campuses was a topic much debated across the country at the time, and Princeton was one of the university campuses soaked deepest in the sauce. They wrote in their study that reunions at the university at that time held the record for the second-highest level of alcohol consumption of any event in the United States other than the Indianapolis 500. So the scientists believed it would be a great place to study a norm, because the culture of excessive drinking would be something new batches of incoming freshmen would have to face year after year.

In the first survey of the campus, they asked students how comfortable they were with the culture of alcohol consumption at Princeton. The psychologists followed up with a question about how comfortable the subjects believed the average student felt about the drinking habits at the university. In that initial study, sure enough, the results came back strongly suggesting that a veil of pluralistic ignorance rested on the heads of the students of Princeton concerning alcohol norms. The majority of the students reported that privately they were much less comfortable with the drinking habits on campus than the majority of students. Not only did most people actually feel similarly uncomfortable privately and assume they were alone in that belief, but the variation in personal comfort levels disappeared when considering the status quo. In other words, the level of discomfort varied when students considered their internal attitudes, but that variability vanished when they imagined how everyone felt, and instead became a communal belief that everyone on campus was equally pleased as punch with the idea of drinking to excess. Prentice and Miller speculated that students tended to see their friends drinking way too much at social gatherings and those students then assumed that their peers must be enjoying themselves, and that, therefore, their friends obviously endorsed the attitude of the majority. The truth, though, was that the students were observing their friends acting comfortable in public with a norm they privately rejected. So, both in small groups and on the campus at large, the norm reinforced itself even though most people disagreed with it.

In 1991 the university handed over a gold mine of data to Prentice and Miller while the researchers continued picking apart the phenomenon. The university instituted a ban on beer kegs. The president of the university announced the ban publicly, and it was repeated on local media over and over again in stories about out-of-control drinking. Like any great symbolic gesture, the ban divided the culture. In interviews and editorials, students and alumni announced their hatred of the keg ban, and protests formed. Even those who had long since graduated organized protests because they felt the ban would ruin their reunions.

For Prentice and Miller, the keg ban presented a great opportunity to study the effects of pluralistic ignorance, and they leapt at it. The psychologists already knew that the majority of students were much less enthusiastic about alcohol than they publicly presented themselves to be. In addition, since most students publicly pretended to be gung ho about jelly shots and keg stands, the majority of students felt personally at odds with the norms of the culture. So, the scientists hypothesized, only a few people would actually assemble to yell and carry signs proclaiming disgust with the university's decision to end keggers forever. Yet, when students saw the outliers protesting and making a great fuss, fueling headlines and nightly news segments, the nonprotesting students felt even more alone than before in their private attitudes. Prentice and Miller started up a new study, this time asking students to compare their private attitudes toward the keg ban to how they assumed the majority of students felt. Once again, pluralistic ignorance showed up in the answers as the majority of students said they personally felt much less negative toward the policy than most other students. The next questions revealed something amazing. When asked if they were likely to attend future reunions, the more a student felt deviant from the presumed norms of the majority, the less attractive the reunions became to him. The study put down on paper one of the craziest side effects of pluralistic ignorance and provided something for all science to ponder and then scratch its head over in delight—something with a capacity to uniquely twist perception. Those who felt estranged were actually in the majority but didn't know it because pluralistic ignorance had scrambled their minds to believe in a majority that didn't exist. The zealotry to which they felt opposed was an illusion, but these students felt themselves ostracized from the university culture—even though their feelings were actually in line with those of the majority of their peers.

Prentice and Miller concluded that their research provided plenty of evidence that you have no idea whether the norms in your culture, subculture, era, or group of friends are real or imagined. The landscape of any social situation is so treacherous that, as they put it, "estimates of the norm are often seriously in error." In their Princeton studies, the students not only presented themselves as supporters of norms they didn't support, but they couldn't see that everyone else was doing the same thing. According to Prentice and Miller, the end result was the perpetuation of a norm that no one in fact supported.

The side effects of this tendency for groups to get reality completely backward can be enormously influential on the course of history. Warping campus culture and increasing the sales of Lambrini is one thing, but pluralistic ignorance can also oppress whole nations and cause social change to stagnate for generations.

A study by the sociologist Hubert J. O'Gorman in 1975, which he later replicated with fellow sociologist Stephen L. Garry, picked apart surveys of American whites during the final years of racial segregation in the United States. Throughout the early half of the twentieth century, it was considered socially acceptable to keep people with light skin and people with dark skin separate on public transportation and in schools, military units, restaurants, bathrooms, cinemas, and even graveyards. It was a part of the beliefs, values, and norms of society, especially in the Deep South, and it was also part of laws and other codes of conduct. As the 1960s began, most Americans saw white people and black people almost as two different species, and the majority of people believed those species shouldn't mix—or so the majority of people believed.

When O'Gorman and Garry took surveys of Caucasians from that time period and plugged the answers into a giant chart for analysis, what they found was astonishing. It turned out that only a small number of white people at the time truly supported segregation. Most people wanted integration, but most people believed that most other people believed differently—classic pluralistic ignorance. O'Gorman and Garry found that the level of pluralistic ignorance varied from region to region. For instance, in the extreme Northeast about 7 percent of people favored segregation, but 19 percent believed the majority disagreed. In the Deep South, 32 percent of people favored segregation, but 61 percent believed the majority of the country was in favor of continuing the policies. Overall, the surveys showed that close to half of all U.S. citizens believed that the majority of the country was in favor of continuing segregation, but in reality the support was there in only about one in five. That level of pluralistic ignorance, speculated the researchers, led to situations in which people might say something like, "Look, I don't have a problem with you eating here, but you know how people are."

The false belief in the majority support for segregation slowed down the process of ending it and swayed policy makers, employers, advertisers, and the rest of society to act as though they lived in a world that wasn't really there. In their study, O'Gorman and Garry showed that whites who were undecided about the issue but who also falsely believed that the majority supported it tended to go with the perceived majority. When asked if white neighborhoods had the right to keep blacks out of vacant houses, the people with strong opinions beforehand fell back on those positions. Segregationists strongly supported the right to say who could and could not live next door based on the color of their skin. Desegregationists strongly opposed the idea. The people on the fence went with what they assumed the majority wanted. They didn't know, however, that most people didn't actually feel that way, and the presumed majority was just a figment of their imaginations. Situations like this, argued the sociologists, continue to enforce norms that most people wish would go away—even today. Pluralistic ignorance keeps people on the fringe, the sort of people who will be phased out by progress, clinging to their outdated beliefs for longer than they should. It keeps their opponents feeling less supported than they truly are while keeping people in the middle favoring the status quo. In the end, a make-believe status quo changes the way everyone acts and thinks. As the sociologists put it, people often "unintentionally serve as cultural carriers of cognitive error."

As the psychologist Leaf Van Boven pointed out in a study published in 2000, pluralistic ignorance doesn't always stall change; it can also lead people to be more politically correct. On a university campus, he observed, people want to appear more tolerant to their peers than they may truly feel. As in the alcohol study, he asked the students at Cornell University how they felt about affirmative action. He found that about a quarter supported it and about half did not. He then asked the same students to estimate what the results of the study would be. They reported that the campus was probably 40 percent in favor and about 40 percent opposed, thus overestimating the support for affirmative action at

Cornell. Boven showed that pluralistic ignorance sways public opinion regardless of what sort of public experiences it. On a predominantly liberal university campus, most people don't want to be seen as racists or lacking in progressive sentiment, so even if they privately harbor doubts about something such as affirmative action, they will censor that opinion when speaking in public. No matter the policy, if there is pressure enough to conform, then people will base their display of support for the given policy on the level of others' public compliance, and thus the policy becomes more and more deeply entrenched in the culture.

Psychologist James Kitts infiltrated vegetarian student cooperatives in which people live and eat together under the norm of a meatless lifestyle. In his 1995 study, he found that most people explained that they would sometimes sneak a piece of beef or chicken when away from the other members, but would never do such a thing in the shared housing, out of a fear of offending others or making them feel sick. Kitts surveyed the population of several of these collectives and combined their answers. Together, the members estimated that about 75 percent of the vegetarians stuck to their diet and avoided beef. The actual number was around 62 percent. When asked about fish, the vegetarians estimated that about 40 percent of their brethren sometimes slipped a bite here and there, but the actual percentage of people sneaking out to eat fish was closer to 60 percent. Kitt's research further supported the idea that pluralistic ignorance can cause any sort of group to remain one way when its members would prefer it to be another. Most people wanted to eat meat occasionally, especially fish, but no one would say so out loud, and so most people thought they were members of a tiny cabal of cheaters.

So why do you do this? What drives you to keep the way you

feel from coming out of your mouth? Well, for one, you fear some sort of social punishment. Many scientists bring up the parable of "The Emperor's New Clothes." In the story by Hans Christian Andersen, a vain emperor hires two tailors who tell him they've made a suit of clothes so fine that it appears invisible to people who are unfit for their job or are very dumb. The trick, of course, is that the tailors haven't made anything at all. All the emperor's lackeys and subjects act as if his clothes were beautiful and amazing out of fear of appearing stupid or unfit, until finally a child points out that the emperor is walking around naked. At that point, everyone sighs in relief and feels safe to say what they were thinking all along. Stories with similar plots to this one go back to antiquity, so the idea has been with us for a long time. You've experienced it yourself, most likely when waiting in line or stuck in a crowded hallway outside a classroom or office. You wonder if a door is locked, or if another class is still in session, but you just join the crowd waiting patiently and say nothing. What you don't know is there was probably just one person waiting at first, and then the second walked up, assumed the first person had a good reason not to go inside, and out of fear of embarrassment the second person joined the first. Then a third did the same, and a fourth, and over time a crowd of pluralistically ignorant people were waiting around out of a shared fear of looking stupid. All it takes is one person to open the door and walk inside for the fear to vanish. Similarly, studies show that people who need help are sometimes left to suffer because everyone in the crowd of onlookers assumes everyone else knows something he does not. One kind soul can get everyone to join in and help. It can't be understated how powerful the fear of embarrassment can be. Describing soldiers facing combat in Vietnam in *The Things They Carried,* Tim O'Brien wrote, "They were afraid of dying but even more afraid to show it," adding later, "They carried the soldier's greatest fear, which was the fear of blushing. Men killed, and died, because they were embarrassed not to."

Sociologists Damon Centola, Robb Willer, and Michael Macy applied game theory to this concept, plugging data into computer models, and showed that unpopular norms are likely to pop up in just about any human social situation in which there is a palpable fear of retribution. As they pointed out, "an outbreak of enforcement" will cascade through a social movement when it is beneficial for members to act or cease to act out of fear. They point out that the literal witch hunts of the early American colonies and the metaphorical witch hunts of the McCarthy era share similarities with the bizarre irony of closeted homosexual men committing acts motivated by homophobia. Politicians known for their antigay legislation have boggled the minds of their constituents by getting caught in gay sex scandals. You might wonder why someone who is homosexual would work so hard to make it difficult to be homosexual, but Centola, Willer, and Macy say it is pretty simple. One of the common strategies to avoid embarrassment and punishment for disagreeing with a norm is actively to enforce it. People often become norm enforcers to prove their loyalty and head off any suspicion. Whenever a person imagines that violating a norm would result in serious consequences, such as eternal damnation in a pit of fiery torture or the complete social abandonment of friends, family, and his brothers and sisters in the church, that person may opt to become an enforcer of norms instead of just simply complying with them. As the researchers put it, "enforcing norms provides a low-cost way to fake sincerity, to signal that one complies—not as an opportunist seeking approval—but as a true believer."

You'll find enforcers wherever there are norms. If drinking on campus is privately shunned but publicly heralded, then the people who are new to the culture and who seek ingratiation will be the most likely to enforce; the result is freshmen who binge more often than finalists. If being openly gay is risky, then people with homosexual feelings may beat up others who are openly homosexual, or try to pass laws that suppress gay rights. If you are an atheist attending Christmas dinner at a church with your fundamentalist family, you might ask to say grace to keep your lack of faith hidden. According to Centola, Willer, and Macy, pluralistic ignorance causes people who feel dangerously deviant to believe the desire among the majority to enforce norms likely matches the level of observable compliance. So, to stay safe, they become enforcers, joining others who may be doing the same thing for the same deluded reasons. What the fearful don't know is that since they're overestimating the level of compliance, the likelihood of suffering the wrath of enforcement should their secret feelings become known is also probably very low. The pattern repeats itself, as it does with a crowd waiting in front of an unlocked door, with each person observing compliance or enforcement, one based on ignorance, the other based on fear, and the net result is the norm enforces itself.

Why is it so hard to see that everyone is holding his tongue for the same reason you are? Why don't you test the waters and ask around every time you encounter one of these situations? In 1987, psychologists Dale Miller and Cathy McFarland decided it was time to answer these questions. They set up an experiment in which they were able to create and eradicate pluralistic ignorance by changing one variable. Miller and McFarland gathered a group of university students and told them that they were taking part in a study about self-concept. Each student met a single researcher one on one when he or she arrived, and the researcher explained that the study was already under way and that the subject would have to wait until the next round. While the students waited to start the fake study, the researcher handed out preparation materials, explaining that everyone else would be required to read the same paperwork before the study began. The materials included an article about theoretical models of how humans construct concepts of the self, an article the scientists had designed to be "virtually incomprehensible." The researcher then told the student she had to leave for a little while, but before she left the room she explained that if the student had any problems understanding the material, to just drop by her office. When she returned each time, the subject was handed a questionnaire and told he or she could be completely honest because total anonymity was guaranteed. Among the items on the questionnaire were the two real questions the researchers were most interested in: How many other people do you think asked for help? and How well did you understand the article? On a scale from one to eleven, most of the respondents said their understanding of the article was about a five, but when asked how many people out of all of those in the study got up and walked down the hall for illumination, the average response was 37 percent. The real number? Zero. There it was: Pluralistic ignorance in the same form as when an instructor asks if anyone in the classroom needs help, or when potential helpers become passive bystanders. In the controlled experiment, each person admitted privately that he or she was having a hard time understanding the article, but as a group the subjects grossly overestimated how many of their peers would be uninhibited enough to ask for help. You are very bad at judging other people's inhibitions from one situation to the next.

The overestimation of the inhibition of others was as Miller and McFarland expected, and it led them to the next stage in their study. In the second version of the experiment, they divided subjects into two conditions, with people in each condition sitting together in units of around eight people. In condition A, the groups received the same treatment as in the first study—if an individual didn't understand the article, he or she could leave the preparation area and get one-on-one help. In condition B, that option was removed—the groups were told that no one was allowed to ask for clarification if he found the material too difficult to understand. As before, no one got up to ask for help in condition A, and since it wasn't allowed, no one asked for help in condition B, either. After some time with the impossible-to-read article, people in both conditions received questionnaires. Each person was asked how much knowledge he now had on the subject compared to other students in his group, how well he understood the article itself compared to his fellow subjects, and how well he thought he might perform up against the other participants in his cluster if asked to write an essay on the topic after reading the article. Participants in both conditions said they understood the article at about the same level as the other participants in their group, but compared with one another, the people in condition A, who had the option to ask for assistance, rated themselves as significantly less knowledgeable than others in their group and predicted their essays would be significantly less thorough than those of their peers. The only variable, according to the researchers, was the fear of embarrassment. People in condition B were just as befuddled by the article, but their personal explanations differed from those of people in condition A. When they wondered about their own understanding and performance in comparison to others, they based it solely on the material. Without anything else for comparison, and as most people do on most things, they rated themselves slightly better than average. People in condition A factored in their own anxieties when considering their understanding of the material. Seeing that no one else had asked for help, the subjects assumed themselves rather dull by comparison; they falsely believed the other people in their group were less inhibited and thus would have asked for help from the experimenter if they hadn't understood the article. People in condition B were prevented from making such assumptions, so the extra layer of negativity never entered their minds.

So, pluralistic ignorance is your crappy ability to predict the inhibition of others combined with your deep, innate drive to seek out the rewards of conformity and to avoid punishment for breaching social norms. On top of that, the people with the most anxiety often become enforcers of norms they disagree with. This leads to what anthropologists Warren Breed and Thomas Ktsanes call a "conservative bias," in the traditional sense of the word, not the modern political sense. Thinking through that bias, most people falsely assume their culture is less progressively tilted than it truly is, and thus the institutions and media of the culture will present themselves as more conservative than necessary. In addition, its programming will consist of content designed to appeal to a public far more prudish than the actual audience consuming it.

Considering all the faces of this psychological beast, how can you use this knowledge to defeat it? Thankfully, science has some suggestions on how to beat your brain.

The feeling that you might be the only person on Earth who feels the way you do is among the most crushing. You may have what looks to the outside world like a great job, and you are fully aware that most of the planet suffers while you piddle around on

Facebook, yet you still feel as if your stomach were full of melted wax every time you start your commute. That sensation is made much worse when you feel too embarrassed to reveal it to your friends. That feeling is more menacing when you fear speaking up. One of the great lessons you can take from the study of pluralistic ignorance is the near certainty that everything you think and feel is right now, at this moment, shared with millions of other people. Whatever angst or shame or doubt burdening you right now is felt in kind by enough of your extended human family at this very second to fill every stadium and concert hall in your country. When the comedian Louis C.K. reveals to his audiences that he sometimes thinks his own children are assholes, that they are not exempt from the normal frustrations he feels toward adults, he mass-produces an epiphanous sigh night after night. His audiences, suffering from pluralistic ignorance, realize in later conversation that their private thoughts about their own children are the majority opinion. It is simply taboo to say so out loud. He extinguished for many people the belief that the majority of parents in American culture in the early twenty-first century truly felt something that the majority was only pretending to feel while in public. Great comedians do that. They fly from city to city blasting apart pluralistic ignorance by moving from one forbidden topic to the next, subverting norms, illuminating audiences to the fact that what each person believes she feels in private and in opposition to her neighbors is, indeed, the true norm.

You can try to do as the Romans do, but remember that the Romans are doing what they think the Romans do, but not even Romans know what the Romans truly believe. Public discourse is the path to beating our brains. The only way out of the loop is to speak up, ask questions, and get a conversation going about what people truly think. Prentice and Miller, the scientists who studied alcohol norms at Princeton, said in their study that wide-net awareness campaigns were the wrong approach to pushing for social change. They said informative public service announcements and consciousness-raising initiatives may be excellent tools for changing private attitudes, but thanks to pluralistic ignorance, those sorts of message-saturation, top-of-mind media-jamming projects are impotent against the perception that the majority still supports the norm in question. Their suggestion? Encourage individuals to speak out and reveal their private thoughts. They, along with Miller and McFarland, advocate support groups and other forms of intimate gatherings in which people are encouraged to open up to others, so the rest of the group can reveal in turn that what everyone thought was their own deviant thoughts or actions or beliefs were not only normal but also the true majority sentiment. In Kitts's study, the one about the vegetarians, he found that the more aberrant your friends and family, the more deviant the people in your inner circles, the less power pluralistic ignorance has over your perceptions. This means that maybe support groups were the old way and the psychedelic mishmash of every human thought palace, belief system, obsession, bend, and fetish on the Internet is the new way. Are you a grown man who loves *My Little Pony*? My friend, you're a Google search away from discovering millions of other Bronies like you. No matter your private, mistakenly deviant ways, you can find your tribe somewhere online, and they probably meet for breakfast once a month.

# 11.

# _The No True Scotsman Fallacy_

---

**THE MISCONCEPTION:** _You honestly define that which you hold dear._

**THE TRUTH:** _You will shift your definitions to protect your ideologies._

If you belong to a group, say, the Leicestershire Trumpet and Crumpet Society, and a member of your group does something despicable, say, robs sixty-four daycare centers at gunpoint while tooting his horn and tossing tiny pancakes into the children's faces, what do you say when the media descend like carrion birds on your public relations fiasco?

The typical response from the typical spokesperson on the typical evening news program is to disavow the suspect. Your spokesperson will go around saying something to the effect of "Well, this certainly is not something a Trumpet and Crumpeteer would ever do. Danforth Minglesnout may claim to be a member of the Leicestershire Trumpet and Crumpet Society, but no true member of our fine brass instrument and griddle cake association would commit such an atrocious crime." By thinking in this way, you can quickly move the furniture around in your mind so that you safely believe the culprit is not one of your own. You refuse to allow it, not even when the court proceedings reveal Minglesnout was one of the Loughborough branch's founding members, not even when the security camera footage shows he was wearing your traditional fedora and cape while playing your group's official call-to-order song, not even when he appears before the judge on national television sporting a tattoo on his neck of a giant trumpet spilling forth an avalanche of steaming crumpets. None of this matters. No true Trumpet and Crumpeteer would rob a daycare center. It's just not what your club is about.

Yet, what are the rules of the Leicestershire Trumpet and Crumpet Society? If Minglesnout was accepted as a member right up until the moment he committed an atrocity, how could it be that no one now claims him as a member of the group? It wasn't as if he traded in his trumpet for a bassoon and filled that bassoon with tea cakes. That would clearly be a violation of the bylaws, and grounds for dismissal, but nothing in the Crumpstitution says a member is to be booted following a criminal offence.

If you belong to an organization or a group or a subculture or a demographic or any other clumping of people into an easier-to-manage category, from time to time people who share membership in that club will make the whole group look bad. When a member of a group to which you belong, or a champion of an ideology you admire, commits an act you consider unacceptable, you revoke her membership on the spot. Not officially, of course, just mentally and on principle. This way you can avoid guilt by association. Someone who believes in your religion just did something incredibly heinous? Well, then he must never have truly believed. He must not truly have been a member of your religion. This defense is called the no true Scotsman fallacy.

The name comes from philosopher Antony Flew. He wrote a book in 1975 called *Thinking About Thinking,* in which he describes a man from Scotland reading about a terrible sex crime in England. The Scotsman proclaims, "No Scotsman would do such a thing." Then, the next day, he reads about an even worse sex crime occurring in Scotland, and he says, "No true Scotsman would do such a thing." Our Scottish friend would rather not believe his Scottish brothers and sisters could be so indecent and cruel, so he creates a fantasy definition that excludes bad people from being like him. Now he can continue to be in a group that does no wrong. You see the problem here?

News pundits commit this fallacy daily. In 2011, Anders Behring Breivik bombed a series of buildings in Oslo, Norway, before traveling to Utøya Island dressed as a police officer and opening fire on a youth camp. He killed seventy-seven people before police could make it to the isolated area by boat. Breivik described himself as a conservative Christian out to stop the "Muslim colonization" of Europe. Despite claiming he was a member of the Knights Templar, he was ruled sane and sentenced in Norwegian court to twenty-one years in prison. Obviously, this guy is not someone you want associated with your faith. During its coverage of the incident, *The New York Times* referred to Breivik as a Christian extremist. He had published a manifesto and set up social media profiles explaining his views. In them, he reiterated that he felt he was committing acts in the name of Christianity on behalf of Christians, just like an old-fashioned Crusader.

Now, obviously, if you were a Christian, you would cringe to learn this guy was going around telling the world he was murdering people in the name of your faith. That's why American right-wing political pundit Bill O'Reilly went on television shortly after and told millions of viewers that "Breivik is not a Christian. That's impossible. No one believing in Jesus commits mass murder. The man might have called himself a Christian on the Net, but he is certainly not of that faith." O'Reilly claimed it was a left-wing conspiracy to make Christians look evil. More likely is that O'Reilly felt personally threatened by the idea that someone of his faith, and of the faith of most of his viewership, could do something so terrible and then claim it was directly motivated by the tenets of that religion. The fact that Breivik claimed over and over again to be a Christian mattered not to O'Reilly, who just couldn't accept it into his worldview, and therefore committed the no true Scotsman fallacy. He created his own definition of what the word *Christian* meant. That new, personal definition made it much easier to sleep in a world fabricated to be less complicated and easier to deal with. In the real world, no one person can follow every rule and fulfill every requirement of his religion all the time. People daily defy the definitions of their labels, though rarely as heinously as Breivik did. Does breaking a code of conduct espoused by your religion retroactively turn all your claims of membership into lies, or do those claims only seem like lies in hindsight? In O'Reilly's world, such people magically flicker out of his faith the moment they do things he wishes they had not.

The motivation for O'Reilly to commit the no true Scotsman fallacy is understandable. You've likely felt the urge to do this every time a news crew has put a microphone in front of someone from your hometown. They always seem to pick the most embarrassing specimen they can find, right? What do you do? I know when I see someone from the Deep South on television acting like Gomer Pyle on meth, I tell people, "Why couldn't they have picked a doctor, or a lawyer, or a professor? That's not a real Southerner."

That's the no true Scotsman fallacy at work. There are plenty of people with the same accent, with the same shade of skin, with the same political affiliation, that we wish didn't represent us when they reach uncomfortable levels of fame. For every American proud of Sarah Palin, there are millions of Republicans who hang their heads in shame when she releases a book. For every fan of *The Big Bang Theory* there are a million nerds who wish they would cancel that show.

The problem is partially one of definitions. What is a liberal? What is a conservative? What is and is not an activist, or a journalist, or an artist? What is dubstep and what is brostep? What is jazz and what is jazz funk grindcore? What is a real hero? What is a real patriot? What is morality or justice? If you make a giant cupcake, is it still a cupcake or is it now a cake cake?

If a Tory champions a Labour policy, or if a dog marries a cat, a common defense mechanism is to say that the very act itself transforms the actor into a nonmember of that club. If a feminist wants to be a stay-at-home mum, is she still a feminist? Some say no; some say yes. The dissenting members gather together, and a new faction is born. Can a vegetarian own a pair of ostrich-hide boots? Time for a split. Does the Bible forbid dancing? Time for a new denomination. Is music made with computers real music? Time for a new genre. The problem with groups and labels is that they encourage you to believe in some sort of homogeneity, some sort of perfect example that demonstrates the tenets and beliefs of a group or a grouping, but when you pluck one member away or one example, you always find a gaggle of exceptions to the rules. The no true Scotsman fallacy is constantly dividing groups into subgroups because some people can't stomach broad definitions.

If you don't like the ending of a movie, or its sequel, you can easily dismiss it by saying the parts you wish didn't exist aren't part of the true canon. Fans of *Star Wars* do this with the prequels. Fans of *The Matrix* do this for the sequels. You do this for real life, too. The parts of the thing you love that you wish weren't around can be deleted from the roll call with the no true Scotsman fallacy. You recoil from the television when you learn a member of your religion has detonated a suicide bomb or been found guilty of molestation. You would rather not believe that you keep company with such a repugnant undesirable. So you just redefine the parameters. If your favorite sports team is shamed by scandal, and your heroes become villains, you understandably shrink away from the news and look for a way to erase the stains on the record of the thing you love. When you finish the sentence "No true so-and-so would . . ." or "No self-respecting such-and-such ever . . ." you are asking the rest of humanity to agree with your new personal definition.

Philosopher Julian Baggini asks in his book *The Duck That Won the Lottery* if alcoholics can consider themselves cured if they have only one or two drinks a week. Does it take total abstinence to consider yourself no longer an alcoholic? That's what Alcoholics Anonymous claims. It says that no truly cured alcoholic would ever have a drink. If while out to dinner with your fruitarian roommate, she asks the waiter for a bowl of pomegranates and pine nuts and he politely explains such off-menu items are not available, would you clutch your chest in shock if she ordered some chicken drumsticks? What if she explained that sometimes she strays, maybe two or three times a year? What makes a fruitarian a fruitarian? Does briefly pausing from a diet really change anything? What if you declared today that you were a fruitarian, but you haven't actually eaten your first all-fruit meal? When do you cross that line?

Definitions are useful, but for most of life there isn't one single agreed-upon-by-all clarification, and even if there is, that thing and its labels will mutate soon enough. Much of what you think are facts about the groups to which you belong and the groups that you see as alien to your ideologies are actually just beliefs. When those beliefs are challenged, you can just step to the side and alter them by editing your definitions with the no true Scotsman fallacy.

The truth is, most things aren't clearly defined, no matter what the dictionary says. You love to define things, to divide and categorize and develop nomenclature. It helps to keep life from being too cluttered, but most things are blurry. Most things exist along a gradient of degrees. The no true Scotsman fallacy steps in when you mistake your personal definition for the official, widely accepted definition. If you think no true Manchester United fan dances in a Gay Pride parade covered in honey and glitter, that's just your definition. If you think no true scientist believes in Bigfoot, that classification belongs to you. When someone reveals your definition to be crappy and inaccurate with a counterexample, you can just regroup and dismiss the challenge with a redefinition.

The definition debate shows how the no true Scotsman fallacy is related to begging the question. In everyday language, the phrase is often used when people mean "raise the question," but that's not the original meaning. Begging the question is another fallacy you drunkenly stumble back on when clumsily defending your opinions. When you beg the question, you assume you already know the truth. You may smile with pride when your mayor says, "We must ensure that it is always possible for people here to make and sell alcoholic mayonnaise, because microbrewed sandwich toppings make for great towns. A town prospers when its citizens know they can ferment oiled egg yolks." Soaring rhetoric like this sounds good, but the sentences are just circling each other. It's no different from saying cake tastes good because it is delicious. The question being begged is, "Who says cake tastes good? Some people hate cake." The question in a begging the question fallacy is always something along those lines. "What proof do you have that your assumption is true? Are there any exceptions?" Begging the question looks like an argument seeking to establish facts, but it is actually a statement of belief. A real argument makes a claim and then supports that claim with a conclusion. Begging the question assumes you already have proof and just need to say so out loud. Wedge issues are magnets for this fallacy. When you hear Americans saying "Abortion is immoral, and should be illegal—even for cows," or "This country was founded by Christians, so the Ten Commandments should appear on every public school desk," those aren't arguments. They are statements that assume something to be true without giving that thing a chance to be disproved before linking it to another assumption.

The most sweeping and stereotypical generalization is to believe that what is unwanted occurs only among the others. You defend the groups you hold dear by suggesting that deviant members of your group have somehow strayed from the true path, but who says what path is true? It's part of the organizational, tribal instinct to draw a border around things, to classify, to create and adhere to nomenclature, to build citadels to ideas and raise the drawbridge.

Remember that definitions are fuzzy and often imprecise, and that which they define is constantly changing. The borders around an idea are permeable and ever-shifting, so what was once excluded may become expected with time, and vice versa. When you commit the no true Scotsman fallacy, you are asking the universe to stand still so that you can be sure your definition is correct now and forever. Not only that, but in an effort to keep pristine the groups to which you belong, the ideas to which you cling, and the institutions to which you pledge allegiance, you use the no true Scotsman fallacy to ensure that those things are exactly as you expect them to be no matter what sort-of-imperfect instance appears. Simply toss out that instance. You can't improve the things you love if you never allow them to be imperfect. Thinking in this way, if you looked hard enough so that you saw every flaw in every example, you would soon find that nothing matched your expectations or deserved your definitions, and the membership of every group and category you hold dear would drop to zero.

# 12.

## The Illusion of Asymmetric Insight

---

**THE MISCONCEPTION:** *You celebrate diversity and respect others' points of view.*

**THE TRUTH:** *You are driven to create and form groups and then believe others are wrong just because they are others.*

In 1954, in eastern Oklahoma, two tribes of children nearly killed each other.

The neighboring tribes were unaware of each other's existence. Separately, they lived among nature, played games, constructed shelters, prepared food—they knew peace. Each culture developed its own norms and rules of conduct. Each culture arrived at novel solutions to survival-critical problems. Each culture named the creeks and rocks and dangerous places, and those names were known to all. They helped each other and watched out for the well-being of the tribal members.

Scientists stood by, watchful, scribbling notes and whispering. Much nodding and squinting took place as the tribes granted to anthropology and psychology a wealth of data about how people build and maintain groups, how hierarchies are established and preserved. They wondered, the scientists, what would happen if these two groups were to meet.

These two tribes consisted of twenty-two boys, ages eleven and twelve, whom psychologist Muzafer Sherif had brought together at Oklahoma's Robbers Cave State Park. He and his team placed the two groups on separate buses and drove them to a Boy Scout camp inside the park—the sort with cabins and caves and thick wilderness. At the park, the scientists put the boys into separate sides of the camp about a half mile apart and kept secret from each group the existence and location of the other group. The boys didn't know one another beforehand, and Sherif believed putting them into a new environment away from their familiar cultures would encourage them to create a new culture from scratch.

He was right, but as those cultures formed, something sinister presented itself. One of the behaviors that pushed and shoved its way to the top of the boys' minds is also something you are fending off at this very moment, something that is making your life harder than it ought to be. We'll get to that in a minute. First, let's get back to one of the most telling and frightening experiments in the history of psychology.

Sherif and his colleagues pretended to be staff members at the camp, similar to camp counselors, so they could record, without interfering, the natural human drive to form tribes. Right away social hierarchies began to emerge in which the boys established leaders and followers and special roles for everyone in between. Norms spontaneously generated. For instance, when one boy hurt his foot but didn't tell anyone until bedtime, it became expected among the group that Rattlers didn't complain. From then on, members waited until the day's work was finished to reveal injuries. When a boy cried, the others ignored him until he got over it.

Regulations and rituals sprouted just as quickly. For instance, the high-status members, the natural leaders in both groups, came up with guidelines for saying grace during meals and correct rotations for the ritual. Within a few days their initially arbitrary suggestions became the way things were done, and no one had to be prompted or reprimanded. They made up games and settled on rules of play. They embarked on projects to clean up certain areas and established chains of command. Slackers were punished; overachievers were praised. Flags were created; signs erected.

Soon the two groups began to suspect they weren't alone. They would find evidence of others. They found cups and other signs of civilization in places they didn't remember visiting. This strengthened their resolve and encouraged the two groups to hold tighter to their new norms, values, rituals, and all the other elements of the shared culture. At the end of the first week, the Rattlers discovered the others on the camp's baseball diamond. From this point forward both groups spent most of their time thinking about how to deal with their newfound adversaries. The group with no name asked about the outsiders. When told the other group called itself the Rattlers, the nameless group's members elected a baseball captain and asked the camp staff if they could face off in a game with the enemy. They named their baseball team the Eagles, after an animal they thought ate snakes.

Sherif and his colleagues had already planned on pitting the groups against each other in competitive sports. They weren't just researching how groups formed but also how they acted when in competition for resources. The fact that the boys were already itching to compete for dominance on the baseball field seemed to fall right in line with their research. So the scientists proceeded to stage two. The two tribes were overjoyed to learn they would not only play baseball but also compete in tug-of-war, treasure hunts, and other summer-camp-themed rivalry. The scientists revealed a finite number of prizes. Winners would receive one of a handful of medals or knives. When the boys won the knives, some would kiss them before rushing to hide the weapons from the other group.

Sherif noted the two groups spent a lot of time talking about how dumb and uncouth the other side was. They called them names, lots of names, and seemed preoccupied every night with defining the essence of their enemies. Sherif was fascinated by this display. The two groups needed the other side to be inferior once the competition for limited resources became a factor, so they began defining them as such. It strengthened their identity to assume that the identity of the enemy was a far cry from their own. Everything they learned about the other side became an example of how not to be, and any similarities tended to be ignored.

The researchers collected data and discussed findings while planning the next series of activities, but the boys made other plans. The experiment was about to spiral out of control, and it started with the Eagles.

One day, some of the Eagles discovered the Rattlers' flag standing unguarded on the baseball field. They discussed what to do and decided it should be ripped from the ground. Once they had it, they decided to burn it. They then put its scorched remains back in place and sang "Taps." Later, the Rattlers saw the atrocity and organized a raid in which they stole the Eagles' flag and burned it as payback. When the Eagles discovered the revenge burning, the leader issued a challenge—a face-off. The two leaders then met, prepared to fight each other in front of the two groups, but the scientists intervened. That night, the Rattlers dressed in war paint and raided the Eagles' cabins, turning over beds and tearing apart mosquito netting. The staff again intervened when the two groups started circling and gathering rocks. The next day, the Rattlers painted with insulting graffiti a pair of blue jeans stolen from the Eagles and paraded it in front of the enemy's camp. The Eagles waited until the Rattlers were eating and conducted a retaliatory raid and then ran back to their cabin to set up defenses. They filled socks with rocks and waited. The camp staff, once again, intervened and convinced the Rattlers not to counterattack. The raids continued, and the interventions, too, and eventually the Rattlers stole the Eagles' knives and medals. The Eagles, determined to retrieve them, formed an organized war party, with assigned roles and planned tactical maneuvers. The two groups finally fought in open combat. The scientists broke up the fight. Fearing the two tribes might murder someone, they moved the groups' camps away from each other.

You probably suspected this was where the story was headed. You know it is possible in the right conditions that people, even children, might revert to savages. You know about the instant coffee version of cultures, too. You remember school. You've worked in a cubicle farm. You've watched Stephen King movies. People in new situations instinctively form groups. Those groups develop their own language quirks, in-jokes, norms, values, and so on. You've probably suspected that economic collapse would lead to a battle over who runs Bartertown. In this study, all they had to do was introduce competition for resources, and summer camp became *Lord of the Flies*.

What you may not have noticed, though, is how much of this behavior is gurgling right below the surface of your consciousness from day to day. You aren't sharpening spears, but at some level you are contemplating your place in society, contemplating your allegiances and your opponents. You see yourself as part of some groups and not others, and like those boys, you spend a lot of time defining outsiders. The way you see others is deeply affected by something psychologists call the illusion of asymmetric insight, but to understand it, let's first consider how groups, like people, have identities. And with both individuals and groups, those identities aren't exactly real.

Hopefully by now you've had one of those late-night conversations fueled by exhaustion, elation, fear, or drugs in which you and your friends finally admitted you were all bullshitting each other. If you haven't, go watch *The Breakfast Club* and come back. The idea is this: You put on a mask and a uniform before leaving for work. You put on another set for school. You have a costume for friends of different persuasions and one just for family. Who you are alone is not who you are with a lover or a friend. You quick-change like Superman in a phone booth when you bump into old friends from school at the supermarket, or the ex in line for a movie. When you part from that person, you quick-change back. The person on your arm forgives you. He or she understands; after all, he or she is also in disguise. It's not a new or novel concept, the idea of multiple identities for multiple occasions, but it's also not something you talk about often. The idea is old enough that the word *person* derives from *persona,* a Latin word for the mask a Greek actor sometimes wore so people in the back rows of a performance could see who he was onstage. This concept—actors and performance, persona and masks—has been intertwined and adopted throughout history. Shakespeare said, "All the world's a stage, and all the men and women merely players." William James said a person "has as many social selves as there are individuals who recognize him." Carl Jung was particularly fond of the concept of the persona, saying it was "that which in reality one is not, but which oneself as well as others think one is." It's an old idea, but you and everyone else seem to stumble onto it in adolescence, forget about it for a while, and suddenly remember again from time to time when you feel like an impostor or a fraud. It's okay; that's a natural feeling, and if you don't step back occasionally and feel funky about how you are wearing a socially constructed mask and uniform you are probably a psychopath.

Social media confound the issue. You are a public relations masterpiece. Not only are you free to create alternate selves for forums, websites, and other digital watering holes, but from one social media service to the next, you control the output of your persona. The clever tweets, the Instagrams of your delectable triumphs with the oven and mixing bowl, the funny meme you send out into the firmament that you check back on for comments, the new thing you own, the new place you visited—they tell a story of who you want to be. They satisfy something. Is anyone clicking on all these links? Is anyone smirking at this video?

The recent fuss over our oversharing culture and over the possible loss of privacy is just noisy ignorance. As a citizen of the Internet, you obfuscate the truth of your character. You hide your fears and transgressions and vulnerable yearnings for meaning, for purpose, for connection. In a world where you can control everything presented to an audience, domestic or imaginary, what is laid bare depends on who you believe is on the other side of the screen. You fret over your father or your aunt asking to be your Facebook friend. What will they think of that version of you? In flesh or photos, it seems built-in, this desire to conceal some aspects of yourself in one group while exposing them in others. You can be vulnerable in many different ways but not all at once it seems.

So you don social masks just like every human going back to

the first campfire. You seem rather confident in those masks, in their ability to communicate and conceal that which you want on display and that which you wish were not. Groups, too, don such masks. Political parties establish platforms, companies give employees handbooks, countries write out constitutions, tree houses post club rules—every human gathering and institution, from a fashion show to the English Defence League, works to remain connected by developing a set of norms and values that signals when they are dealing with members of the in-group and identifies others as part of the out-group. The peculiar thing, though, is that once you feel included in a human institution or ideology, you can't help but see outsiders through a warped lens called the illusion of asymmetric insight.

How well do you know your friends? Pick one out of the bunch, someone you interact with often. Do you see the little ways he lies to himself and others? Do you secretly know what is holding her back, but also recognize the beautiful talents she doesn't appreciate? Do you know what he wants, what he is likely to do in most situations, what he will argue about and what let slide? Do you notice when she is posturing and when she is vulnerable? Do you know the perfect gift for him? Do you wish she had never gone out with so-and-so? Do you sometimes say with confidence, "You should have been there. You would have loved it," about things you enjoyed for him by proxy? Research shows you probably feel all these things and more. You see your friends, your family, your coworkers and peers, as semipermeable beings. You label them with ease. You see them as the artist, the grouch, the slacker, and the overachiever. "They did what? Oh, that's no surprise," you say about them. You know who will watch the meteor shower with you and who will pass. You know whom to ask about spark plugs and whom to ask about planting a vegetable garden. You can, you believe, put yourself in their shoes and predict their behavior in just about any situation. You believe every person except you is an open book. Of course, the research shows they believe the same thing about you.

In 2001, Emily Pronin and Lee Ross, along with Justin Kruger and Kenneth Savitsky, conducted a series of experiments exploring why you see people this way. In the first experiment, they had people fill out a questionnaire asking them to think of a best friend and rate how well they believed they knew him or her. They showed the subjects a series of photos of an iceberg submerged in varying levels of water and asked them to circle the one that corresponded to how much of the "essential nature" they felt they could see of their friends. How much, they asked, of your friend's true self is visible and how much is hidden below the surface? They then had the subjects take a second questionnaire that turned the questions around, asking them to put themselves in the minds of their friends. How much of their own iceberg did they think their friends could see? Most people rated their insight into their best friend as keen. They saw more of the iceberg floating above the water line. In the other direction, they felt the insight their friends possessed of them was lacking; most of their own self was submerged and invisible to their friends. You believe you see more of other people's icebergs than they see of yours; meanwhile, they think the same thing about you.

The same researchers also asked people to describe a time when they felt most like themselves. Most subjects (78 percent) described something internal and unobservable, such as the feeling of seeing their child excel or the rush of applause after playing for an audience. When asked to describe when they believed friends or relatives were most illustrative of their personalities, they described internal feelings only 28 percent of the time. Instead, they tended to describe actions: Tom is most like Tom when he is telling a dirty joke, or Jill is most like Jill when she is rock climbing. You can't see internal states of others, so you generally don't use those states to describe their personalities.

When they had subjects complete words with some letters missing (such as *g–l*, which could be *goal, girl, gall, gill,* etc.) and then ask how much the subjects believed those word-completion tasks revealed about their true selves, most people said they revealed nothing at all. When the same people looked at other people's word completions, they said things such as "I get the feeling that whoever did this is pretty vain, but basically a nice guy." They looked at the words and said the people who filled them in were nature lovers, or having their periods, or were positive thinkers, or needed more sleep. When the words were their own, they meant nothing. When they were others', they pulled back a curtain.

When Pronin, Ross, Kruger, and Savitsky moved from individuals to groups, they found an even more troubling version of the illusion of asymmetric insight. They had subjects identify themselves as either liberals or conservatives and, in a separate run of the experiment, as either pro-abortion or anti-abortion. The groups filled out questionnaires about their own beliefs and how they interpreted the beliefs of their opposition. They then rated how much insight their opponents possessed. The results showed liberals believed they knew more about conservatives than conservatives knew about liberals. The conservatives believed they knew more about liberals than liberals knew about conservatives. Both groups thought they knew more about their opponents than their opponents knew about themselves. The same was true of the pro-abortion and anti-abortion groups.

The illusion of asymmetric insight makes it seem that you know everyone else far better than they know you, and not only that, you know them better than they know themselves. You believe the same thing about groups of which you are a member. As a whole, your group understands outsiders better than outsiders understand your group, and you understand the group better than its members know the group to which they belong.

The researchers explained that this could be how you arrive at believing your thoughts and perceptions are true, accurate, and correct, therefore if someone sees things differently from you or disagrees with you in some way, it is the result of a bias or an influence or a shortcoming. You often feel the other person must have been tainted in some way, otherwise he would see the world the way you do—the right way. The illusion of asymmetrical insight clouds your ability to see the people you disagree with as nuanced and complex. You tend to see yourself and the groups you belong to in shades of gray, but others and their groups as solid and defined primary colors lacking nuance or complexity.

The two tribes of children in Oklahoma formed because groups are how human beings escaped the Serengeti and built pyramids and invented Pot Noodles. All primates depend on groups to survive and thrive, and human groups thrive most of all. It is in your nature to form them. Sherif's experiment with the boys at Robbers Cave State Park showed how quickly and easily you do so and how your innate drive to develop and observe norms and rituals will express itself even in a cultural vacuum. But there is a dark side to this behavior. As psychologist Jonathan Haidt says, our minds "unite us into teams, divide us against other teams, and blind us to the truth." It's that last part that keeps getting you into trouble. Just as you don a self, a persona, and believe it to be thicker and harder to see through than those of your friends, family, and peers, you, too, believe that the groups to which you belong are more complex, more diverse, and more granular than are groups of which you could never imagine yourself a member. When you feel the warm comfort of belonging to a team, a tribe, a group—to a party, an ideology, a religion, or a nation—you instinctively turn others into members of out-groups, into outsiders. Just as soldiers come up with derogatory names for enemies, every culture and subculture has a collection of terms for outsiders so as to better see them as a single-minded collective. You are prone to forming and joining groups and then believing your group is more diverse than outside groups.

In a political debate, you feel that the other side just doesn't get your point of view, and if they could only see things with your clarity, they would understand and fall naturally in line with what you believe. They must not understand, because if they did, they wouldn't think the things they think. By contrast, you believe you totally get their point of view and you reject it. You don't need to hear them elaborate on it because you already know it better than they do. So each side believes it understands the other side better than the other side understands both its opponents and itself.

The research suggests that you and the rest of humanity will continue to churn into groups, banding and disbanding, and the beautiful collective species-wide macromonoculture imagined by the most utopian of dreams might just be impossible unless alien warships lay siege to our cities. In Sherif's study, he was able to reintegrate the boys of the Robbers Cave experiment somewhat by telling them the water supply had been sabotaged by vandals. The two groups were able to come together and repair it as one. Later he staged a problem with one of the camp trucks and was able to get the boys to work together to pull it with a rope until it started. They never fully joined into one group, but the hostilities eased enough for both groups to ride the same bus together back home. Had the study continued, they might have dissolved back into one unit. It seems that peace is possible when we face shared problems, but for now we need to be in our tribes. It just feels right.

You pick a team, and like the boys at Robbers Cave, you spend a lot of time talking about how stupid and uncouth the other side is. You, too, can become preoccupied with defining the essence of your enemy. You, too, need the other side to be inferior, so you define it as such. You start to believe your persona is actually your identity, and the identity of your enemy is actually his persona. You see yourself in a game of self-deluded poker and assume you are impossible to read while everyone else has obvious tells.

You are succumbing to the illusion of asymmetric insight, and as part of a flatter, more connected, always-on world, you will be tasked with seeing through this illusion more and more often as you are presented with more opportunities than ever to confront and define those who you feel are not in your tribe. Your ancestors rarely made any contact with people of opposing views with anything other than the end of a weapon, so your natural instinct is to assume anyone not in your group is wrong just because she is not in your group. Just a small amount of exposure to the opposition, especially if you are forced to cooperate with it, can allay those feelings.

Research by psychologist Steven Sloman and marketing expert Phil Fernbach shows that people who claim to understand complicated political topics such as cap and trade and flat taxes tend to reveal their ignorance when asked to provide a detailed explanation without the aid of Google. Though people on either side of an issue may believe they know their opponents' positions, when put to the task of breaking it down they soon learn that they have only a basic understanding of the topic being argued. Stranger still, once subjects in such studies recognize this, they reliably become more moderate in their beliefs. Zealotry wanes; fanatical opposition is dampened. The research suggests simply working to better explain your own opinion saps your fervor. Yet that same research shows the opposite effect when subjects are asked to justify their positions on a contentious issue. Justification strengthens a worldview, but exploration weakens it.

# 13.

## *Enclothed Cognition*

---

**THE MISCONCEPTION:** *Clothes as everyday objects are just fabrics for protection and decoration of the body.*
**THE TRUTH:** *The clothes you wear change your behavior and can either add or subtract from your mental abilities.*

Imagine this. Halloween is approaching, and you are shopping for a costume. You hear about a great new place that is super cheap and lets you mix and match any costumes in the shop. When you arrive, you open the door to discover one giant room with no shelves or aisles, just a big pile of clothes and accessories in the center and some changing rooms in the corner. You dig through the pile, giggling and watching as everyone tries on hats and buckles up holsters and asks how they look in wigs.

In a situation like this, do you think you would be satisfied drawing out random trousers and shirts to go along with unassociated trinkets and footwear? If you showed up at the party with one piece of clothing from eleven different costumes, what would you tell people when they asked, "So, what are you supposed to be?"

If such a terrible free-market experiment existed, the likely result would be that people would just go searching for matching items, slowly assembling pirate costumes and witch ensembles. You, and everyone else, would have no problem picking through a pile of Halloween clothing to successfully assemble costumes because clothes have meaning beyond their utility. At Halloween, or at a science fiction convention, or at a business meeting, clothes are more than protection from the elements.

All you have to do is watch an episode of *Mad Men* or browse through a photo gallery from a science-fiction convention to understand the power clothing has over the human mind. Clothes are one of the most obvious differences between you and your primate cousins, which means the motivation to create and wear clothing rests somewhere in that 4 percent difference between your DNA and a chimpanzee's. This is not so strange an idea. If you take enough objective steps back and then squint hard, you'll realize you are looking at a form of technology—an artificial enhancement of the human body. Clothes allow you the ability to survive in colder climates, or escape the appetites and anger of insects. Clothing protects you from harm and makes it possible to do all sorts of things better than if you were nude, and some estimates suggest your ancestors donned apparel beginning about 650,000 years ago. That means clothing was one of the first things humans and human ancestors made by hand. It isn't too much of a stretch to speculate that, along with weapons and tools, clothing was among the first art forms and among the first items to materialize as physical representations of the evanescent internal world of the human mind. Clothes would be left behind by the dead, would vary by culture and individual, would represent mastery of technique or a lack thereof, and could communicate class, status, roles, intent, and all sorts of other things. Clothes, in other words, were likely among the first items in all of human history to be charged with symbolism and to communicate ideas from one person to another independent of their creator.

You may have noticed that heads of state and heads of corporations tend to wear the same thing no matter in what country those states and corporations operate. Around the world, when it is time to get down to business, men and women wear business suits. China, France, the United States, Singapore, Bavaria—it doesn't matter; only a handful of people, such as monks and cardinals, still wear attire unique to their culture when on official errands. An article in *The Economist* traced the origin of the modern suit back to the 1600s, when British monarchs declared an early version of the outfit the official dress of courtiers to indicate to the masses that even the royalty was taking measures to cut costs in the aftermath of the Great Plague of London. Commoners, ahem, followed suit, and it became the apparel of gentlemen throughout Europe. The downgraded elegance of the court's attire was still tight and rather dandy by today's standards, but as the military version became looser and looser, to accommodate the functionality required for uniforms—riding a horse, shooting a gun, standing at attention—so did the civilian's business suit. Over time, neckerchiefs became cravats and cravats became ties, and as the world got better acquainted, other cultures adopted the slacks and sports coat. It is now an international symbol, no different from a collection of letters representing a sound representing a concept. With their long history, suits are now particularly adept at influencing others. Communicating this message is so valuable that women now wear variations on the traditional male business suit, and with good reason. Studies show the more masculine a woman's attire in Western society, the better her chances of getting hired when compared with women who wear more feminine clothing in a job interview. The suit has transcended whatever original function it once served to become a costume, and as with any costume, its value is in what it communicates. If you want to present yourself as a responsible and dependable member of society who gets things done in a professional manner so that you nab that job, you'd damn well better show up to the interview in a suit.

Clothes communicate ideas, but how? Well, the answer has to do with the wiring inside that furry coconut between your shoulders.

It is unusual to find human beings sitting in empty rooms with barren walls. A room devoid of all decoration, painted stark white, is a metaphor for madness. You tend to fill up any living or working space with photos and art, artifacts and souvenirs. Cubicles accumulate the ephemera of the occupant's personality, and the interior of a home expands to project that which the owner finds beautiful and expressive, that which demonstrates the ideas the owner admires. As George Carlin put it, when you get down to it, a house is just "a pile of stuff with a cover on it." You can't help it. Wherever you go, you amass objects. When someone passes away, those things remain wherever that person spent time, and standing among it, you can feel her presence because human beings pump meaning into their environments. Every surface, every wall, buzzes with meaning thanks to objects placed there with intent and purpose. Even inside a theme restaurant where the interior walls look like a tornado whipped through a glue factory before obliterating an antiques roadshow, there is a method to the madness. Wherever people linger, you will find objects as symbols posted in plain sight in order to communicate meaning.

Symbols are a big part of your life thanks to the associative architecture of your brain. When I write a terrible romance novel line such as "It should have been obvious she was born in Africa, she had a beautifully long, slender neck not unlike a . . ." you can finish my sentence because your brain long ago formed a connection to the words *long, slender, neck,* and *Africa.* Neuroscientists call this a semantic net—every word, image, idea, and feeling is associated with everything else, like an endless tree growing in every direction at once. When you smell popcorn, you think of the cinema. When you hear a Christmas song, you think of Christmas trees. In his book *Brain Bugs,* Dean Buonomano discusses something called the Baker/baker phenomenon, in which you are much more likely to remember a brief acquaintance's profession after a few days than you will his name. In a study into this odd quirk, researchers had some people read a list of names and professions. The results showed that it was much easier for most people to remember later that a person worked as a baker than it was to remember that a person's last name was Baker. As Buonomano explains, the name Baker and the word *baker,* although differentiated only by a single capital letter, are members of two completely different semantic webs. One connects only to every other Baker you've met in your life. The other connects to carrot cake and puffy hats and Lorraine Pascale and thousands of other ideas. The network there is much richer, and thus, when you are stumped, there are many more routes you can take down the associative web of memory to fill in the blank regarding what someone does for a living. That's why you have a bad memory for some things and not for others. As Buonomano puts it, "complaining you have a bad memory for names or numbers is a bit like whining about your smartphone functioning poorly underwater." The syrupy muck beneath your scalp works best with associations, synthesis, and pattern recognition, and works worst with numbers, lists, measurements, statistics, and similarly hard-edged logic tasks.

Because your semantic memory is more like a network of nodes than a cabinet of files, you are highly susceptible to a psychological phenomenon called priming. Every idea you experience now unconsciously influences all the ideas you experience later. Those ideas then influence your behavior without your realizing it. In studies in which people unscramble sentences about rudeness, those people will later be much more likely to interrupt experimenters after being placed in frustrating situations. People primed by solving puzzles that include words associated with the elderly will temporarily walk more slowly after the task. In one study, subjects asked to imagine how cool it would be to become university professors outperformed others who were not primed in that way in a game of Trivial Pursuit. Priming is one of the fundamental drivers of your behavior, and it isn't limited to simple symbols and images. Studies in which people are asked to hold either a cold or warm beverage show that those same people will react differently to strangers. Subjects who hold a cold coffee cup report back that new people they meet while holding the beverage seem reserved and standoffish. Subjects in that same study who held a warm coffee said the people they met seemed sociable and outgoing. Everything else was made identical to both groups, including the strangers. The only difference was the temperature of the cup the subjects were asked to hold. Psychologists call this embodied cognition—your physical state is translated into words, and those words initiate a cascade of associations. If you begin a conversation while feeling the sensation of warm or cold, it can prime all the varied things you feel when you use the words *warm* and *cold* to describe another person.

All these factors—the symbolic power of clothing, priming, embodied cognition—didn't really come together in psychological research until Hajo Adam and Adam Galinsky, psychologists at Northwestern University, published the results of a study in 2012 that introduced a new term into the scientific lexicon: *enclothed cognition*.

Adam and Galinsky knew that previous research into the effects of clothes on the mind tended to focus on either priming or deindividuation. Psychologists Mark Frank and Thomas Gilovich showed in 1988 that sports teams tended to be more aggressive when players wore black uniforms. Black-wearing teams, across several sports, also tended to rack up more penalties over time compared with teams wearing any other color. Frank and Gilovich's research showed that when a team changed its uniforms to predominantly black, the average number of penalties per game increased immediately. In any sport that rewards aggressive play, you can rank all the teams in order of how many penalties each team received in the course of a season, and the teams with the black attire will clump up at one end. The researchers also found that it wasn't just that players were more bloodthirsty when draped in black, but referees were more likely to notice infractions and penalize players when those players wore black uniforms. In another study, by psychologists Barbara Fredrickson, Stephanie Noll, Tomi-Ann Roberts, Diane Quinn, and Jean Twenge in 1998, women who wore one-piece swimsuits while working on maths problems performed significantly worse than men in swimming trunks and women in jumpers.

Adam and Galinsky weren't satisfied with the literature on clothing, and felt that there was something deeper at work than just priming, so they devised a clever series of experiments. In one, they divided subjects into two groups. One group slipped into lab coats and another remained in the clothes they were already wearing. Members of both groups then worked on a Stroop test. The Stroop test is an exam in which you must identify the color ink used to print a word. You first read words such as *red, blue,* and *green* written in ink matching the color's name. Next, you read the same words in ink that doesn't match. So, for instance, at first the word *blue* is written in blue ink, but in the next run of the test the word *blue* might be written in pink. It's a fun test because no matter how witty or nimble your mind, the nonmatching portion is pretty difficult, at least hard enough to slow you down in a measurable way. So how did the two groups perform on this task? When the colors didn't match the words, the people wearing the lab coats made half as many errors as the people wearing street clothes. There it was—enclothed cognition, a state similar to embodied cognition but unique to clothing. The findings suggested that the physical act of wearing a lab coat actually made the subjects better at a test of attention and sharpness. The wearer embodied the symbolic nature of her guise.

Their next experiment was even better. This time Adam and Galinsky split people into three groups. One group wore white coats, and the scientists told them it was the same coat that doctors wore. Another group wore the same white coats, but the scientists told them they were painters' smocks. In a third group, the scientists presented a coat described as the sort a medical doctor would wear and asked the subjects to write an essay on what images and ideas a doctor's coat conjured up when they considered its meaning. This third group then moved on to the next task with the coat lying on a desk nearby. Members of all three groups then looked at photos positioned side by side, each with four minor difficult-to-spot differences. The psychologists measured how long it took the subjects to find the disparities and how many they found in each set. This is where the most interesting aspect of enclothed cognition appeared. The people who wore what they believed was a painter's smock spotted the fewest differences in the photos. The people who merely thought deeply about a doctor's coat spotted more, and the people who wore what they assumed was a doctor's white coat spotted the most. Priming alone was not as powerful as actually putting on the coat, but even more astounding was that the same clothes can affect you more or less powerfully depending on the symbolic meaning you ascribe to those threads.

The white lab coats pinged the semantic nets of each person in the study, but like the Baker/baker experiment, when a person believed the coat was that of a painter, the web of ideas and associations that flooded into his unconscious was completely different from those of a person who believed she was wearing what doctors wear. For most people, the network of concepts that emerge when pondering a doctor's costume is richer and more powerful than the network surrounding the ideas, schemas, memories, and other assorted concepts related to painters and painting. One symbol is more potent than the other. Priming you to think about doctors is a compelling enough experience to influence you to outperform people who believe they are wearing painters' smocks, but if you go a step further and slip your arms into what you believe to be a doctor's coat, feel it against your skin, notice its weight as you move around, the effect is far more powerful. Adam and Galinsky showed that enclothed cognition isn't just priming. It is something more. They wrote in their study that they speculated the uniforms worn by police, judges, priests, firefighters, soldiers, sports teams, doctors, and so on may do more than communicate the role played by the wearer to other members of society. Those clothes may also strongly alter the wearers' attitudes and behaviors, making them more courageous or ethical or aggressive or compassionate or attentive.

Research has long suggested that clothes aren't completely inanimate or inert, at least not inside the brains of humans. Looking at garments sets in motion a cascade of associations that can and do affect your perceptions and behaviors. Ball gowns, high-heel shoes, fedoras, and burqas—these are not simple objects, but symbols with the power to influence you and others. From Nazi uniforms to Superman's tights, in the grand masquerade, every costume communicates something. The most recent research suggests that this sensation can be taken to even greater heights.

Adorning yourself in symbolic garb affects you on a deeper level than just looking at it when empty or draped over the shoulders of another. As if their fibers were enchanted, the things you wear cast a spell over your persona. The trick is that it's you who is doing the enchanting, and you do it unconsciously. The brain under a wizard's hat is different from one under a cowboy hat or a tiara or a yarmulke or a helmet, not because those objects are infused with a power that radiates into your cerebrum, but because the architecture of your memory won't allow any object to be neutral, whether you notice or not. Symbols, like rituals, are important not because they encourage superstitious behavior or obsolete beliefs, but because they naturally plug into the way your brain works. Everything has a symbolic power, a communicative potential to evoke memories and ideas in your brain like a beehive reacting to a thrown rock.

Use that knowledge to beat your brain, and know that when you feel uncomfortable in a tuxedo or a cocktail dress, part of that feeling comes from resisting the spell of the garment powered by the concepts it primes in your network of self while you remain enclothed. Know, too, that when you want some of the magic associated with fashion, wearing those objects can make you more alert, more assertive. A person wearing glasses both looks and feels smarter, but stranger still, there is evidence to suggest that that person will perform better on tests of intelligence. But also beware. The negative concepts associated with a costume are equally influential. When shrouded in the gowns of evil, their power to affect others seeps into your skin, and we don't yet know the strength or duration of the poison.

# 14.

## *Deindividuation*

---

**THE MISCONCEPTION:** *People who riot and loot are scum who were just looking for an excuse to steal and be violent.*

**THE TRUTH:** *Under the right conditions, you are prone to losing your individuality and becoming absorbed into a hive mind.*

When a crowd gathers near a suicidal jumper, something terrible is unleashed.

In Seattle in 2001 a twenty-six-year-old woman who had recently ended a relationship held up traffic for a little too long as she considered the implications of leaping to her death. As cars began to back up on the bridge and the motorists became irate, the drivers started yelling, "Jump, bitch, jump!" until she did.

Cases like this aren't unusual.

In 2008 a seventeen-year-old man jumped from the top of a car park in England after three hundred or so people chanted for him to go for it. Some took photos and recorded video before, during, and after. The crowd dispersed, the strange spell broken. The taunters walked away wondering what had come over them. The other onlookers vented their disgust on social media.

In San Francisco in 2010 a man stepped onto the ledge of his apartment window and contemplated dropping from the building. A crowd gathered below and soon started yelling for him to jump. They even tweeted about it. He died on impact fifteen minutes later.

One comment in *The San Francisco Examiner* read, "i was there and im traumatized. the guys next to me were laughing telling him to jump and videotaping the whole thing. i'm still young and in high school and this is gunna stick with me for the rest of my life. there was a total lack of respect for the poor man and people were laughing when he jumped."

Police and firefighters are well aware of this tendency for crowds to gather and taunt. This is why they tape off potential suicide scenes and get the crowd out of shouting distance. It takes only one person to get a crowd going. If you lose your sense of self, feel the power of a crowd, and then get slammed by a cue from the environment, your individuality may evaporate.

Within a crowd many will retain their sense of right and wrong. Some are able to maintain their composure. Many who witnessed these events felt terrible about what happened and condemned those who encouraged the jumpers. What they didn't realize, and what the people yelling didn't anticipate, was the predictability and regularity of the behavior.

This is going to be hard to believe, but this sort of behavior could be inside you as well. Under the right circumstances, you, too, might yell, "Jump!" To understand why, let's go shopping for costumes.

As mentioned in the previous chapter on enclothed cognition, Halloween is a fantastic playground for cultural norms to clash and crack. Costumes and chocolate, parents and children, the revelry and irreverence directed toward evil and death and hauntings—it is a day to pull back from standards, the rules of proper and normal behavior, and experiment with surrogate selves. In the United States, Halloween is very popular, with total sales each year around $6 billion. Of that, costumes make up more than $2 billion. Across the country, people recede into anonymity and become absorbed by characters who will be shed the next day. Halloween is fun because it feels good to drop the heft of your flesh-and-blood identity from time to time no matter how old you are. The fantasy is something that kids wearing clown shoes in pursuit of sweets and adults shifting aside Guy Fawkes masks to accommodate Jager shots can both appreciate. Halloween isn't Mardi Gras or Carnival where just about anything goes, but it is truly the only holiday in the United States where everyone agrees to tilt their heads in wonder and let a giant swath of weird things slide.

A great costume can draw attention to the garments of individuality you wear every other day simply by replacing them. Halloween gives you an opportunity to play around with the roles, labels, and characters we all know are in some ways fabrications, mutually accepted fibs required to get by in a complex social game. The mask you wear to work or to a family reunion or out on a first date is not so much different from the one you wear heading out to plead for Snickers or dance to digital mixtapes. These shades of self you've molded and honed over the years started out awkward and blunt, obvious and tacky. As you approached adolescence, you tried on a variety of personae until one fit. You may have pierced body parts or tattooed areas you could cover up when needed. You may have singled out some celebrity or fictional character and cherry-picked from her wardrobe, stealing a bit of her magic in the hope you could add it to yours. Through each season of your life, you sharpen your image and polish your patina until you have a sense of the individual you claim to be. Still, it's always fun to role-play and hit Reset, and Halloween is one of the few widely accepted times you get to do this in front of everyone you know. In many ways, it is a holiday celebrating anonymity through experimentation with individuality.

It was this muted sense of self that, in the late 1970s, led a group of psychologists to turn Halloween into a controlled study of the human mind. Arthur Beaman, Edward Diener, and Soren Svanum traveled to a nice neighborhood in Seattle, Washington, and picked out twenty-seven homes that would become makeshift laboratories. The researchers wanted to see if the anonymity of Halloween costumes would affect the behavior of children as they gallivanted from secret lab to secret lab. The researchers placed inside the entrance to each home a bowl of sweets, a mirror, and a festive Halloween decoration in which a scientist watched through a peephole as children arrived throughout the evening. Yes, it was a bit creepy. Unfortunately, there wasn't a side study into how difficult it would be to hold back the urge to leap out and scream at children while wearing a lab coat and waving a clipboard.

A woman greeted the children throughout the night, and when the tykes presented their trick-or-treat bargains, she told them each could have only one treat. She then walked away, leaving them to sort out their tiny moral codes. Half the time the woman at the door asked the children to say their names and where they lived before leaving them. If the children arrived with adults, they were omitted from the results. The psychologists wondered if the kids would take only one piece, thinking there were no adults around to exact punishment or express disappointment in their gluttony. Would they react differently when alone or in groups? Would saying their names remind them of the people behind the masks? Once the kids were primed to remember their identity, or if they saw their reflection in the mirrors, would it remind them who they were? In the end, the mirror wasn't the determining factor. What made the most difference was whether they had said their names and whether they were alone or in a group.

If they had to say their names and were also alone, less than 10 percent of children cheated. In a group, about 20 percent of those who revealed their identity disobeyed the host. More of the anonymous children stole sweets when alone—20 percent. In a group, close to 60 percent of the anonymous stole sweets. The results suggested that the power of their anonymity was magnified in the presence of others. When the children were left unmasked by giving their names, the cheating in a group rose a bit. When their masks were on, it was turbocharged. The kids who felt most anonymous, and the most protected by the shared anonymity of the group, were also the most likely to break the rules and take more sweets. With anonymity set to maximum, many kids tried to take all the sweets they could.

This study is one of many showing that your identity can spring a leak in the presence of others, and the more others there are, the more you dissolve into the collective will of the group. Looting, rioting, lynchings, beatings, war, chasing a monster with torches—the switch is always there, and it doesn't take much to flip it.

Psychologists call this phenomenon deindividuation. In certain situations, you can expect to be deindividualized. Unlike conformity, in which you adopt the ideas and behaviors of others for acceptance and inclusion, deindividuation is mostly unconscious, and more likely to lead to mischief. As psychologist David G. Myers writes, it is "doing together what you would not do alone." Think back to when you got into the most trouble as a teenager. Chances are, you were in a group and became seduced by the collective will of your peers. There may have been influencers, instigators, or natural leaders, but in the end, everyone in your circle probably dissolved into the mind of the unit. When the headteacher, parent, or police officer asked, "What were you kids thinking?" you had no answer, because there wasn't one. You were just reacting, moving as a herd.

In 1969, psychologist Philip Zimbardo had female university students deliver painful electric shocks to other female students. Half the students giving the shocks were randomly selected to wear big hoods and roomy lab coats during the experiment, in addition to numbered tags. The other half remained unmasked and wore tags revealing their names. Zimbardo told the soon-to-be torturers he was studying creativity under stress, and as a woman on the other side of a one-way mirror took a test, they were to deliver shocks to see if it affected her performance. The women riding the lightning were actually actors and only pretended to writhe in agony.

Zimbardo made sure the subjects knew it was going to hurt by giving each one a sample of 75 volts of pain. In addition, to provide motivation, he had the subjects watch a taped interview with the two test takers in which one seemed friendly and sweet, but the other was rude and mean. Zimbardo didn't tell the girls in either group, masked or unmasked, how often to zap the test takers or for how long. They didn't have to shock at all if they didn't want to. They also didn't talk to each other during the experiment. He wanted to eliminate as best he could obedience to authority and peer pressure. The only factors in play were anonymity and deindividuation. In groups of four, the students sat down and began to torment the test takers.

In each run of the experiment, the women hidden behind hoods and lab coats shocked the test takers twice as often. It didn't matter if the test takers seemed nice or mean; each actor got just as much juice from the hooded women. As the test continued, the shocks got more frequent and lasted longer. All the while, the actors on the other side of the mirror pretended to be in terrible pain.

The women whose faces could be seen shocked the nice actor less often than the unpleasant one, and this, according to Zimbardo, was the most interesting finding. The deindividuation, the anonymity afforded by the hoods, allowed a terrible behavior usually held back by social norms to run free without regard to fairness or justice. Without consequences, the excitement of having control over another person fed on itself. As Zimbardo said, the escalation was driven by a positive-feedback loop of arousal. The more they shocked, the more excited the subjects got. The more excited they got, the more often they shocked. Although no one in the experiment refrained from shocking the test takers, those who weren't masked made a distinction between the woman who deserved her comeuppance and the one who didn't.

Strangely enough, this same experiment was conducted with Belgian soldiers, and when they wore the hoods, they shocked the test takers less. In their case, the uniforms they wore already promoted deindividuation, but the hoods isolated them. Among other soldiers each was part of a unit, a group. Under the hood, he was one person again. Zimbardo wrote in his book *The Lucifer Effect,* "The banality of evil shares much with the banality of heroism. Neither attribute is the direct consequence of unique dispositional tendencies; there are no special inner attributes of either pathology or goodness residing within the human psyche or the human genome."

Zimbardo conducted another experiment, and like the Seattle researchers, he used the wonderful built-in anonymity of Halloween as a tool. He observed as primary school children played games to win tokens they could turn in at the end in exchange for prizes. The kids had a choice of games to play. Some games were competitive but nonaggressive, while others were one-on-one duels such as extracting a beanbag from a tube. The children played these games at a Halloween party both in and out of costume. During the first round, the teacher told the children the costumes were on their way. When the costumes had supposedly arrived, the kids competed again with their identities concealed. Once the competition was over, the teachers said another class needed the costumes, so the children went through the games one more time unmasked. The amount of time the children spent playing the aggressive games, pushing and shoving and yelling, doubled once the costumes were on, going from 42 percent to 86 percent. When the costumes came off, it dropped back to 36 percent. When in costume, under the spell of deindividuation, the kids wanted to go head to head and fight, even though those games took longer and yielded far fewer tokens. As soon as the costumes were removed, they returned to more civil behavior.

Every time you wade into a crowd or don a concealing garment, you risk deindividuation, and it often brings out the worst in you. When you step back and see yourself as the perpetrator, you act as though your reputation and position in society were at stake. When you have no identity, when you are nameless, faceless, and free from retribution, the chains of inhibition fall from your brain.

What hides inside you, held back by inhibition, and how would it manifest itself if freed? Would you yell for someone to jump to her death while tweeting about it and taking photos? Sitting there now, you think there is no way you could do such a thing, but right now you are an individual with social chains binding both the darkest evil and the brightest good in your heart. You can't truly predict what would happen if the three ingredients of deindividuation were added to your consciousness: anonymity, group size, and arousal.

If you recall, arousal can come from a stirring speech, a mind-melting concert with an intense light show, a dangerous enemy pressing forward on your position, or any number of things that get your attention and won't let it go. Chanting, singing, dancing, and other ritualistic, repetitive group activities are particularly effective at focusing your attention and distracting you from the boundaries of your head and body. Your focus and emotional response build and build until the fragile container holding your persona shatters, and not only do your emotions diffuse among the many, but so do your morals and sense of responsibility toward your actions. You no longer feel accountable for your deeds, good or bad, but instead imagine a future in which the group will be praised or blamed for what you did together. It is at this point when you feel fully anonymous. The finely crafted individuality you usually enjoy is suppressed, and the cues from your environment steer you and the others in your group. If you are at Woodstock in 1969, you may feel saturated with love and belonging and come away from the experience with a sense of wonder and joy, in addition to whatever else you end up putting in your body. If you are at Woodstock in 1999, you may feel enraged and aggressive and come away from the experience with broken ribs and a criminal record. In each situation, a giant crowd of people followed the natural path to deindividuation. They became aroused, lost their selves, and then went with the cues from their environment.

Deindividuation is usually promoted in any organization where it is important to reduce inhibition and get you to do things you might not do alone. Soldiers and police don uniforms, warriors wear face paint, gangs have colors and dances and rituals. Businesses spend millions on team building in an effort to instill a deindividualized sense of worth. Celebrations by groups of football supporters have more potential to get out of hand than a party where no one feels absorbed by a group or protected by its norms.

Deindividuation takes away your inhibitions, your sense of self, and your fear of accountability, but this isn't necessarily a bad thing. The same force that influences otherwise rational people to loot and vandalize and invade Poland can also lead to prosocial behaviors. If you are surrounded by positive cues, deindividuation could lead you to work harder in an exercise class, or pitch in at a homeless shelter, or help build a house. People who forget their sense of self and work together to save a life or search for a missing child show that deindividuation is a neutral force of the human will. When Web communities such as 4chan or Reddit assemble into an anonymous collective to exact revenge, it often ends in actual justice. Once deindividuation kicks in, the cues from the environment shape the resulting behavior. The norms of the mob, good or evil, replace the norms of everyday life.

Robert D. Johnson and Leslie Downing showed in 1979 how manipulating environmental cues could change the behavior of deindividualized people. Their study was much like Zimbardo's in that subjects were instructed to shock other people trying to learn a task. In their study, the people delivering the shocks wore either Ku Klux Klan robes or nurses' uniforms. The subjects in the KKK costumes shocked more than control groups, and those in nurses' uniforms shocked less. Psychologists Steven Prentice-Dunn and C. B. Spivey showed in a series of studies in the late 1980s and early '90s that a deindividualized person could be swayed to donate more money than normal if the cues in his environment were prosocial. The deindividuation that occurs at the Super Bowl, the church sermon, the prison riot, and the revolutionary uprising is the same—the behavior that follows is not.

Keep in mind how prone you are to deindividuation and in what situations you are most susceptible to it. Anything from binge drinking to singing hymns can decrease your awareness of self. Add to this the diffusion of responsibility and anonymity that comes from being within a group, living in a large city, sitting in a darkened room, or wearing a mask, and all it takes is a heightened state of arousal for you to become permeable, vulnerable to whatever cues grab your attention. Know, too, that chat rooms, comment threads, and message boards are perfect breeding grounds for deindividuality. The more anonymity a user is allowed, the more powerful the effect of being protected by the group. The tone and tenor of the conversations therein, and the meatspace ramifications of their collective efforts, will reflect the cues provided by the website.

Deindividuation pervades virtual worlds, and the results are mixed. Download the virtual world *Second Life* and take a stroll. Sooner or later you'll end up in a sex dungeon. Play any game on Xbox Live, and someone will eventually claim to have carnal knowledge of your mother. You can thank anonymity and deindividuation for both. The comments under a YouTube video may make you weep for the species, but remember that the same force that built and maintained concentration camps also pushed soldiers onto Omaha Beach.

If you want to promote deindividuation for a good cause either in the analog world or a digital one, help people in your group feel safe from judgment, and provide prosocial cues. If, instead, you want to discourage deindividuation in yourself and others, you must eliminate anonymity and avoid dehumanizing labels. The more you feel personal accountability, the more restraint you will show.

If nothing else, remember that if you want to throw a badass party where inhibitions fade and hijinks ensue, turn down the lights, turn up the music, and, if appropriate, wear costumes.

# 15.

# *The Sunk Cost Fallacy*

---

**THE MISCONCEPTION:** *You make rational decisions based on the future value of objects, investments, and experiences.*

**THE TRUTH:** *Your decisions are tainted by the emotional investments you accumulate, and the more you invest in something, the harder it becomes to abandon it.*

You can learn a lot about dealing with loss from a video game called *FarmVille*.

You have probably heard of this game. In 2010 one in five Facebook users had a *FarmVille* account. The barrage of updates generated by the game annoyed other users so much it forced the social network to change how users sent messages. At its peak, 84 million people played it, a number greater than the population of Italy.

*FarmVille* accounts have steadily shrunk since then. About 50 million people were still playing in early 2011, still impressive considering the fantasy megagame *World of Warcraft* boasted about a quarter as many players at the same time. In late 2012 Zynga, the company behind the game, launched *FarmVille 2*, and by January of 2013 more than 42 million people had joined up to try it out.

A game with this many players must promise potent, unadulterated joy, right? Actually, the lasting appeal of *FarmVille* has little to do with fun. To understand why people commit to this game and what it can teach you about the addictive nature of investment, you must first understand how your fear of loss leads to the sunk cost fallacy.

In psychologist Daniel Kahneman's book *Thinking Fast and Slow*, he writes about how he and his colleague Amos Tversky, through their work in the 1970s and '80s, uncovered the imbalance between losses and gains in your mind. Kahneman explains that since all decisions involve uncertainty about the future, the human brain you use to make decisions has evolved an automatic and unconscious system for judging how to proceed when a potential for loss arises. Kahneman says organisms that placed more urgency on avoiding threats than they did on maximizing opportunities were more likely to pass on their genes. So, over time, the prospect of losses has become a more powerful motivator on your behavior than the promise of gains. Whenever possible, you try to avoid losses of any kind, and when comparing losses to gains you don't treat them equally. The results of their experiments and the results of many others who've replicated and expanded on them have teased out an inborn loss aversion ratio. When offered a chance to accept or reject a gamble, most people refuse to make a bet unless the possible payoff is around double the potential loss.

Behavioral economist Dan Ariely adds a fascinating twist to loss aversion in his book *Predictably Irrational*. He writes that when factoring the costs of any exchange, you tend to focus more on what you may lose in the bargain than on what you stand to gain. The "pain of paying," as he puts it, arises whenever you must give up anything you own. The precise amount doesn't matter at first. You'll feel the pain no matter what price you must pay, and it will influence your decisions and behaviors.

In one of his experiments, Ariely set up a booth in a well-trafficked area. Passersby could purchase chocolates—Hershey's Kisses for one penny a piece or Lindt Truffles for fifteen cents each. The majority of people who faced this offer chose the truffles. It was a fine deal considering the quality differences and the normal prices of both items. Ariely then set up another booth with the same two choices but lowered the price by one cent each, thus making the Kisses cost nothing and the truffles cost 14 cents each. This time, the vast majority of people selected the Kisses instead of the truffles.

If people acted on pure mathematical logic, explained Ariely, there should have been no change in the behavior of the subjects. The price difference was the same. But you don't think in that way. Your loss aversion system is always vigilant, waiting on standby to keep you from giving up more than you can afford to spare, so you calculate the balance between cost and reward whenever possible. He speculates that this is why you accumulate free tchotchkes you don't really want or need and why you find it so tempting to accept shady deals if they include free gifts or choose decent services that offer free shipping over better services that do not. When anything is offered free of charge, Ariely believes your loss aversion system remains inactive. Without it, you don't weigh the pros and cons with as much attention to detail as you would if you had to factor in potential losses.

This is why marketing and good salesmanship are all about convincing you that what you want to buy is worth more than what you must pay for it. You see something as a good value when you predict the pain of loss will be offset by your joy of gain. If the salesman does his job well, somewhere in your jumbled perception you feel you won't lose at all. Emotionally, you will come out ahead. Unless you are buying something just to show others how much money you can burn, you avoid cringing when you fork over your earnings.

When you lose something permanently, it hurts. The drive to mitigate this negative emotion leads to strange behaviors. Have you ever gone to see a movie only to realize within fifteen minutes or so that you are watching one of the worst films ever made, but you sit through it anyway? You don't want to waste the money, so you slide back in your chair and suffer. Maybe you once bought nonrefundable tickets to a concert, and when the night arrived, you felt sick or tired or hungover. Perhaps something more appealing was happening at the same time. Still, you went to the concert anyway, even though you didn't want to, in order to justify spending money you knew you could never get back. What about that time you made it back home with a box of spicy chicken wings, and after the first bite you suspected they might have been filled with salsa-infused dog food, but you ate them anyway, not wanting to waste either money or food? If you've experienced a version of any of these, you've fallen victim to the sunk cost fallacy.

Sunk costs are payments or investments that can never be recovered. An android with fully functioning logic circuits would never make a decision that took sunk costs into account, but you would. As an emotional human, your aversion to loss often leads you right into the sunk cost fallacy. A confirmed loss lingers and grows in your mind, becoming larger in your history than it was when you first felt it. Whenever this clinging to the past becomes a factor in making decisions about your future, you run the risk of being derailed by the sunk cost fallacy.

Hal Arkes and Catherine Blumer created an experiment in 1985 that demonstrated your tendency to go fuzzy when sunk costs come along. They asked subjects to assume they had spent one hundred dollars on a ticket for a ski trip in Michigan, but soon after found a better ski trip in Wisconsin for fifty dollars and bought a ticket for this trip, too. They then asked the people in the study to imagine they learned the two trips overlapped and the tickets couldn't be refunded or resold. Which one do you think they chose, the one-hundred-dollar good holiday or the fifty-dollar great one?

More than half of the people in the study went with the more expensive trip. It may not have promised to be as much fun, but the loss seemed greater taking the cheaper holiday. That's the fallacy at work, because the money is gone no matter what. You can't get it back. The fallacy prevents you from realizing the best choice is to do whatever promises the better experience in the future, not that which negates the feeling of loss in the past.

Kahneman and Tversky also conducted an experiment to demonstrate the sunk cost fallacy. See how you do with this one. Imagine you go see a movie that costs ten pounds for a ticket. When you open your wallet or purse you realize you've lost a ten-pound note. Would you still buy a ticket? You probably would. Only 12 percent of subjects said they wouldn't. Now imagine you go to see the movie and pay ten pounds for a ticket, but right before you hand it over you realize you've lost the ticket. Would you go back and buy another one? Maybe, but it would hurt a lot more. In the experiment, 54 percent of people said they would not. The situation is exactly the same—you lose ten pounds and then must pay ten pounds to see the movie—but the second scenario feels different. It seems that the money was assigned to a specific purpose and then lost, and loss sucks. This is why *FarmVille* is so addictive that people have lost their jobs over it.

*FarmVille* is a valuable tool for understanding your weakness in the face of loss. The sunk cost fallacy is the engine that keeps *FarmVille* running, and the developers behind *FarmVille* know this. *FarmVille* is free, and the first time you log on you are transported to a patch of grass where you float above an abeyant young farmhand eager to get to work. His will is your will, and his world is empty save the land ready to be plowed and a crop of vegetables ready to be picked. Wading into the experience, you feel the game designers have made every attempt to turn your head toward the screen in the least obtrusive but most insidious way possible. It is all your choice, they seem to be saying; no one is forcing you to proceed. Here, harvest these beans. Hey, why not plant some seed? Oh, look, you could plow a patch of land, you know, if you want. A loading bar appears and then quickly fills as you watch your grinning Aryan-ish avatar with his messy-on-purpose haircut virtually dirty his digital overalls. The cheery music, which sounds like a cyborg interpretation of clumsily extracted memories from the brain of a reanimated Old West piano player, drones on and on. The moment the loop restarts is difficult to pinpoint.

Within a few minutes, you've done everything that can be done on your first garden, but there are hints all over the screen portending a fully functioning Texas-ranch-size megafarm should you plant your seeds well. Once you learn you must wait at least an hour or so to continue, you start clicking around and find you have coins and cash that can be spent on trees, plants, seeds, an impressive bestiary of jaunty fantastical creatures, and a bevy of clothes, devices, buildings, and props. You have just enough currency when the game starts to buy a caramel apple tree or some honeybees, but the nice stuff, such as pink tractors and magic waterfalls, will have to wait until you've played the game awhile. If you stay vigilant, checking back throughout the day to see how close your strawberries are to being ripe or if a wandering animal has visited your feed trough, you can earn more virtual currency and advance in levels and unlock more stuff. You'll need to plant and plow and harvest to advance, most of which is also an investment in something that must be harvested . . . later.

This is the powerful force behind *FarmVille*. Playing *FarmVille* is a commitment to a virtual life form. Your neglect has consequences. If you don't return, your investments die and you will feel like you've wasted your time, virtual money, and effort. You must return, sometimes days later, to reap the reward of the time and virtual money you are spending now. If you don't, not only do you not get rewarded, but you also lose your investments. To stave off these feelings, you can pay *FarmVille* real-world money or participate in offers from its advertisers to negate the need to tend to certain things, reverse the death of crops, or expand your farm ahead of schedule. You can also ask your friends to help, since the game has tendrils reaching deep into Facebook.

Although all these strategies will keep the fallacy at bay for a few days, they also feed it. The urge to stay the course and keep your farm flourishing gets more powerful the more you invest in it, the more you ask others for help, the more time you spend thinking about it. People set alarms to wake up in the middle of the night to keep their farm alive. You continue to play *FarmVille* not to have fun but to avoid negative emotions. It isn't the crop you are harvesting, but your fallacy. You return and click to patch cracks in a dam holding back something icky in your mind: the sense you wasted something you can never get back.

To say that *FarmVille* has been successful is a silly sort of understatement. It has led to the creation of a whole new genre of entertainment. Hundreds of millions of dollars are being generated by social gaming, and like so many profitable businesses, someone is hedging their bets against a predicable weakness in your behavior in order to turn a profit. *FarmVille* players are mired in a pit of sunk costs. They can never get back the time or money they've spent, but they keep playing to avoid feeling the pain of loss and the ugly sensation that waste creates.

You may not play *FarmVille,* but there is probably something similar in your life. It could be a degree you want to change, or a career you want to escape, or a relationship you know is rotten. You don't stick with it, or return to it over and over again, to create good experiences and pleasant memories but to hold back the negative emotions you expect to feel if you accept the loss of time, effort, money, or whatever else you have invested.

If you dropped your mobile phone over the edge of a cruise ship, you would need James Cameron's unmanned submarine fleet to find it again. Sure, you could spend a small fortune to retrieve it, but you wouldn't throw good money after bad. When the argument is laid out like this, logical and rational and easy to pick apart, you can pat yourself on the back for being such a reasonable human. Unfortunately, the sunk costs in life aren't always so easy to see. When something is gone forever it can be difficult to realize it. The past isn't as tangible a concept as the sea floor, yet it is just as untouchable. What is left behind is just as irretrievable.

Sunk costs drive wars, push up prices in auctions, and keep failed political policies alive. The fallacy makes you finish the meal when you are already full. It fills your home with things you no longer want or use. Every garage sale is a funeral for someone's sunk costs.

The sunk cost fallacy is sometimes called the Concorde fallacy when it is used to describe an escalation of commitment. This is a reference to the construction of the first commercial supersonic airliner. Early on, the project was predicted to be a failure, but everyone involved kept going. Their shared investment built a hefty psychological burden that outweighed their better judgments. After losing an incredible amount of money, effort, and time, they didn't want to just give up.

It is a noble and exclusively human proclivity, this desire to persevere, the will to stay the course—studies show lower animals and small children do not commit this fallacy. Wasps and worms, rats and raccoons, toddlers and tykes—they do not care how much they've invested or how much goes to waste. They can only see immediate losses and gains. As an adult human being, you have the gift of reflection and regret. You can predict a future place where you must admit your efforts were in vain, your losses permanent, and when you accept the truth, it is going to hurt.

# 16.

# *The Overjustification Effect*

---

**THE MISCONCEPTION:** *There is nothing better in the world than getting paid to do what you love.*

**THE TRUTH:** *Getting paid for doing what you already enjoy will sometimes cause your love for the task to wane because you attribute your motivation as coming from the reward, not your internal feelings.*

Money isn't everything. Money can't buy happiness. Don't live someone else's dream. Figure out what you love and then figure out how to get paid to do it.

Maxims like these waft out of the collective sighs of well-paid boredom around the world and get routinely polished for presentation in graduation speeches and church sermons. Money, fame, and prestige—they dangle just outside your reach it seems, encouraging you to lean farther and farther over the edge, to study longer and longer, to work harder and harder. When someone reminds you that acquiring currency while ignoring all else shouldn't be your primary goal in life, it feels good. You retweet it. You post it on your wall. You forward it, and then you go back to work.

If only science had something concrete to say about the whole thing. All these living greeting cards dispensing wisdom are great and all, but what about really putting money to the test? Does money buy happiness? In 2010, scientists published the results of a study looking into that very question.

The research, by Daniel Kahneman and Angus Deaton, published in the *Proceedings of the National Academy of Sciences*, analyzed the lives and incomes of nearly half a million randomly selected U.S. citizens. They dug through the subjects' lives searching for indicators of something psychologists call "emotional well-being," a clinical term for how often you feel peaks and valleys such as "joy, stress, sadness, anger and affection" and to what degree you feel those things daily. In other words, they measured how happy or sad people were over time compared with how much cash they brought home. They did this by checking if the subjects were consistently able to experience the richness of existence, to taste the poetic marrow of life.

The researchers discovered that money is indeed a major factor in day-to-day happiness. No surprise there. You need to make a certain amount, on average, to be able to afford food, shelter, clothing, entertainment, and the occasional Apple product, but what spun top hats around the country was their finding that, beyond a certain point, your happiness levels off. The happiness that money offers doesn't keep getting more and more potent—it plateaus. The research showed that a lack of money brings unhappiness, but an overabundance does not have the opposite effect.

According to the research, in modern America the average income required to be happy day to day, to experience "emotional well-being" is about $75,000 a year. According to the researchers, past that point, adding more to your income "does nothing for happiness, enjoyment, sadness, or stress." A person who makes, on average, $250,000 a year has no greater emotional well-being, no extra day-to-day happiness, than a person making $75,000 a year. In Kentucky it is a bit less, in Chicago a bit more, but the point is there is evidence for the existence of a financiohappiness ceiling. The super-wealthy may believe they are happier, and you may agree, but you both share a delusion.

If you don't already have it, money can improve your life and make you happier, but once you have enough to go to Pizza Express on Tuesday night without worrying about paying the water bill that month, you're good to go. Or, as Henry David Thoreau once said, "A man is rich in proportion to the number of things which he can afford to let alone." In the modern United States the ability to let most things alone, according to Kahneman and Deaton's research, costs about $75,000 a year.

If you find that hard to believe, you aren't the only one. A study in 2011 at Cornell University asked Americans which they would rather have, more money or more sleep. Most people said more money. In a choice between either $80,000 a year, normal work hours, and about eight hours of sleep a night versus $140,000 a year, routine overtime, and six hours of nightly sleep—the majority of people went with the cash. It's unfortunate, because although it looks good on paper and feels right in your gut, the research has never agreed. No matter how you turn it, the science says that once your basic needs are taken care of, money and other rewards don't make you happier, and you can appreciate why after examining a psychological jewel called the overjustification effect. To understand it, we must travel to 1973, when a group of psychologists poisoned a few children's love of drawing in the name of science.

Throughout the twentieth century, as psychology came into its own as a scientific discipline, many psychologists emerged from the halls of academia and ascended to the rank of celebrity after delivering open-palmed scientific slaps to the face of mankind. Sigismund Freud got people talking about the unconscious and the malleable, hidden world of desires and fears. Carl Jung put the ideas of archetypes, introversion, and extroversion into our vocabulary. Abraham Maslow gave us a hierarchy of needs, including hugs and sex. Timothy Leary fed Harvard students psychedelic mushrooms and advocated that an entire generation should use LSD to "turn on, tune in, and drop out." There are many more, but in the 1970s, B. F. Skinner was the rock star of psychology. Skinner and his boxes made the cover of *Time* magazine in 1971 underneath the ominous proclamation WE CAN'T AFFORD FREEDOM. His research into behaviorism had made its way into the public consciousness, and he was intent on using his celebrity to convince all of humanity there was no such thing as free will. You've seen his findings in practice. The Supernanny and the Dog Whisperer reward desired behavior and either punish or ignore undesired behavior—and they get impressive results. Skinner could make birds do figure eights on his command, or train them to pilot guided missiles. He invented climate-controlled baby boxes in which infants never cried. He created teaching machines that still influence user interfaces today. But he also scared a romantic generation of freedom seekers into thinking freedom might be an illusion.

Skinner said all human thoughts and behaviors were just reactions to stimuli—conditioned responses. To believe as Skinner did is to believe everything you do is part of seeking a reward or avoiding a punishment. Your entire life is just a stack of evolutionarily selected-against quirks and desires seasoned with programmed interests and fears. There is no free will. There is no one in control.

Those things are illusions, side effects of a complex nervous system observing its own actions and cognitions. In light of this, Skinner advocated we build a society through setting goals and then condition people toward those goals through positive reinforcement. Skinner didn't trust human beings not to be lazy, greedy, and violent. Humans, he said, were inclined to seek and reinforce status through institutions, class warfare, and bloodshed. People can't be trusted with freedom, he told the world. Psychology could instead design systems to condition people toward positive goals that ensured the best possible quality of life for all.

As you might imagine, the proclamation that humans have no soul, or at least no special spark, caused a great deal of consternation. Many psychologists resisted the idea that you are nothing more than chemical reactions on top of physical laws playing themselves out no differently than rocks crashing down the side of a mountain or a tree converting sunlight and carbon dioxide into wood. Skinner claimed that what goes on inside your head is irrelevant; that the environment, the stuff outside your skull, determines behavior, thoughts, emotions, beliefs, and so on. It was a bold and terrifying claim to many, so science set about the task of picking it apart.

Among those who wanted to know if the mind was just a pile of reactions to rewards and punishments were psychologists Mark Lepper, Daniel Greene, and Richard Nisbett. They wondered if thinking about thinking played a bigger role than the behaviorists suggested. In their book, *The Hidden Costs of Reward,* they detail one experiment in particular that helped pull psychology out from under what they called Skinner's "long shadow."

In 1973, Lepper, Greene, and Nisbett met with teachers of a preschool class, the sort that generates a steady output of macaroni art and paper-bag vests. They arranged for the children to have a period of free time in which the tots could choose from a variety of fun activities. Meanwhile, the psychologists would watch from behind a one-way mirror and take notes. The teachers agreed, and the psychologists watched. To proceed, they needed children with a natural affinity for art. So as the kids played, the scientists searched for the ones who gravitated toward drawing and coloring activities. Once they identified the artists of the group, the scientists watched them during free time and measured their participation and interest in drawing for later comparison.

They then divided the children into three groups. They offered Group A a glittering certificate of awesomeness if the artists drew during the next fun time. They offered Group B nothing, but if the kids in Group B happened to draw, they received an unexpected certificate of awesomeness identical to the one received by Group A. The experimenters told Group C nothing ahead of time, and later the scientists didn't award a prize if those children went for the colored pencils and markers. The scientists then watched to see how the kids performed during a series of playtimes over three days. They awarded the prizes, stopped observations, and waited two weeks. When they returned, the researchers watched as the children faced the same choice as before the experiment began. Three groups, three experiences, many fun activities—how do you think their feelings changed?

Well, Group B and Group C didn't change at all. They went to the art supplies and created monsters and mountains and houses with curlicue smoke streams crawling out of rectangular chimneys with just as much joy as they had before they met the psychologists. Group A, though, did not. They were different people now. The children in Group A "spent significantly less time" drawing than did the others, and they "showed a significant decrease in interest in the activity" as compared to before the experiment. Why?

The children in Group A were swept up and overpowered, their joy perverted by the overjustification effect. The story they told themselves wasn't the same story the other groups were telling themselves. Self-perception theory says you observe your own behavior and then, after the fact, make up a story to explain it. That story is sometimes close to the truth, and sometimes it is just something nice that makes you feel better about being a person. For instance, remember the Stanford University experiment on the Benjamin Franklin effect, in which people were paid for turning wooden knobs round and round for an hour? Some were paid well, and some were paid very little, but both were asked to lie about their experience to a stranger and then to rate the experience honestly. The people paid a pittance reported that the study was a blast. The people paid well reported that it was awful. Subjects in both groups lied to the person after them, but the people paid well had a justification, an extrinsic reward to fall back on. The other group had no safety net, no outside justification, so they invented one inside. To keep from feeling icky, they found solace in an internal justification—they thought, You know, it really was fun when you think about. If you recall, that's called the insufficient justification effect, the yang to overjustification's yin. They told themselves stories that differed based on the size of their rewards and whether they felt extrinsically or intrinsically motivated. You are driven at the fundamental level in almost everything you choose to do by either intrinsic or extrinsic goals.

Intrinsic motivations come from within. As Daniel Pink explained in his excellent book *Drive,* those motivations often include mastery, autonomy, and purpose. There are some things you do just because they fulfill you, or they make you feel that you are becoming better at a task, or that you are a master of your destiny, or that you play a role in the grand scheme of things, or that you are helping society in some way. Intrinsic rewards demonstrate to you and others the value of being you. They are blurry and difficult to quantify. Charted on a graph, they form long slopes stretching into infinity. You strive to become an amazing cellist, or you volunteer in the campaign of an inspiring politician, or you build the starship *Enterprise* in *Minecraft*.

Extrinsic motivations come from without. They are tangible baubles handed over for tangible deeds. They usually exist outside of you before you begin a task. These sorts of motivations include money, prizes, and grades or, in the case of punishment, the promise of losing something you like or acquiring something you do not. Extrinsic motivations are easy to quantify, and can be demonstrated in bar graphs or tallied on a calculator. You work a double shift for the overtime pay so you can make rent. You put in the hours to become a doctor hoping your father will finally deliver the praise for which you long. You say no to the cheesecake so you can fit into that dress at the Christmas party. If you can admit to yourself that the reward is the only reason you are doing what you are doing—the sit-ups, the spreadsheet, the speed limit—it is probably extrinsic. Whether a reward is intrinsic or extrinsic helps determine the setting of your narrative—the marketplace or the heart. As Dan Ariely writes in his book *Predictably Irrational,* you tend to unconsciously evaluate your behavior and that of others in terms of social norms or market norms. Helping a friend move for free doesn't feel the same as helping a friend move for fifty pounds. It feels wonderful to slip into the same bed with your date after getting to know him and staying up one night making butterscotch crepes and talking about the differences and similarities between *Breaking Bad* and *The Wire,* but if after all that he tosses you a hundred pounds and says, "Thanks, that was awesome," you will feel crushed by the terrible weight of market norms. Payments in terms of social norms are intrinsic, and thus your narrative remains impervious to the overjustification effect. Those sorts of payments come as praise and respect, a feeling of mastery or camaraderie or love. Payments in terms of market norms are extrinsic, and your story becomes vulnerable to overjustification. Marketplace payments come as something measurable, and in turn, they make your motivation measurable when before it was nebulous, up for interpretation and easy to rationalize.

The children in the experiment who fell out of love with art did so not because they received a reward but because of the deal they struck with the experimenters. After all, the children in Group B got the same reward and kept their desire to draw. No, it wasn't the prize but the story they told themselves about why they chose what they chose, why they did what they did. During the experiment, Group C thought, I just drew this picture because I love to draw! Group B thought, I just got rewarded for doing something I love to do! Group A thought, I just drew this to win an award! When all three groups were faced with the same activity, Group A was faced with a metacognition, a question, a burden unknown to the other groups. These children asked themselves why they would draw if there was no reward. Thinking about thinking changes things. Extrinsic rewards can steal your narrative. As Lepper, Greene, and Nisbett wrote, "engagement in an activity of initial interest under conditions that make salient to the person the instrumentality of engagement in that activity as a means to some ulterior end may lead to decrements in subsequent, intrinsic interest in the activity." In other words, if you are offered a reward to do something you love and then agree, you will later question whether you continue to do it for love or for the reward.

In 1980, David Rosenfield, Robert Folger, and Harold Adelman revealed a way you can defeat the overjustification effect. Seek employers who dole out rewards—paychecks, bonuses, promotions, etc.—based not on quotas or tasks completed but instead on competence. They ran an experiment in which they told subjects the goal was to find fun and interesting ways to improve vocabulary skills in schools. They placed participants in two categories and two groups per category. In one category, subjects would be paid for being good at their task. In the other category, the subjects would be paid for completing a task. The subjects received twenty-six dice with letters on their faces instead of dots and a stack of index cards each with thirteen random letters. The subjects hit a timer and used their dice to make words from the letters on the cards. Once they had used nine letters or spent a minute and a half trying, they moved on to the next index card and kept repeating until the experiment ended. It was difficult but fun, and as the players kept going, they started to improve in their abilities.

In the payment-for-competence category, Group A was told they were being paid based on how well they did compared with the average score. In Group B, the subjects were told they would be compared with the average, but there was no mention of any reward. In the payment-for-completion category, the scientists told Group C each completed puzzle would increase their payout, and Group D was told they would be paid by the hour. After the games, the experimenters pretended to tally up the subjects' scores and showed groups A and B how well they did. No matter how they actually performed, the scientists told half of groups A and B that they'd done poorly and half that they were amazing at the game. Groups C and D, the ones who were paid for completions, were also split. Half got low pay, and half high pay. The subjects then filled out a questionnaire and sat alone in a room with the dice and cards for three minutes. During that alone time the real study began. The scientists wanted to see who would keep playing the game for fun and for how long.

The people in groups A and B, the ones who were paid for being better than average, picked up the game and played it for more than two minutes, but slightly less than that if they had been told they weren't that good. The people in groups C and D, the ones paid for completions, didn't play it for fun for as long as did the people in the competency groups, and they tended to play longer the less they were paid.

The results of the study suggested that when you get rewarded based on how well you perform a task, as long as those reasons are made perfectly clear, rewards will generate that electric exuberance of intrinsic validation, and the higher the reward, the better the feeling and the more likely you will try harder in the future. On the other hand, if you are getting rewarded just for being a warm body, no matter how well you do your job, no matter what you achieve, the electric feeling is absent. In those conditions, greater rewards don't lead to more output, don't encourage you to strive for greatness. Overall, the study suggested rewards don't have motivational power unless they make you feel competent. Money alone doesn't do that. With money, when you explain to yourself why you worked so hard, all you can come up with is "to get paid." You come to believe you are being coerced, paid off, bought out. In the absence of what the scientists called "competency feedback," there is no story to tell yourself that paints you as a badass. Quotas and overtime and hourly pay don't offer such indications of competency. Bonuses based on reaching a specific number of completions or reaching a quantified goal make you feel like a machine. If you pay people to complete puzzles instead of paying them for being smart, they lose interest in the game. If you pay children to draw, fun becomes work. Payment on top of compliments and other praise and feeling good about personal achievement are powerful motivators, but only if they are unexpected. Only then can you continue to tell the story that keeps you going; only then can you still explain your motivation as coming from within.

Consider the story you tell yourself about why you do what you do for a living. How vulnerable is that tale to these effects?

Maybe your story goes like this: Work is just a means to an end. You go to work; you get paid. You exchange effort for survival tokens and the occasional steampunk thong from Etsy. Work is not fun. Work pays bills. Fun happens at places that are not work. Your story is in no danger if that's how you see things. In an environment like that, Skinner's assumptions hold true: You will work only as hard as is necessary to keep getting paychecks. If offered greater rewards, you'll work harder for them. Maybe your story goes like this, though: I love what I do. It changes lives. It makes the world a better place. I am slowly becoming a master in my field, and I get to choose how I solve problems. My bosses value my efforts, depend on me, and offer praise. In this scenario, rewards just get in the way of your job. As Kahneman and Deaton's study about happiness showed, once you earn enough to be happy day to day, motivation must come from something else. Kahneman and Deaton's research seems to suggest that the only material reward worth seeking once you have a bed, running water, and access to microwave popcorn, are tributes—symbols of your merit, stuff that demonstrates your effectance to yourself and others. Ranks, degrees, gold stars, trophies, Nobel Prizes, and Academy Awards—these are shorthand indicators of your competence. Those rewards amplify your internal motivations; they build your self-esteem and strengthen your feelings of self-efficacy. They show you've leveled up in the real world. Achievement unlocked. They help you construct a personal narrative you enjoy telling.

The overjustification effect threatens your fragile narratives, especially if you haven't figured out what to do with your life. You run the risk of seeing your behavior as motivated by profit instead of interest if you agree to get paid for something you would probably do for free. Conditioning will not only fail; it will also pollute you. You run the risk of believing that the reward, not your passion, was responsible for your effort, and it will be a challenge to generate future enthusiasm. It becomes more and more difficult to look back on your actions and describe them in terms of internal motivations. The thing you love can become drudgery if that which can't be measured is transmuted into something you can plug into your tax return.

# 17.

## *The Self-Enhancement Bias*

---

**THE MISCONCEPTION:** *You set attainable goals based on a realistic evaluation of your strengths and weaknesses.*

**THE TRUTH:** *You protect unrealistic attitudes about your abilities in order to stay sane and avoid despair.*

Take a deep, deep breath.

No, really. Go ahead and take in as much air as you can.

Keep going. Come on, just a little bit more. Okay. Let it out.

Did you feel like you couldn't quite breathe in as much as you could probably hold? Now take a deep breath and then breathe out as much air as you can. Keep pushing it out. A little more—try to get every last puff out of your body. Okay, grab your breath and look around to see if anyone is calling for paramedics or police.

You may have noticed at some point in your life that it is impossible to completely inflate or deflate your lungs. You don't have complete control over your body in this regard. Your brain doesn't trust you with that much responsibility. Most of your organs do their business without any direct input from your whims, and it's a good thing, too. It would probably be a bad idea to hand the keys to the pancreas over to a person who routinely forgets his phone at restaurants. You are allowed to mess with only a handful of the bazillions of processes swirling and spinning and streaming throughout your body. One of those functions under partial control is breathing, and most of the time you leave it to your automatic systems to handle. Still, when you do take control and do silly things such as hold your breath or try to completely exhale because some book asked you to, there are behavioral safeguards in place to prevent you from popping your alveoli or emptying so much air from your body that the tiny bits collapse and stick together. There is a respiration inhibition module in your brain that prevents you from damaging your lungs with your free will. Not literally, of course, but it is useful to imagine such a thing since the results are the same.

Your body also resists excessive self-doubt. When the giant boot of reality begins to press down on you, a series of defense mechanisms pushes back. Just as your body resists your attempt to empty all the air from your lungs with its respiration inhibition module, you also keep yourself motivated thanks to a sort of despair-inhibition module. It is a pretty complicated piece of mental machinery full of what psychologists call positive illusions. These illusions serve as a system of checks and balances running in the background at all times. Taken together, they form your self-enhancement bias—the rosy glasses through which you see yourself.

Shelley Taylor and Jonathon Brown made positive illusions famous among psychologists with their research on cancer patients in the 1980s. Before them, the widely held assumption in mental health was that the more accurate your perception and cognitions, the happier you became. Such was the mantra of the humanist psychologists—Abraham Maslow and his hierarchy of needs, Carl Rogers and his person-centered therapy. In the 1940s and '50s, Maslow and Rogers championed a view that preferred to see human beings as something more than just molecules of meat. They felt it was wrong to assume you could approach the mind as a biological machine that could be repaired and improved at the level of its cogs and gears. Instead, they advocated something that still reverberates in the public consciousness today: a holistic approach to mental health. They saw you as a creature with a sense of self and a desire for improvement of that self. To reach that goal you need first to satisfy biological needs, they said, and once your most basic needs are met, your final hurdle is to become the best possible version of yourself. That final goal was called self-actualization, and in that state, they said, you would become completely honest with yourself and others. Rogers called the gap between how you see yourself and how you really are incongruence. He believed that the more you moved toward congruence, toward matching reality with your subjective experience, the happier you would become. You would no longer lie about your abilities or hide your shortcomings, but instead would be a totally open book during both introspection and conversation.

The idea that people would be happier if they maintained a constant state of realism is a beautiful sentiment, but Taylor and Brown found just the opposite. They presented a new theory that suggested that well-being came from unrealistic views of reality. They said you reduce the stress of terminal illness or a high-pressure job or unexpected tragedy by resorting to optimism and delusion. Your wildly inaccurate self-evaluations get you through rough times and help motivate you when times are good. Indeed, later research backed up their claims, showing that people who are brutally honest with themselves are not as happy day to day as peo-.ple with unrealistic assumptions about their abilities. People who take credit for the times when things go their way but who put the blame on others when they stumble or fall are generally happier people.

Your explanatory style exists along a gradient. At one end is a black swamp of unrealistic negative opinions about life and your place in it. At the other end is an overexposed forest of unrealistic positive opinions about how other people see you and your own competence. Right below the midpoint of this spectrum is a place where people see themselves in a harsh yellow light of objectivity. Positive illusions evaporate there, and the family of perceptions mutating off the self-serving bias cannot take root. About 20 percent of all people live in that spot, and psychologists call the state of mind generated by those people depressive realism. If your explanatory style rests in that area of the spectrum, you tend to experience a moderate level of depression more often than not because you are cursed to see the world as a place worthy neither of great dread nor of bounding delight, but just a place. You have a strange superpower—the ability to see the world closer to what it really is. Your more accurate representations of social reality make you feel bad and weird mainly because most people have a reality-distortion module implanted in their heads; sadly, yours is either missing or malfunctioning. The notion of depressed realism has its naysayers, but meta-analysis of the last few decades of research still favors the concept. It also shows that even if you are one of those people who seem to have misplaced their rose-tinted glasses, you can't eliminate positive illusions entirely. They may shrink up to dehydrated specks and look tiny alongside their giant delusional counterparts inside your most optimistic peers, but they don't completely disappear. To be a person is to be irrationally positive about your ability to understand and affect the world around you.

Taylor and Brown revealed a new side to the research of well-being, and found that you maintain happiness under the spell of three broad positive illusions: illusory superiority bias, an unrealistically positive view of yourself; the illusion of control, the belief that you have command over the chaos that awaits you every day; and optimism bias, the belief in a future that can't possibly be as great as you expect it to be. Let's take a look at these in action, starting with the illusory superiority bias.

Have you ever had the thought while stuffed into an airplane or pressed against strangers on the tube that you are probably the dumbest person in the room? What about at a shopping center near the holidays, people bumping into you, children screaming, long lines of angry shoppers huffing and loudly answering phones using the latest pop music hits to signal incoming calls—in that environment, do you have a gut feeling that you would struggle in a game of Trivial Pursuit with the average shopper? How about opening night of a blockbuster movie? Do you sit in a crowd listening to people having casual conversations about their sister-in-law's hemorrhoid operation and, upon comparison with the people around you, see yourself as below average in the realms of politeness and consideration?

Imagine in any one of these scenarios that you had every person in the room take an IQ test. Where do you think you would rank compared with others in the group? Near the top? Near the bottom? What if you compared your driving skills with those of everyone else on the road during your typical morning commute? Imagine we created a graph that judged the cooking ability of every person you went to school with on a scale from one to ten. Where do you think you would fall on that scale? Most people put themselves slightly above average, so in this imaginary experiment—unless you know you are a terrible or an excellent cook—you likely thought you were about a six.

The illusory superiority bias allows you to move through airports and cinemas unhindered by the burden of realistic analysis. This is an enchantment generated by the brain that allows you to judge yourself in a light more positive and less harsh than the one you shine on others, and the end result is that you tend to see yourself as unique and apart from the crowd, and you tend to see the crowd as homogeneous and a bit dull. You may even wonder sometimes how everyone around you can be so stupid when it seems so easy to be, you know, smart like you.

Chances are you see yourself as slightly above average in most categories, and way above average in a few. When you compare yourself to an imaginary average person, you see yourself as superior in just about every category. The irony, of course, is that in most airports, tube carriages, cinemas, and shopping centers, the majority of the people squirming inside are thinking the same thing. The research suggests that the average person thinks she is not the average person. She thinks most people are dumb, and that she is not like most people.

The second major positive illusion is the illusion of control. Studies into its power go back all the way to the beginning of psychology, but the landmark paper was published in 1975. Ellen Langer showed that although you are fully aware of the difference between skill and luck, you have a hard time separating them in retrospect. Langer's studies had people play betting games. In one, two people sat across from each other. Each chose one card from a shared deck. Each then wagered a small sum of money and turned over his card. The person with the higher-value card won whatever amount he'd bet, but the loser had to pay the money he'd gambled to the researchers. What the subjects didn't know was that the person they were playing against was an actor instructed to behave timid for some people and confident for others. The timid actor arrived late, pretended to have a twitch, and wore an ill-fitting sports coat. The confident actor was on time, initiated a conversation, wore a fitted coat, and called for the scientists to hurry up and start the study. Who won and lost in the card game was completely random. It was a game of pure chance, yet Langer noted that subjects tended to make larger bets when they believed the other person playing the game was nervous, and they made smaller bets when the other person seemed sure of himself. Even though they knew full well they had no way of knowing what cards would come up, because the game was pure luck, their confidence in their chances of winning changed depending on whether they believed the other person playing was strong or weak. It was as if, with nothing else to go on, they compared their illusion of control with that of the other person and bet cautiously in the presence of someone who seemed more confident in his delusions.

In another study, Langer's team asked people on their lunch breaks at the Southern New England Telephone Company if they would mind helping in some marketing research on a new product. The people who agreed were then shown into a room housing a bizarre piece of scientific equipment—a large wooden box with parallel metal strips running across the top. The researchers told the subjects that it was a new game, and the object was to guess which of the three metal strips would set off a buzzer when it made contact with a metal pen. They asked one group of subjects to take the metal pen and place it on one of the strips, and then run that pen from one end of the strip to the other. Only one of the strips, the researchers explained, would cause the box to make a sound, and the strip was chosen at random by an apparatus in the box. Another group was told all the same things, but a researcher used the pen to touch the path chosen by the subject, instead of the subjects using the pen themselves. People in both groups were further divided into two subgroups each, one that was allowed to mess around with the box for a few minutes while the scientists pretended to repair the machine, and another that had to choose a strip right away. Langer asked each person right before she picked a metal strip how confident she felt that she would guess the strip that would make the buzzer go off.

The results? The people who had time to play around with the machine and who also got to hold the pen were the most confident. The people who let the researcher do the work and who had to begin immediately felt the least confident. Even though the outcome was completely random, and the subjects were fully aware of the randomness, their confidence differed depending on how much direct contact and previous familiarity they had with the mystery box.

The illusion of control persists like the other positive illusions because you need to feel as though you can push against the world and notice it move. Without that belief, your spirit dwindles quickly, as Langer showed in her later studies in which permanent residents of nursing homes tended to live shorter lives and develop more illnesses when they were no longer allowed to choose their activities or arrange furniture to their liking.

The third great positive illusion is optimism bias, the mental construct that provides smokers the belief they'll be among those who escape cancer, motorists the confidence they can speed during rainstorms, couples the certainty they will die hand in hand behind a white picket fence, and immigrants the beamish tenacity to open a new business in a down economy. No matter the statistical odds, no matter how many examples to the contrary you've seen in your life, you have a tendency to believe everything will work out in the end, and it is hard to argue with this approach to life when you consider the alternative. The bias, however, disappears when you observe others. You believe your heart will stay strong until you are in your nineties, but that your cousin who buys chicken-fried steaks in bulk is headed for an early grave. The bias also prevents you from buying a fire extinguisher for your kitchen, or going to get a regular checkup. Your optimism bias keeps you looking to the horizon with growing expectation and glee. As psychologist Tali Sharot says, research shows you prefer Friday more than Sunday because Fridays are filled with optimistic daydreams about what may come, and Sundays are filled with the constant unwanted encroachment of realistic expectations of what is going to happen on Monday. In one of her studies, she asked people to say how likely they felt it was that they would get cancer. She then explained that science suggests that their chance of getting cancer over their lifetime was about 30 percent. People who guessed higher than 30 percent initially and then heard the truth dropped their estimates to something close to the average. People who guessed lower than 30 percent and then heard the realistic estimate barely raised their assumed chances at all. This, according to Sharot, is why warning labels and government adverts rarely work on you. The odds, you think, are always in your favor. The labels are for other people.

These three positive illusions require constant upkeep. You

hold them together with three supporting delusions called confirmation bias, hindsight bias, and self-serving bias. They serve as a sort of pump plugged into your consciousness that constantly pushes away negativity and sucks in positive thoughts. Not everyone has a fully functional pump, but most do. If yours is working properly, it churns day and night, helping you survive a world determined to prove you are not as awesome as you think you are.

Confirmation bias, something you've seen mentioned several times in this book, is the tendency to notice and remember when information and events match your expectations and confirm your beliefs, but to ignore and forget when the world challenges your preconceived notions. It is why streetlights always seem to flicker when you walk under them, or why it seems to rain every time you wash your car, or why your friend with the tickets always seems late. The truth is that you only notice when the streetlight flickers, when it rains after a wash, and when your flakey friend keeps you waiting. When those things don't happen they become what psychologists call nonevents. Nonevents are a waste of attention and memory, so they don't stick. If you never look for disconfirmation of your beliefs, especially the ones that make you feel special and above average, you can proceed unchallenged and deluded.

When you are presented with new information or an outcome you could not possibly have foretold, you have a tendency to look back on your memories and assume that, back before you knew what was going to happen, you accurately predicted what has just now unfolded. That's your hindsight bias at work, making you constantly feel like you knew what was going to happen all along. You might never know about this bias unless you catch yourself in the act in a diary or some old text message. It makes the past seem inevitable, and causes you to believe the future is predictable. Yet predictions of the future are monumentally terrible. Just look at old science fiction movies. From flying cars to cities on the moon, science fiction movies rarely get the future right. There is no Internet on *Star Trek,* no smartphones in *Blade Runner.* Your brain is just as bad as any science fiction movie when it comes to predicting your own future. The difference is that movies leave behind a perfect record of their failure. You don't.

When things are going your way, you have no problem calling attention to your own contributions to good fortune. If you win a game, or get promoted, or make an excellent grade, you tend to attribute that success to your skills, talent, effort, and preparation. If you fail, though, or get passed over, you have a habit of looking for something outside yourself to blame—a mean boss, a crappy team, a confusing teacher—whatever it takes to keep yourself from blame. This self-serving bias provides you with credit for all the things in life that worked out in your favor, and it absolves you of responsibility for those times you fell short. The self-serving bias makes it difficult for you to acknowledge the help of others, or luck, or an unfair advantage. It isn't a malicious defect of your personality; it's just your brain's way of framing things so that you don't stop moving forward. If you fail the tests that would have made you a doctor, lawyer, engineer, or dog groomer, you protect your ego by noticing all the factors in between you and your goals. That way, you can try again with the gumption and certainty required to accomplish such difficult objectives.

The positive illusions and their helpers form a supercluster of delusion that thumps in the psyche of every human. Together, illusory superiority bias, the illusion of control, optimism bias, confirmation bias, hindsight bias, and self-serving bias combine like Voltron into a mental chimera called self-enhancement bias. It works just as the name suggests—it enhances your view of your self. If you drive, you probably see yourself as a competent, considerate, skillful driver, especially compared with the morons and assholes you face on the road on a daily basis. If you are like the typical subject, you believe you are slightly more attractive than the average person, a bit smarter, a smidgen better at solving puzzles and figuring out riddles, a better listener, a cut above when it comes to leadership skills, in possession of paramount moral fiber, more interesting than the people passing you on the street, and on and on it goes.

A report in 2010 published in the *British Journal of Social Psychology* suggests that you even see yourself as more human than other people. The findings predict that no matter what country you come from, no matter your culture, if aliens chose you to represent the entire species as Earth's ambassador, you would feel as though you could fulfill that role better than most. When asked, most people said they exhibited the traits that make humans unique in the animal kingdom more than the average person. In 2010, UCLA researchers conducted a survey of more than 25,000 people ages 18–75 and found that the majority rated their own attractiveness as about a seven out of ten. This suggests that the average person thinks he is a little better looking than the average person. About a third of the people under 30 rated themselves as somewhere around a nine. That sort of confidence is fun to think about considering that it is impossible for everyone to be better-looking than half the population. A survey conducted by American Viewpoint in 2010 showed that 80 percent of American parents believe childhood obesity is a growing problem, but 84 percent of those same Americans said their own children were at a healthy weight, even though the Centers for Disease Control and Prevention estimated that about a third of all U.S. children are obese. When psychologists asked professors at the University of Nebraska to rate their own teaching abilities, 94 percent said they were better than the average teacher.

You don't have to be a mathematician to see a major problem here. Every person's assumptions about being above average can't be true. There can't be an average unless some people sit in the middle of a bell curve and others fall to either side. Statistically speaking, if you had a perfect measure of your abilities you would see that you fall into the average category for most things, but you have a very hard time believing this is true.

In 1998, psychologist Joachim Krueger and his colleagues asked a group of subjects to take a look at a list of adjectives. The words described personality types: words such as *domineering, outspoken, nervous,* and *intellectual*. The subjects then rated how accurately they believed those words described them, and how accurately the words described an average person. For example, think of the word *perfectionist*. On a scale from one to ten, how much of a perfectionist do you think you are? Now, on a scale from one to ten, rate an imaginary average human being the same age and gender as you. The next part of the study then asked the same people to rate those traits on a scale of desirability, with one being a quality society generally shunned and nine being something everyone should aspire to add to his or her charms. Consider your answer. Now, how would you rate perfectionism on a scale of desirability? Most of the subjects in the study rated the traits they believed they possessed as the sort of traits society values most. The traits they believed the average person possessed were rated as the least desirable. If you believe you are more of a perfectionist than the average person, you also tend to believe that society loves sticklers more than it does people without strict standards. On the other hand, if you despise people who believe there is such a thing as absolute control, and prefer a loose and free approach to solving problems, that's the sort of trait you assume the rest of the world admires.

Not only do you see yourself as above average, but you also see the ways in which you exceed the average person as being the best attributes of humanity. According to Krueger, one of your most reliable strategies for pumping up your sense of self-worth is simply to alter the way you see your own traits. If you transform your traits into virtues and the traits of the average person into vices, you can step out of the door sparkling and beautiful with no need for change. That effect can be reduced, though, as the experimenters in the study discovered. When they asked subjects to put themselves in other people's shoes and think about how individuals with dissimilar personality traits might rate themselves and others, a small epiphany routinely sparked, and the tendency to be biased toward self-enhancement diminished. As with most biases, all it took was a pause for reflection to trump the default settings of the mind.

So, why is it, then, that you so rarely pause to reflect? What keeps the self-enhancement bias and all its positive illusions thriving in your mind? Why would such an obviously impossible set of beliefs persist in the heads of just about every conscious person?

Scientists can't say for sure why these biases and illusions about how awesome you are exist, but most speculation on the issue suggests that for something like this to be so ubiquitous among human minds, it must have served an adaptive purpose in your ancestors. As your ability to think and reason evolved, you also developed the power to obfuscate the truth lest you see through the illusions of life and became despondent. Your ancestors slept on dirt and were pummeled like Rocky Balboa minute by minute with a steady flow of harassment from an unforgiving and indifferent world. Nature never gave up, and it makes sense that your species developed mechanisms to ensure you couldn't be kept down.

Some researchers have posited that the overconfident invaders of the jungles and savannah may have been so bold and intimidating that when they charged into the camps of their enemies, they tended to do better than the more timid and shy among them. There are psychologists who believe that morale is nothing more than a cluster of positive illusions; and morale is generally considered more important in combat than anything else. Confidence in battle and in courtship is certainly an important starting point for understanding where self-enhancement bias came from. These, though, may just be variations on a more fundamental truth. The general speculation is that over the last few million years, the primates who survived long enough to become your grandparents were the ones who didn't give up when all hope was lost.

In a 2011 article published in *Nature* by Dominic Johnson and James Fowler, the two social scientists presented compelling speculation as to how positive illusions may have formed and why they continue to persist. They contend that, in the long run, over the course of most of human history, in the situations people would have often faced before the modern age, overconfidence fed a suite of other traits that have kept humans from fading into the fossil record. Traits such as ambition, resolve, and group morale pushed human beings to cross oceans and tame crops. When the wind crushed those ships to splinters against impartial rocks, and those crops withered under an unsympathetic sun, your ancestors' positive illusions kicked in, biasing the downtrodden to see things in such a way that led to persistence, no matter how futile it must have seemed at times.

Johnson and Fowler point out that your potential ancestors who led lives based on realistic expectations didn't survive. Positive illusions must have been a better alternative. They speculated that early humans competed with one another for resources, and if both parties were completely honest about themselves and their opponents, they could just glance at the other person, correctly estimate who would win in a dispute, and then yield without any confrontation.

Imagine you want access to a watering hole, but a nasty person arrives at this place at the same time as you and refuses to share. This person looks like he might be a bit stronger than you, but you can't be sure. He might be bluffing. If you are totally honest with yourself, you'll walk away, and thus possibly remove yourself from the gene pool. If, instead, you feel slightly overconfident given what you know about the other person, you might stand your ground, or go for some sort of bluff yourself. When Johnson and Fowler plugged these strategies into a computer program and had simulated opponents face off in a struggle for limited resources, they found that, over several thousand generations, those who were slightly overconfident started to outperform those with other evaluations of themselves. As long as the reward was worth fighting for, and both sides were naive about what they were up against, overconfidence won. Those who routinely overestimated their abilities never turned away from disputes in which it seemed like a toss-up as to who could win, and they sometimes won even when they were the underdog because the other party didn't call their unwitting bluff. The more uncertain the computer opponents were, the more advantageous it became to be overconfident.

You have the capacity to rationally judge the risks and benefits, the costs and rewards, of complex systems, but in a pinch you can fall back on a simple and reliable shortcut: just be slightly and blindly overconfident. The best bluff, it turns out, is the one in which even the bluffer is unaware of the cards he is holding. If you could accurately assess the odds against you—whether those odds took the shape of a hunting expedition, a one-on-one fight, or the job market for philosophy majors—you would probably turn away from the struggle more often than not. There is always plenty of evidence that the odds are not in your favor, enough to deter you from trying just about everything in life. Luckily for you, most of the time you have no idea what you are getting into, and you greatly overestimate your chances for success. It makes sense that primates like you would have evolved a fondness for delusions of grandeur. That's the sort of attitude that gets you out of caves and beds. The relentless bombardment of challenges and tribulations makes it very difficult to be a person, whether you must fend off rabid beavers or ravenous debt collectors. Those who tried just a few percentage points harder, who persevered just a smidge longer, defeated nature more often than the realists. You've inherited a tendency to thrash against the odds, to be optimistic in the face of futility.

On average, positive illusions work, but left unchecked, they can lead to terrible decisions and policies. Overconfidence is a powerful tool to drive behaviors and encourage perseverance against strife and uncertainty in both your personal life and in the lives of nations and institutions. Occasionally, though, that same emotional state can mutate into hubris and blind ambition. History is littered with the bodies, both real and metaphorical, of self-enhancement biases. The same irrational, unrealistic overconfidence swimming in your nervous system can be disastrous should you find yourself leading millions or tending to their investments.

Your evolved response is to allow your brain to trick you into doing what maximizes fitness in your species, even though that benefit shows up only over the course of millions of lifetimes. In an isolated instance, in a specific situation, overconfidence may not be the best state of mind, and the behaviors that spring from that sort of reality assessment may not be the best actions in the great multiple-choice exam of life. When you dissolve that situation into the billions that humans faced over their journey into modernity, though, it averages out to be the preferred route to just about every destination. In short, your brain fiddles with your emotions to get you to do what usually works by suggesting that you are more awesome than you actually are, even in scenarios in which that would be a terrible mistake. Sometimes you pause, think, and reject the suggestion. Sometimes you don't. As some experts have pointed out, this general strategy matured among small societies without the ability to prevent or cause great harm. Modern society is large and complex, with institutions wielding great power over the lives of many. This is why Johnson and Fowler added a dire parting shot in their predictions. Since you are programmed to become increasingly overconfident the less you understand about any given scenario, you can expect to find the most destructive overconfidence in places that are exceedingly complicated and unpredictable. Their examples include governments, wars, financial markets, and natural disasters.

If you want to see positive illusions causing harm in a more domestic realm, look no further than social media. Services such as Twitter and Facebook magnify the scope of natural tendencies. You use social media to adapt social norms to the new levels of expression just as people did when it became possible to see cities they would never visit or talk over wires with people they would never

meet. The desire to boost your self-esteem through positive illusions is one of the most obvious and ubiquitous elements of the
social media landscape. In those worlds, you choose what to show
other people and what to censor.

Heavy social media use skews strongly toward younger people
at the moment, although there are people of every age managing a
public persona through online media, status updates, and eternally
malleable profiles. For some, that world makes them feel like stars
of small-scale reality programming. If you have younger friends
and relatives in your update streams, you've probably noticed their
overactive urge to duckface, turn up the contrast, and shoot
their faces with cameras awkwardly perched somewhere behind their heads. It's all about self-esteem, and the drive to maintain high self-esteem can lead to strange choices.

For instance, imagine you are walking in a park, admiring the
song of an unseen bird while watching light dance on a lake across
the peaks of wind-pushed ripples, when you notice out of the corner of your eye a coppery lamp lying on its side. You pick it up,
realizing instantly that this is not some ornate crack pipe—no,
this is an object of quality and value. A little polish and maybe this
thing will . . . whoa! As you buff it with the cuff of your sleeve, a
vortex of magical dust and vapor surrounds you, and out of the
fractalized tendrils of smoke a blue-skinned, legless djinni comes
forth grinning and smelling of fresh-baked brownies.

The djinni offers you a reward for freeing him from the lamp
through your concentrated scrubbing. Unfortunately, he's just a
multiple-choice wish granter, and says you may choose only one
item among four choices: an extra paycheck; obligation-free fantasy sex with the partner of your choice; a gourmet meal comprised
of as many delights as you can imagine; or a nice, heartfelt compli-

ment. What would you choose? A version of these choices appeared in a psychological study conducted by Brad Bushman, Scott Moeller, and Jennifer Crocker published in 2010. As part of a series of experiments exploring self-esteem, they asked university students to rate a variety of things the average person desires—food, sex, money, friendship, compliments—and asked the subjects to say how strongly they wanted those things and how much they tended to like them. The clear winner? Compliments. In studies of secondary school and university-age people, boosts to self-esteem were found to be usually more attractive and beguiling than the sort of things older people see as proper rewards. When you ask a person in the first quarter of her life what she would rather have—sex, pizza, or a positive comment about her—the majority of people tend to go for the kind words, even if the subject had not enjoyed the other options in a very long time. The same researchers found in another study that this tendency to prefer boosts to self-esteem over other rewards diminishes over time, but it doesn't completely go away.

Some researchers, such as psychologist Jean Twenge, say this new world where compliments are better than sex and pizza, in which the self-enhancing bias has been unchained and allowed to gorge unfettered, has led to a new normal in which the positive illusions of several generations have now mutated into full-blown narcissism. In her book *The Narcissism Epidemic,* Twenge says her research shows that since the mid-1980s, clinically defined narcissism rates in the United States have increased in the population at the same rate as obesity. She used the same test used by psychiatrists to test for narcissism in patients and found that, in 2006, one in four U.S. university students tested positive. That's real narcissism, the kind that leads to diagnoses of personality disorders. In her estimation, this is a dangerous trend, and it shows signs of acceleration. Narcissistic overconfidence crosses a line, says Twenge, and taints those things improved by a skosh of confidence. Over that line, you become less concerned with the well-being of others, more materialistic, and obsessed with status in addition to losing all the restraint normally preventing you from tragically overestimating your ability to manage or even survive risky situations. In her book, Twenge connects this trend to the housing market crash of the mid-2000s and the stark increase in reality programming during that same decade. According to Twenge, the drive to be famous for nothing went from being strange to predictable thanks to a generation or two of people raised by parents who artificially boosted self-esteem to 'roidtastic levels and then released them into a culture filled with new technologies that emerged right when those people needed them most to prop up their self-enhancement biases. By the time Twenge's research was published, reality programming had spent twenty years perfecting itself, and the modern stars of those shows represent a tiny portion of the population who not only want to be on those shows, but who also know what they are getting into and still want to participate. Producers with the experience to know who will provide the best television entertainment to millions then cull that small group. The result is a new generation of celebrities with positive illusions so robust and potent that the narcissistic overconfidence of the modern American teenager by comparison is now much easier to see as normal.

The desire to see yourself as better than average and more competent, skilled, intelligent, and beautiful than you truly are is likely embedded in your psyche as a by-product of millions of years of forging ahead against the same odds of survival that have erased 99 percent of all species that once roamed this planet. Still, that overconfidence gets tempered by a number of things following your birth.

Life experience, of course, can enhance or suppress those feelings. Your parents' choices in how they styled your upbringing are major factors as well. Your generational attitudes drastically affect the way you go about self-enhancing. A girl raised in an orphanage in 1850, for instance, would probably use different aspects of life to judge her self-esteem than a girl brought up in 2012 competing in gymnastic sports. Aside from all these factors, the culture in which you develop and grow exerts tremendous influence. In the late twentieth-century United States, individuality and self-reliance was instilled in most citizens, while in Japan most people were encouraged to consider their interdependence and community ties. Cross-cultural studies by psychologists Hazel Markus and Shinobu Kitayama in the 1990s showed that many Asian cultures actively suppress the urge to self-enhance. As they put it, the Western concept of "the squeaky wheel gets the grease" is seen in Eastern cultures as "the nail that stands out gets pounded down." American self-help techniques, they point out, ask people to do things such as look in the mirror and say, "I am beautiful," one hundred times before leaving the house, while in Japan, workers gladly do things such as hold hands and tell coworkers that *they* are beautiful. Markus and Kitayama point out that in such a culture, people tend to become more confident after subsequent failures than they do following easy, first-time successes. Self-esteem comes from fitting in and contributing to the well-being of the whole. A person in such a culture, they say, doesn't feel the gut punch of disappointment if their personal accomplishments never set them apart or don't generate individual praise or fame. Disapproval in the eyes of others is given much more weight than praise, because praise is less reliable, less likely to be honest. As Markus and Kitayama put it, "Those with interdependent selves will typically not claim they are better than others" and will feel icky if a sense of superiority does waft into their heads. You've probably noticed shades of Eastern attitudes in Western cultures. Subcultures and political camps will often laud the sort of sensibility that leads to drum circles and communal ownership and that coincides with a sense of diminished self-enhancement and more focus on interdependence. People in those subcultures may even adopt some of the philosophical and religious views of Asian societies. Likewise, opposing camps offer an alternative view, admiring individuality and personal liberty to a degree that stimulates feelings of self-enhancement in a far more magnified way.

A century of experimental data points to a central fact about your day-to-day experience and behavior: You are deeply invested in self-confidence. The higher your baseline self-esteem, the more protective you become of it. It waxes and wanes throughout your day and throughout your life, but a general feeling of being able to take on the world keeps you going. You feel effective. You feel you have some sort of control over your environment. You feel as though you have choices, and those choices can make your life better. Psychologists call that sense of control over your destiny self-efficacy. The famous psychologist B. F. Skinner said that your core personality developed around tiny science experiments you conducted throughout childhood. He saw a pattern in behavior he called responses and reinforcers. Imagine, as a kid, that you played around on a piano during a holiday party one year and everyone came into the room to listen, and then everyone clapped and laughed and praised you. Skinner said that added some points to your feelings of efficacy. You might try that again in a similar situation in the future, and if it worked again, you would add it to your bag of tricks for getting attention. Over time, he believed, you learn that a wide variety of situations and behaviors will get you attention and praise or some other reward, and you begin to position yourself to always be in situations that allow for such an exchange with the outside world. You build a sense of self-confidence around those actions and situations you can be fairly certain will provide you a return or, as he put it, a reinforcer. This is why, he said, you decide to skip some gatherings and attend others. This is why you become fast friends with some people, and others turn you off within seconds. You tend to protect a bubble you've created and nurtured your entire life, a bubble of positive illusions that make you feel good about yourself. Those good feelings bleed into your sense of control and your general attitude when facing unfamiliar problems. Self-esteem and self-efficacy work together to get you out of bed in the morning and keep you going back for more punishment from the unforgiving world.

The studies into self-enhancement show that there is no one set level of confidence in all human beings. Instead, people make a wide variety of nuanced and complex assumptions about their abilities and self-worth. As with most aspects of the mind, there is a spectrum out there in the real world, and you fall somewhere along it, but when you take humanity as a whole and average out the temperaments, most people rate themselves a tad bit above average. Chances are, you do the same thing when it comes to the more nebulous and desirable aspects of the self, whatever you believe those aspects to be. Your opinions on what makes for an above-average, covetable persona are deeply influenced by your culture and the era in which you live, but the factory settings in your comparison-to-other-people introspection module seem to be set slightly above the midpoint. Knowing this, you can predict how you and others will attack difficult and convoluted issues, and maybe you can come to less-dumb conclusions and develop thoroughly non-dumb plans of action. Know that the people who do beat all the odds, who do persevere after being knocked down over and over again, end up being the only people left to compare yourself against. They are the people who tell inspirational stories of overcoming great odds and never giving in to doubt. The other people, the ones who tried and failed, the ones who make up the true majority—they don't get invited to speak at university graduations.

This mass of delusions was a useful evolutionary trick for your people. It is difficult to be a person hurtling through space on a hostile rock with only a handful of friends. It is hard even if you are fortunate enough to live in a wealthy, educated, industrialized nation in the twenty-first century and be born into a family who lives above the poverty line. In such a place, you live like a king compared with billions of less fortunate people. If you are living in such a wonderful place, think about all the complaining and sadness you've felt and witnessed. The gulf between what you want and what you have, the sudden loss of a loved one, the yearning for love and the pining for it when unrequited—no matter how good you've got it, you are no stranger to tears. Obviously, owning a brain is not easy. It is a testament to the weirdness of our pursuit of happiness and fulfillment to realize how well we get by in the face of so much strife—real or imagined. Self-enhancement bias and all its positive illusions temper the trials and tribulations of many people on this planet struggling with poverty and war, hunger and disease. In Phnom Penh and in Calcutta, a series of rubbish heaps stretch out like low mountain ranges, and every day, large crowds of children gather to pick at the fresh rubbish as it spills from the back of giant trucks. The children scavenge all day, often barefoot, choking in the haze generated by nearby fires. There are places where, right now, people go to work every day worried about sniper fire and suicide bombers. In many places, the water runs brown and meals are not guaranteed.

Throughout human history there have been periods in which people bore tremendous burdens and slogged through what seemed like insurmountable misery. From concentration camps to death marches, to plagues and wars, people who share the same basic mind as you have suffered and survived horrific events. Likewise, you share something amazing with those who live daily under the yoke of terrible oppression. Should you be plucked from your cozy place in this world and assume their plight, should your will be tested at the intensity of so many before you, one constant is sure: You will be resilient. You won't give up.

## ACKNOWLEDGMENTS

This book would not have been possible without the support of my wife, Amanda, who sat with me night after night as I talked with my mouth full discussing these studies. Those conversations, and the back and forth during them, showed me how it could fit together in interesting ways so I could tell fun stories about the human mind. She kept track of the sources as I wrote, and she kept my friends and family assured that I would eventually come out of my writing room and join them for a drink. Thank you so much.

Thank you, Erin Malone. You have been my champion for a while now. Thank you for yanking me into the life of a writer and believing in the concept for this book and its predecessor back when it was a quirky blog. You've opened all the doors I thought were forever locked. You're good people.

Patrick Mulligan, you were an amazing editor. You not only told me to go read David Foster Wallace and Harold Bloom, but you corrected me when I got Voltron's enemies mixed up. You've been extremely encouraging, and you immediately got where I was coming from and made sure I was true to the voice that made this possible. Thank you for pulling this together.

Jessica Sindler, my other tremendous editor, you received the strangest e-mail during copyediting, and I thank you for being so understanding. The day before I turned in the final edits a tornado destroyed our house. I saved a copy of the manuscript in Dropbox. A minute later, my wife and I were in our hallway on the floor. This sentence was written after retrieving the manuscript from the cloud and finishing it from a laptop at a relative's house. I e-mailed Jessica, and she moved the deadline. Thank you, again. We both now have an awesome writing story.

Jenna Dolan, thank you for correcting tenses and asking me why I did so many stupid things. This book is so much better thanks to your efforts.

Of course, my parents are the real reason I'm able to write these thank-you notes. Jerry and Evelyn, thank you for allowing an only child to stay blissfully unaware of the world of adults for as long as you did, and then telling him the truth about it when he finally asked.

Growing up in the Deep South, you meet plenty of home-grown philosophers and armchair psychologists who refuse to stay in their homes or their chairs. In every petrol station, every diner, at every coffee break, they stand around telling you how it is. There is a truck stop where I've bought breakfast many times, and old men sit inside at hand-me-down fast-food tables to chew on biscuits and complain about politicians. Sometime back, someone hung a sign above them that reads, HUNTERS, FISHERMEN AND OTHER LIARS GATHER HERE. That's true. The fact that they announce it in factory-produced, flame-engraved letters on a wooden sign is a precious thing to me. Southerners love bullshittery, and they are masters of it. It's the first thing a Southerner notices when traveling far from home. Yankees seem quaintly unaware of how terrible they are at bullshitting.

With their baked-in mastery of rhetoric and nimble-as-aballerina storytelling prowess, an educated Southerner is an astounding creature. A well-read, worldly man or woman of the hills and hollows can see through the absurdity of existence like no one else. They have a way about them. They walk a path. Once you've met a few of these people you can't help but want a piece of their magic. You will know when you've met the genuine article because you'll forever aspire to their aloof genius.

I've had the pleasure of being a student to one such person.

He lives in Jones County, in Mississippi. He flies airplanes, photographs weddings, and plays Led Zeppelin on an acoustic guitar at his desk amid a collection of religious artifacts from around the world. He studied to become a fire-and-brimstone preacher, and ended up a philosophy professor coaxing silly ideas out of the heads of the children of farmers, truck drivers, and all the rest of several generations of kids. His name is Ronald Bishop, and I will never be as cool as that man.

Is he deeply religious? I think so, but he also welcomed Christopher Hitchens to campus so Hitchens could give a lecture deep in enemy territory. Is he in love with Immanuel Kant and Bertrand Russell? I think he is, but when he took me and my wife to a philosophy conference, he ended up leaving early so we could go to a juke joint in Columbus, Mississippi, to hear real blues.

Bishop taught the first philosophy class I ever took, and like most people where I grew up, there was nothing like that in high school. It was the first time I heard of Plato's Cave and the death of Socrates. It was definitely the first time I heard someone ask a group of people if free will was real or just wishful thinking. Every class with Bishop ended up with a dozen people shaking their heads and challenging the professor, and he stood up there with his silver bowl cut and cherubic grin just soaking in the ignorance. He loved it. He loved being the first person to shake up beliefs most Southerners never question. For most people who took Bishop's class, that would be their one and only exposure to philosophy, and he knew it. I wish you could have been there all the times he made hard-core Baptists gasp and strict Pentecostals squirm in their blue-jean skirts. "If God is omnipotent and omniscient, why does he allow evil?" he might ask. "How do you know you aren't just a brain in a jar?" You can imagine the answers. Bishop started the arguments most polite people ignore, and his students loved him for it because he didn't accuse them of being trapped in dogma or tradition or superstition. He just encouraged them to replace certainty with curiosity. The people most shaken by his assertions were the most eager to return.

Bishop convinced me that the world was way, way bigger than I thought it was (and that I was way, way smaller than I believed). So, I thank you, Ronald Bishop. You showed me a better way to be bullheaded without becoming a doryphore. This book was possible because you, with all your education and rhetorical brilliance, knew that you were not so smart, and that brought me around to the truth that neither was I.

## SOURCES

### *Introduction — Self-Delusion*

"Dartmouth Football: Season by Season Results: 1940–59."
*Dartmouth Sports*. Dartmouth College, Aug. 30, 2006. Web:
Aug. 2012, www.dartmouthsports.com/ViewArticle.dbml
?SPSID=48870.

Hastorf, Albert H., and Hadley Cantril. "They Saw a Game: A
Case Study." *Journal of Abnormal and Social Psychology* 49, no.
1 (1954): 129–34.

Maisel, Ivan. "1951 Heisman Winner Dick Kazmaier." *ESPN*.
ESPN Internet Ventures.Web: Aug. 2012, espn.go.com/ncf/
features/heisman/_/year/1951/set/3.

Simons, Daniel J., and Christopher F. Chabris. "What People
Believe About How Memory Works: A Representative
Survey of the U.S. Population." *PloS ONE* 6, no. 8 (2011):
E22757.

### *1. Narrative Bias*

Abumrad, Jad, and Robert Krulwich. "Where Am I?" Audio
blog post *Radiolab*. WNYC, May 5, 2006. Web: May 2012,
www.radiolab.org/2006/may/05/.

"Acting Irrationally." *Mr. Hoye's TOK Website*. Web: May 2012.

Carey, Benedict. "This Is Your Life (And How You Tell It)." *The
New York Times,* May 22, 2007. Web: May 2012, www.nytimes

.com/2007/05/22/health/psychology/22narr.html
?pagewanted=all.

Eagleman, D. *Incognito: The Secret Lives of the Brain*. New York: Pantheon, 2011.

Fiala, Brian, and Shaun Nichols. "Confabulation, Confidence, and introspection." *Behavioral and Brain Sciences* 32, no. 2 (2009): 144.

Fleming, Jim. "The Examined Life." Audio blog post *To the Best of Our Knowledge (TTBOOK)*. Wisconsin Public Radio, May 29, 2011. Web: tunein.com/topic/?topicId=39415622.

Hirstein, William. *Brain Fiction: Self-Deception and the Riddle of Confabulation*. Cambridge, MA: MIT Press, 2004.

Hitt, Jack. "This Is Your Brain on God." *Wired,* Nov. 1999. Web: May 2012, www.wired.com/wired/archive/7.11/persinger.html.

Hood, Bruce M. *The Self Illusion: How the Social Brain Creates Identity*. Oxford: Oxford University Press, 2012.

Joseph, R. "Confabulation and Delusional Denial: Frontal Lobe and Lateralized Influences." *Journal of Clinical Psychology* 42, no. 3 (1986): 845–60.

McAdams, Dan P., Michelle Albaugh, Emily Farber, Jennifer Daniels, Regina L. Logan, and Brad Olson. "Family Metaphors and Moral Intuitions: How Conservatives and Liberals Narrate Their Lives." *Journal of Personality and Social Psychology* 95, no. 4 (2008): 978–90.

McRaney, David. "Episode Three: Confabulation with V. S. Ramachandran." Audio blog post, *You Are Not So Smart*, May 30, 2012. Web: http://youarenotsosmart.com/2012/05/30/yanss-podcast-episode-three/

Pantel, Johannes. "*Brain Fiction: Self-Deception and the Riddle of Confabulation*." Review in *American Journal of Psychiatry* 163 (2006): 559.

Parfit, Derek. *Reasons and Persons*. Oxford [Oxfordshire]: Clarendon, 1984.

Pearn, J., and C. Gardner-Thorpe. "Jules Cotard (1840–1889): His Life and the Unique Syndrome Which Bears His Name." *Neurology* 58, no. 9 (2002): 1400–403.

Ramachandran, V. S. "Self-awareness: The Last Frontier." January 10, 2009. Web: http://integral-options.blogspot.com/2009/01/vs-ramachandran-self-awareness-last.html.

Rawlence, Christopher, and Emma Crichton-Miller. "Secrets of the Mind." *Nova*. PBS. October 23, 2001.

Rokeach, Milton. *The Three Christs of Ypsilanti*. New York: New York Review Books, 2011.

Sacks, Oliver W. *The Man Who Mistook His Wife for a Hat and Other Clinical Tales*. New York: Perennial Library, 1987.

Tversky, Amos, and Daniel Kahneman. "Judgments of and by Representativeness." *Judgment Under Uncertainty: Heuristics and Biases*. Eds. Daniel Kahneman, Paul Slovic, and Amos Tversky. Cambridge: Cambridge University Press, 1982, pp. 84–99.

Whinnery, James E., and Angela M. Whinnery. "Acceleration-Induced Loss of Consciousness: A Review of 500 Episodes." *Archives of Neurology* 47, no. 7 (1990): 764–76.

## 2. The Common Belief Fallacy

Anderson, Chuck. "Rags to Rats? Is Spontaneous Generation Possible?" *Discovery News*. 2006. Web: http://www.discoverynews.us/DISCOVERY%20MUSEUM/SciencePavilion/RAGS_to_RATS.html.

Conant, James Bryan, ed. *The Overthrow of Phlogiston Theory: The Chemical Revolution of 1775–1789*. Cambridge, MA.: Harvard University Press, 1950.

LaBossiere, Michael. *42 Fallacies*. Amazon Digital Services, 2010. Kindle edition.

Levine, Russell, and Chris Evers. *The Slow Death of Spontaneous Generation (1668–1859)*. Access Excellence @ the National Health Museum Resource Center. Web: http://www

.accessexcellence.org/RC/AB/BC/Spontaneous_Generation
.php

*Encyclopædia Britannica*, s.v. "Spontaneous Generation," accessed
March 28, 2013, http://www.britannica.com/EBchecked/
topic/560859/spontaneous-generation.

## 3. The Benjamin Franklin Effect

Batson, C. Daniel, Diane Kobrynowicz, Jessica L. Dinnerstein,
Hannah C. Kampf, et al. "In a Very Different Voice:
Unmasking Moral Hypocrisy." *Journal of Personality and
Social Psychology* 72, no. 6 (1997): 1335–348.

Cacioppo, John T., Joseph R. Priester, and Gary G. Berntson.
"Rudimentary Determinants of Attitudes: II. Arm Flexion and
Extension Have Differential Effects on Attitudes." *Journal of
Personality and Social Psychology* 65, no. 1 (1993): 5–17.

Festinger, Leon, and James M. Carlsmith. "Cognitive
Consequences of Forced Compliance." *Journal of Abnormal
and Social Psychology* 58, no. 2 (1959): 203–10.

Franklin, Benjamin. *The Autobiography of Benjamin Franklin*. Ed.
Frank Woodworth Pine. Garden City, NY: Garden City Pub.,
1916.

Jecker, Jon, and David Landy. "Liking a Person as a Function of
Doing Him a Favour." *Human Relations* 22, no. 4 (1969): 371–78.

Myers, D. G. *Social Psychology*. New York: McGraw-Hill, 2005.

Schopler, John, and John S. Compere. "Effects of Being Kind or
Harsh to Another on Liking." *Journal of Personality and Social
Psychology* 20, no. 2 (1971): 155–59.

Tavris, Carol, and Elliot Aronson. *Mistakes Were Made (But Not
by Me): Why We Justify Foolish Beliefs, Bad Decisions, and
Hurtful Acts*. Orlando, FL: Harcourt, 2007.

Wicker, Allan W. "Attitudes Versus Actions: The Relationship of
Verbal and Overt Behavioral Responses to Attitude Objects."
*Journal of Social Issues* 25, no. 4 (1969): 41–78.

## 4. The Post Hoc Fallacy

ADA Accessibility Guidelines for Buildings and Facilities (ADAAG). September 2002 edition. Web: http://www.access -board.gov/adaag/html/adaag.htm

Adams, Cecil. "Do 'Close Door' Buttons on Elevators Ever Actually Work?" *The Straight Dope*. November 7, 1986. Web: http://www.straightdope.com/columns/read/595/do-close-door-buttons-on-elevators-ever-actually-work.

Arabe, Katrina C. "'Dummy' Thermostats Cool Down Tempers, Not Temperatures." *ThomasNet News,* Apr. 11, 2003. Web: Sept. 2012, news.thomasnet.com/IMT/2003/04/11/dummy_thermosta/.

Associated Press. "Power Balance: Bracelets Don't Work." ESPN, Jan. 4, 2011. Web: Sept. 2012, sports.espn.go.com/nba/news/story?id=5989365.

Bathe, Carrlyn. "The Ice Crew's Lucky Charms." *FOX Sports West,* Mar. 8, 2012. Web: Sept. 2012, www.foxsportswest .com/03/08/12/The-Ice-Crews-Lucky-Charms/landing_kings .html?blockID=683256.

Beecher, Henry, K. "The Powerful Placebo." *The Journal of the American Medical Association* 159, no. 17(1955): 1602–6.

Brice, S. R., B. S. Jarosz, R. A. Ames, J. Baglin, and C. Da Costa. "The Effect of Close Proximity Holographic Wristbands on Human Balance and Limits of Stability: A Randomised, Placebo-Controlled Trial." *Journal of Bodywork and Movement Therapies* 15, no. 3 (2011): 298–303.

Callahan, Gerry. "Cheers Wade's World Back in Town."*Boston Herald,* May 21, 1993, Sports sec.: 112.

Damisch, L., B. Stoberock, and T. Mussweiler. "Keep Your Fingers Crossed!: How Superstition Improves Performance." *Psychological Science* 21, no. 7 (2010): 1014–20.

"Goran Ivanisevic Quotes." *Goran Online*. Web: Sept. 2012, www.goranonline.com/gi_quotes.html.

Hutson, Matthew. "In Defense of Superstition." *The New York Times,* Apr. 8, 2012: SR5. Web: www.nytimes.com/2012/04/08/opinion/sunday/in-defense-of-superstition.html.

Kaptchuk, Ted J., Elizabeth Friedlander, John M. Kelley, M. Norma Sanchez, Efi Kokkotou, Joyce P. Singer, Magda Kowalczykowski, Franklin G. Miller, Irving Kirsch, and Anthony J. Lembo. "Placebos Without Deception: A Randomized Controlled Trial in Irritable Bowel Syndrome." *PLoS One* 5, no. 12 (2010): E15591.

Lockton, Dan. "Placebo Buttons, False Affordances and Habit-Forming." *Design with Intent.* WordPress, Jan. 10, 2008. Web: Sept. 2012, architectures.danlockton.co.uk/2008/10/01/placebo-buttons-false-affordances-and-habit-forming/.

Luo, Michael. "For Exercise in New York Futility, Push Button." *The New York Times,* Feb. 27, 2004. Web: Sept. 2012, www.nytimes.com/2004/02/27/nyregion/for-exercise-in-new-york-futility-push-button.html.

Murdoch, Jason. "Superstitious Athletes." *CBC Sports,* May 10, 2005. Web: Sept. 2012, www.cbc.ca/sports/columns/top10/superstition.html.

"Power Balance Band Is Placebo, Say Experts." *BBC News Wales,* Nov. 22, 2010. Web: Sept. 2012, www.bbc.co.uk/news/uk-wales-11805616.

"Power Balance Endorsers, Athletes Who Wear Power Balance Bands." *AthletePromotions.* Web: Sept. 2012, www.athletepromotions.com/power-balance-band-endorsements.php.

Sandberg, Jared. "Employees Only Think They Control Thermostat." *The Wall Street Journal,* Jan. 15, 2003. Web: Sept. 2012, online.wsj.com/article/SB1042577628591401304.html.

Stech, Katy. "Power Balance Sold to Chinese Manufacturer." *The Wall Street Journal, Bankruptcy Beat* (blog), Jan. 11, 2012. Web: Sept. 2012, blogs.wsj.com/bankruptcy/2012/01/11/power-balance-sold-to-chinese-manufacturer/.

Tritrakarn, Thara, Jariya Lertakyamanee, Pisamorn Koompong, Suchai Soontrapa, Pradit Somprakit, Anupan Tantiwong, and Sunee Jittapapai. "Both EMLA and Placebo Cream Reduced Pain during Extracorporeal Piezoelectric Shock Wave Lithotripsy with the Piezolith 2300." *Anesthesiology* 92, no. 4 (2000): 1049–54.

"Wade Boggs." *Baseball Library*. Ed. Richard Lally. The Idea Logical Company, Inc. Web: Sept. 2012, www.baseballlibrary.com/chronology/.

## 5. The Halo Effect

Abikoff, Howard, Mary Courtney, William E. Pelham, and Harold S. Koplewicz. "Teachers' Ratings of Disruptive Behaviors: The Influence of Halo Effects." *Journal of Abnormal Child Psychology* 21, no. 5 (1993): 519–33.

Brewer, Gayle. "Height, Relationship Satisfaction, Jealousy, and Mate Retention." *Evolutionary Psychology* 7, no. 3 (2009): 477–89.

Chilton, Martin. "Hollywood's Shortest Actors." *Telegraph,* June 15, 2011. Web: June 2012, www.telegraph.co.uk/culture/film/film-news/8577019/Hollywoods-shortest-actors.html.

Clifford, Margaret M., and Elaine Walster. "The Effects of Physical Attractiveness on Teacher Expectations." *Sociology of Education* 46, no. 2 (1973): 248–58.

Dion, Karen, Ellen Berscheid, and Elaine Walster. "What Is Beautiful Is Good." *Journal of Personality and Social Psychology* 24, no. 3 (1972): 285–90.

Eagly, Alice H., Richard D. Ashmore, Mona G. Makhijani, and Laura C. Longo. "What Is Beautiful Is Good, But . . . : A Meta-analytic Review of Research on the Physical Attractiveness Stereotype." *Psychological Bulletin* 110, no. 1 (1991): 109–28.

Efran, M. "The Effect of Physical Appearance on the Judgment of Guilt, Interpersonal Attraction, and Severity of

Recommended Punishment in a Simulated Jury Task."
*Journal of Research in Personality* 8, no. 1 (1974): 45–54.

Foster, Glen, and James Ysseldyke. "Expectancy and Halo Effects as a Result of Artificially Induced Teacher Bias."
*Contemporary Educational Psychology* 1, no. 1 (1976): 37–45.

Harmon, David. "5 Things More Likely Than a Shark Attack." *The Diving Blog,* Oct. 4, 2010. Web: June 2012, www .thedivingblog.com/5-things-more-likely-than-shark-attack/.

Judge, Timothy A., and Daniel M. Cable. "The Effect of Physical Height on Workplace Success and Income: Preliminary Test of a Theoretical Model." *Journal of Applied Psychology* 89, no. 3 (2004): 428–41.

Kahneman, Daniel. *Thinking, Fast and Slow*. New York: Farrar, Straus and Giroux, 2011.

Kaplan, Robert M. "Is Beauty Talent? Sex Interaction in the Attractiveness Halo Effect." *Sex Roles* 4, no. 2 (1978): 195–204.

Landy, David, and Harold Sigall. "Beauty Is Talent: Task Evaluation as a Function of the Performer's Physical Attractiveness." *Journal of Personality and Social Psychology* 29, no. 3 (1974): 299–304.

Levitt, Steven D., and Stephen J. Dubner. *Freakonomics: A Rogue Economist Explores the Hidden Side of Everything*. New York: William Morrow, 2005.

Moore, F. R., D. Filippou, and D. I. Perrett. "Intelligence and Attractiveness in the Face: Beyond the Attractiveness Halo Effect." *Journal of Evolutionary Psychology* 9, no. 3 (2011): 205–17.

Nisbett, Richard E., and Timothy D. Wilson. "The Halo Effect: Evidence for Unconscious Alteration of Judgments." *Journal of Personality and Social Psychology* 35, no. 4 (1977): 250–56.

Reinemeyer, Erika. "Edward Lee Thorndike (1874–1949)." *History of Psychology Archives*. Muskingum College, May 1999. Web: June 2012, www.muskingum.edu/~psych/psycweb/ history/thorndike.htm.

Rincon, Paul. "Newborns Prefer Beautiful Faces." *BBC News,*
June 9, 2004. Web: June 2012, news.bbc.co.uk/2/hi/science/
nature/3631018.stm.

Rolirad, Larry S. "Size Does Matter: Kerry to Win Easily . . ."
*Hackwriters,* 2004. Web: June 2012, www.hackwriters.com/
tall.htm.

Sigall, Harold, and Nancy Ostrove. "Beautiful but Dangerous:
Effects of Offender Attractiveness and Nature of the Crime
on Juridic Judgment." *Journal of Personality and Social
Psychology* 31, no. 3 (1975): 410–14.

Slater, Alan. "Visual Perception in the Newborn Infant: Issues
and Debates." *Intellectica* 1, no. 34 (2002): 57–76.

Thorndike, E. L. "A Constant Error in Psychological Ratings."
*Journal of Applied Psychology* 4, no. 1 (1920): 25–29.

Uva, Michael. "Essential Equipment." *The Grip Book,* 4th ed.
Burlington, MA: Focal, 2010, p. 37.

World Health Organisation Statistical Information System.
"Mortality Statistics: Fall on and from Stairs and Steps (Most
Recent) by Country." *NationMaster,* Jan. 2004. Web: June
2012, www.nationmaster.com/graph/mor_fal_on_and_fro_
sta_and_ste-mortality-fall-stairs-steps.

## 6. Ego Depletion

Banja, John D. *Medical Errors and Medical Narcissism*. Sudbury,
MA: Jones and Bartlett, 2004.

Baumeister, Roy, and John Tierney. "The Authors of *Willpower*
Answer Your Questions." Interview, *Freakonomics,* Sept. 22,
2011. Web: Apr. 2012, www.freakonomics.com/2011/09/22/
the-authors-of-willpower-answer-your-questions/.

————. *Willpower: Rediscovering the Greatest Human Strength*.
New York: Penguin, 2011.

Baumeister, Roy F., C. Nathan DeWall, Natalie J. Ciarocco, and
Jean M. Twenge. "Social Exclusion Impairs Self-regulation."

*Journal of Personality and Social Psychology* 88, no. 4 (2005): 589–604.

Baumeister, Roy F., Ellen Bratslavsky, Mark Muraven, and Dianne M. Tice. "Ego Depletion: Is the Active Self a Limited Resource?" *Journal of Personality and Social Psychology* 74, no. 5 (1998): 1252–265.

Beedie, C. J., and A. M. Lane. "The Role of Glucose in Self-control: Another Look at the Evidence and an Alternative Conceptualization." *Personality and Social Psychology Review* 16, no. 2 (2012): 143–53.

Bloom, Harold. "Freud, The Greatest Modern Writer." *The New York Times,* March 23, 1986. Web: http://www.nytimes. com/1986/03/23/books/freud-the-greatest-modern-writer .html?pagewanted=all.

Carey, Benedict. "Analyze These." *The New York Times,* Apr. 25, 2006. Web: Apr. 2012, www.nytimes.com/2006/04/25/health/ psychology/25freud.html?pagewanted=print.

Danziger, Shai, Jonathan Levav, and Liora Avnaim-Pesso. "Extraneous Factors in Judicial Decisions." Ed. Daniel Kahneman. *Proceedings of the National Academy of Sciences of the United States of America* 108, no. 17 (2011): 6889–892.

Floyd, Barbara. *From Quackery to Bacteriology: The Emergence of Modern Medicine in 19th Century America*. University of Toledo, Feb. 1995. Web: April 2012, www.utoledo.edu/ library/canaday/exhibits/quackery/quack1.html.

Gailliot, Matthew T., Roy F. Baumeister, C. Nathan DeWall, Jon K. Maner, E. Ashby Plant, Dianne M. Tice, Lauren E. Brewer, and Brandon J. Schmeichel. "Self-control Relies on Glucose as a Limited Energy Source: Willpower Is More Than a Metaphor." *Journal of Personality and Social Psychology* 92, no. 2 (2007): 325–36.

Goodall, J. "Social Rejection, Exclusion, and Shunning Among the Gombe Chimpanzees." *Ethology and Sociobiology* 7, nos. 3–4 (1986): 227–36.

Gorlick, Adam. "Need a Study Break to Refresh? Maybe Not, Say Stanford Researchers." *Stanford News,* Stanford University, Oct. 14, 2010. Web: Apr. 2012, news.stanford.edu/news/2010/october/willpower-resource-study-101410.html.

Hagger, Martin S., Chantelle Wood, Chris Stiff, and Nikos L. D. Chatzisarantis. "Ego Depletion and the Strength Model of Self-control: A Meta-analysis." *Psychological Bulletin* 136, no. 4 (2010): 495–525.

Holmes, Oliver Wendell. *Medical Essays, 1842–1882.* Boston: Houghton Mifflin, 1891.

Inzlicht, Michael, and Brandon J. Schmeichel. "What Is Ego Depletion? Toward a Mechanistic Revision of the Resource Model of Self-control." *Perspectives on Psychological Science* 7, no. 5 (2012): 450–63.

Job, V., C. S. Dweck, and G. M. Walton. "Ego Depletion—Is It All in Your Head?: Implicit Theories About Willpower Affect Self-Regulation." *Psychological Science* 21, no. 11 (2010): 1686–693.

Leher, Jonah. "The Willpower Trick." *Wired Science,* Jan. 9, 2012. Web: Apr. 2012, www.wired.com/wiredscience/2012/01/the-willpower-trick/.

"Medical Class of 1889." University of Pennsylvania University Archives and Records Center. Web: Apr. 2012, www.archives.upenn.edu/histy/features/1800s/1889med/med1889entry.html.

Muraven, Mark, and Owen Flanagan. "The Mechanisms of Self-control: Lessons from Addiction." Lecture. The Oxford Centre for Neuroethics, University of Oxford. May 13, 2010. *The Science Network,* May 13, 2010. Web: Apr. 2012, thesciencenetwork.org/programs/the-mechanisms-of-self-control-lessons-from-addiction.

Muraven, Mark, and Roy F. Baumeister. "Self-regulation and Depletion of Limited Resources: Does Self-control Resemble a Muscle?" *Psychological Bulletin* 126, no. 2 (2000): 247–59.

Muraven, Mark, Dianne M. Tice, and Roy F. Baumeister. "Self-control as a Limited Resource: Regulatory Depletion Patterns." *Journal of Personality and Social Psychology* 74, no. 3 (1998): 774–89.

"Overview: Medicine 1800–1899." BookRags. Web: Apr. 2012, www.bookrags.com/research/overview-medicine-1800-1899-scit-051234/.

Tice, Dianne M., Roy F. Baumeister, Dikla Shmueli, and Mark Muraven. "Restoring the Self: Positive Affect Helps Improve Self-regulation Following Ego Depletion." *Journal of Experimental Social Psychology* 43, no. 3 (2007): 379–84.

Tierney, John. "Do You Suffer From Decision Fatigue?" *The New York Times,* Aug. 21, 2011. Web: Apr. 2012, www.nytimes.com/2011/08/21/magazine/do-you-suffer -from-decision-fatigue.html?pagewanted=all. A version of this article appeared in print on August 21, 2011, on page MM33 of *The New York Times Magazine* with the headline "To Choose Is to Lose."

Vohs, Kathleen D., Brian D. Glass, W. Todd Maddox, and Arthur B. Markman. "Ego Depletion Is Not Just Fatigue: Evidence from a Total Sleep Deprivation Experiment." *Social Psychological and Personality Science* 2, no. 2 (2011): 166–73.

Wegner, Daniel M., David J. Schneider, Samuel R. Carter, and Teri L. White. "Paradoxical Effects of Thought Suppression." *Journal of Personality and Social Psychology* 53, no. 1 (1987): 5–13.

Wootton, David. *Bad Medicine: Doctors Doing Harm Since Hippocrates*. Oxford: Oxford University Press, 2006.

Wrangham, Richard W. *Chimpanzee Cultures*. Cambridge, MA:

Harvard University Press in cooperation with the Chicago Academy of Sciences, 1996.

## 7. The Misattribution of Arousal

Cooper, Joel, Mark P. Zanna, and Peter A. Taves. "Arousal as a Necessary Condition for Attitude Change Following Induced Compliance." *Journal of Personality and Social Psychology* 36, no. 10 (1978): 1101–106.

Dutton, Donald G., and Arthur P. Aron. "Some Evidence for Heightened Sexual Attraction Under Conditions of High Anxiety." *Journal of Personality and Social Psychology* 30, no. 4 (1974): 510–17.

Forster, Jens. "How Body Feedback Influences Consumers' Evaluation of Products." *Journal of Consumer Psychology* 14, no. 4 (2004): 416–26.

Gilbert, Daniel. "Family, Friends and Lovers." *This Emotional Life*. Public Broadcasting Service (PBS), Jan. 2010.

Gilovich, Thomas. *How We Know What Isn't So*. Noew York: Free Press, 1993.

Graham, James M. "Self-expansion and Flow in Couples' Momentary Experiences: An Experience Sampling Study." *Journal of Personality and Social Psychology* 95, no. 3 (2008): 679–94.

Munger, Dave. "'Just Smile, You'll Feel Better!' Will You? Really?" *ScienceBlogs,* Apr. 6, 2009. Web: July 2011, scienceblogs.com/cognitivedaily/2007/11/27/just-smile-youll-feel-better-w/.

Myers, D. G. *Social Psychology.* New York: McGraw-Hill, 2005.

Reisenzein, Rainer. "The Schachter Theory of Emotion: Two Decades Later." *Psychological Bulletin* 94, no. 2 (1983): 239–64.

Strack, F., L. L. Martin, and S. Stepper. (1988). "Inhibiting and Facilitating Conditions of the Human Smile: A Nonobtrusive

Test of the Facial Feedback Hypothesis." *Journal of Personality and Social Psychology* 54, no. 5 (1988): 768.

Wells, Gary L., and Richard E. Petty. "The Effects of Over Head Movements on Persuasion: Compatibility and Incompatibility of Responses." *Basic and Applied Social Psychology* 1 no. 3 (1980): 219–30.

"Where the Body Goes, the Mind Follows." *Tools for Changing the World*. WordPress, May 9, 2011. Web: July 2011, toolsforchangingtheworld.com/where-the-body-goes-the-mind-follows/.

## 8. The Illusion of External Agency

Brickman, Philip, Dan Coates, and Ronnie Janoff-Bulman. "Lottery Winners and Accident Victims: Is Happiness Relative?" *Journal of Personality and Social Psychology* 36, no. 8 (1978): 917–27.

Gertner, Jon. "The Futile Pursuit of Happiness." *The New York Times,* Sept. 7, 2003. Web: Aug. 2012, www.nytimes.com/2003/09/07/magazine/the-futile-pursuit-of-happiness.html?pagewanted=all&src=pm.

Gilbert, Daniel. *Stumbling on Happiness*. New York: Knopf, 2006.

———. "The Surprising Science of Happiness." *TED Talks*. Sept. 2006. Web: Aug. 2012, www.ted.com/talks/dan_gilbert_asks_why_are_we_happy.html.

Gilbert, Daniel T., and Jane E. J. Ebert. "Decisions and Revisions: The Affective Forecasting of Changeable Outcomes." *Journal of Personality and Social Psychology* 82, no. 4 (2002): 503–14.

Gilbert, Daniel T., Elizabeth C. Pinel, Timothy D. Wilson, Stephen J. Blumberg, and Thalia P. Wheatley. "Immune Neglect: A Source of Durability Bias in Affective Forecasting." *Journal of Personality and Social Psychology* 75, no. 3 (1998): 617–38.

Gilbert, Daniel T., Ryan P. Brown, Elizabeth C. Pinel, and Timothy D. Wilson. "The Illusion of External Agency."

*Journal of Personality and Social Psychology* 79, no. 5 (2000): 690–700.

Metcalfe, Janet, Teal S. Eich, and Alan D. Castel. "Metacognition of Agency across the Lifespan." *Cognition* 116, no. 2 (2010): 267–82.

Schwartz, Barry. *The Paradox of Choice: Why More Is Less*. New York: Ecco, 2004.

Wilson, Timothy D., and Daniel T. Gilbert. "Affective Forecasting: Knowing What to Want." *Current Directions in Psychological Science* 14, no. 3 (2005): 131–34.

## 9. The Backfire Effect

Biggs, John. "Study Finds That We Still Believe Untruths Even After Instant Online Corrections." TechCrunch RSS. N.p., 24 Jan. 2013. Web. 11 Feb. 2013.

Committee on Psychosocial Aspects of Child and Family Health. "Guidance for Effective Discipline." *Pediatrics* 101, no. 4 (1998): 723–28.Web: June 2011, pediatrics.aappublications .org/content/101/4/723.full.

Cook, John, and Stephen Lewandowsky. *The Debunking Handbook*. St. Lucia, Australia: University of Queensland, 2011.

Davies, Gavyn. "Can Two Different Numbers Be the Same?" *The Guardian,* June 21, 2006.Web: June 2011, www.guardian .co.uk/commentisfree/2006/jun/22/comment.tvandradio.

Dunbar, Kevin N., Jonathan A. Fugelsang, and Courtney Stein. "Do Naïve Theories Ever Go Away? Using Brain and Behavior to Understand Changes in Concepts." In *Thinking with Data*. Eds. Marsha C. Lovett and Priti Shah. New York: LEA, 2007, pp. 193–206.

Ditto, Peter H., and David F. Lopez. "Motivated Skepticism: Use of Differential Decision Criteria for Preferred and Nonpreferred Conclusions." *Journal of Personality and Social Psychology* 63, no. 4 (1992): 568–84.

Garrett, R. Kelly, and Brian E. Weeks. "The Promise and Peril of Real-Time Corrections to Political Misperceptions," Ohio State University School of Communication (Jan. 2013, PDF).

Gilbert, Daniel. "I'm O.K., You're Biased." *The New York Times,* April 16, 2006. Web: June 2011, www.nytimes .com/2006/04/16/opinion/16gilbert.html?pagewanted=all.

Gilliam, Franklin D., Jr. "The "Welfare Queen" Experiment: How Viewers React to Images of African-American Mothers on Welfare." *Nieman Reports* 53, no. 2 (Summer 1999): 49–52.

Hulsizer, Michael R., Geoffrey D. Munro, Angela Fagerlin, and Stuart P. Taylor. "Molding the Past: Biased Assimilation of Historical Information." *Journal of Applied Social Psychology* 34, no. 5 (2004): 1048–74.

Krugman, Paul. "Republicans and Race." *The New York Times,* Nov. 19, 2007. Web: June 2011, www.nytimes.com/2007/11/19/ opinion/19krugman.html.

Lehrer, Jonah. "Why We Don't Believe in Science." *The New Yorker,* June 7, 2012. Web: Dec. 2012, www.newyorker.com/ online/blogs/frontal-cortex/2012/06/brain-experiments-why- we-dont-believe-science.html.

"Literally Unbelievable." Hudson Hongo. Web: June 2011, www .hudsonhongo.com/2011/05/20/literally-unbelievable/.

Lord, Charles G., Lee Ross, and Mark R. Lepper. "Biased Assimilation and Attitude Polarization: The Effects of Prior Theories on Subsequently Considered Evidence." *Journal of Personality and Social Psychology* 37, no.11 (1979): 2098–109.

Marquand, Robert. "Osama Bin Laden Conspiracy Theories Race Across the World." *Christian Science Monitor,* May 3, 2011. Web: June 2011, www.csmonitor.com/World/ Europe/2011/0503/Osama-bin-Laden-conspiracy-theories- race-across-the-world.

Morales, Lymari. "Obama's Birth Certificate Convinces Some,

but Not All, Skeptics." Gallup, May 13, 2011. Web: June 2011, www.gallup.com/poll/147530/obama-birth-certificate-convinces-not-skeptics.aspx.

"More Say There Is Solid Evidence of Global Warming." Pew Research Center for the People and the Press. Oct. 15, 2012. Web: Dec. 2012, www.people-press.org/2012/12/17/pew-research-year-in-review/prc_12-12-24_yearreview12/.

Munro, Geoffrey D. "The Scientific Impotence Excuse: Discounting Belief-Threatening Scientific Abstracts." *Journal of Applied Social Psychology* 40, no. 3 (2010): 579–600.

Nyhan, Brendan, and Jason Reifler. "When Corrections Fail: The Persistence of Political Misperceptions." *Political Behavior* 32, no. 2 (2010): 303–30.

Pariser, Eli. "When the Internet Thinks It Knows You." *The New York Times,* May 22, 2011, Sec. A: 23.Web: June 2011, www.nytimes.com/2011/05/23/opinion/23pariser.html.

Paul, Pamela. "Is Spanking O.K.?" *Time,* May 8, 2006: W1–W3.Web: June 2011, www.time.com/time/magazine/article/0,9171,1191825,00.html.

Reber, R. "Effects of Perceptual Fluency on Judgments of Truth." *Consciousness and Cognition* 8, no. 3 (1999): 338–42.

Salzberg, Steven. "Anti-vaccine Movement Causes the Worst Whooping Cough Epidemic in 70 Years." *Forbes,* July 23, 2012. Web: Dec. 2012, www.forbes.com/sites/stevensalzberg/2012/07/23/anti-vaccine-movement-causes-the-worst-whooping-cough-epidemic-in-70-years/.

Schwarz, Norbert, Lawrence J. Sanna, Ian Skurnik, and Carolyn Yoon. "Metacognitive Experiences and the Intricacies of Setting People Straight: Implications for Debiasing and Public Information Campaigns." *Advances in Experimental Social Psychology* 39 (2007): 127–61.

"'Welfare Queen' Becomes Issue in Reagan Campaign." *The New York Times,* Feb. 15, 1976, p. 51.

## 10. *Pluralistic Ignorance*

Breed, Warren, and Thomas Ktsanes. "Pluralistic Ignorance in the Process of Opinion Formation." *Public Opinion Quarterly* 25, no. 3 (1961): 382–92.

Centola, Damon, Robb Willer, and Michael Macy. "The Emperor's Dilemma: A Computational Model of Self-enforcing Norms." *American Journal of Sociology* 110, no. 4 (2005): 1009–40.

Ferrante-Wallace, Joan. *Sociology: A Global Perspective*. Belmont, CA: Wadsworth/Thomson Learning, 2003.

Katz, Daniel, Floyd Henry Allport, and Margaret Babcock Jenness. *Students' Attitudes: A Report of the Syracuse University Reaction Study.* Syracuse, NY: Craftsman, 1931.

Kitts, James A. "Egocentric Bias or Information Management? Selective Disclosure and the Social Roots of Norm Misperception." *Social Psychology Quarterly* 66, no.3 (2003): 222–37.

Miller, Dale T., and Cathy McFarland. "Pluralistic Ignorance: When Similarity Is Interpreted as Dissimilarity." *Journal of Personality and Social Psychology* 53.2 (1987): 298-305. Print.

O'Gorman, Hubert J. "The Discovery of Pluralistic Ignorance: An Ironic Lesson." *Journal of the History of the Behavioral Sciences* 22, no. 4 (1986): 333–47.

———. "Pluralistic Ignorance and White Estimates of White Support for Racial Segregation." *The Public Opinion Quarterly* 39, no. 3 (1975): 313–30.

Prentice, Deborah A., and Dale T. Miller. "Pluralistic Ignorance and Alcohol Use on Campus: Some Consequences of Misperceiving the Social Norm." *Journal of Personality and Social Psychology* 64, no. 2 (1993): 243–56.

Schanck, Richard Louis. "A Study of a Community and Its Groups and Institutions Conceived of as Behaviors of Individuals." *Psychological Monographs* 43, no.2 (1932): I-133.

## 11. The No True Scotsman Fallacy

"Anders Behring Breivik." *The New York Times,* Times Topics, Aug. 24, 2012. Web: Sept. 2012, topics.nytimes.com/top/reference/timestopics/people/b/anders_behring_breivik/index.html.

Baggini, Julian. *The Duck That Won the Lottery: 100 New Experiments for the Armchair Philosopher.* New York: Plume, 2008.

Fogarty, Mignon. "Begs the Question." *Grammar Girl: Quick and Dirty Tips for Better Writing.* August 19, 2008. Web: http://grammar.quickanddirtytips.com/begs-the-question.aspx.

Krepel, Terry. "Sorry, O'Reilly: Anders Breivik Is A Christian." *Media Matters for America.* July 27, 2011. Web: http://mediamatters.org/blog/2011/07/27/sorry-oreilly-anders-breivik-is-a-christian/183298.

Mirkinson, Jack. "Bill O'Reilly: Media Labeling Norway Killer Breivik 'Christian' Because 'They Don't Like Christians.'" *The Huffington Post,* July26, 2011. Web: Sept. 2012, www.huffingtonpost.com/2011/07/26/bill-oreilly-media-breivik-christian_n_909498.html.

## 12. The Illusion of Asymmetric Insight

Bracegirdle, Ian. "Greek Masks: The Rich History." *Mask and More Masks.* WebRing. Web: Aug. 2011, www.mask-and-more-masks.com/greek-masks.html.

Haidt, Jonathan. "The Moral Roots of Liberals and Conservatives." *TED Talks.* Filmed March 2008. Posted September 2008. Web: http://www.ted.com/talks/jonathan_haidt_on_the_moral_mind.html.

Johnston, Dan, Ph.D. "Persona—The Mask We Wear." *Awakenings: Lessons for Living.* Web: Aug. 2011, www.lessons4living.com/persona.htm.

Pronin, E., D. Y. Lin, and L. Ross. "The Bias Blind Spot:

Perceptions of Bias in Self Versus Others." *Personality and Social Psychology Bulletin* 28, no.3 (2002): 369–81.

Pronin, Emily, Justin Kruger, Kenneth Savtisky, and Lee Ross. "You Don't Know Me, but I Know You: The Illusion of Asymmetric Insight." *Journal of Personality and Social Psychology* 81, no.4 (2001): 639–56.

Pronin, Emily, Thomas Gilovich, and Lee Ross. "Objectivity in the Eye of the Beholder: Divergent Perceptions of Bias in Self Versus Others." *Psychological Review* 111, no. 3 (2004): 781–99.

Sherif, Muzafer, O. J. Harvey, B. Jack White, William R. Hood, and Carolyn W. Sherif. *Intergroup Conflict and Cooperation: The Robbers Cave Experiment*. Norman, OK: University Book Exchange, 1961. *Classics in the History of Psychology*. York University, Toronto. Web: Aug. 2011, psychclassics.yorku.ca/.

Sloman, Steven, and Philip M. Fernbach. "I'm Right! (For Some Reason)." *The New York Times*. October 19, 2012. Web: http://www.nytimes.com/2012/10/21/opinion/sunday/why-partisans-cant-explain-their-views.html?_r=0.

## 13. Enclothed Cognition

Adam, Hajo, and Adam D. Galinsky. "Enclothed Cognition." *Journal of Experimental Social Psychology* 48, no. 4 (2012): 918–25.

Bargh, John A., Mark Chen, and Lara Burrows. "Automaticity of Social Behavior: Direct Effects of Trait Construct and Stereotype Activation on Action." *Journal of Personality and Social Psychology* 71, no. 2 (1996): 230–44.

Buonomano, Dean. *Brain Bugs: How the Brain's Flaws Shape Our Lives*. New York: W.W. Norton, 2011.

Dijksterhuis, Ap, and Ad Van Knippenberg. "The Relation Between Perception and Behavior, or How to Win a Game of Trivial Pursuit." *Journal of Personality and Social Psychology* 74, no. 4 (1998): 865–77.

Forsythe, Sandra M. "Effect of Applicant's Clothing on

Interviewer's Decision to Hire." *Journal of Applied Social Psychology* 20, no. 19 (1990): 1579–595.

Frank, Mark G., and Thomas Gilovich. "The Dark Side of Self- and Social Perception: Black Uniforms and Aggression in Professional Sports." *Journal of Personality and Social Psychology* 54, no. 1 (1988): 74–85.

Fredrickson, Barbara L., Tomi-Ann Roberts, Stephanie M. Noll, Diane M. Quinn, and Jean M. Twenge. "That Swimsuit Becomes You: Sex Differences in Self-objectification, Restrained Eating, and Math Performance." *Journal of Personality and Social Psychology* 75, no. 1 (1998): 269–84.

Myers, D. G. *Social Psychology*. New York : McGraw-Hill, 2005.

"Suitably Dressed." *The Economist*. Dec. 16, 2010. Web: Apr. 2012, www.economist.com/node/17722802.

Williams, L. E., and J. A. Bargh. "Experiencing Physical Warmth Promotes Interpersonal Warmth." *Science* 322, no. 5901 (2008): 606–7.

Zimbardo, Philip G. "The Human Choice: Individuation, Reason, and Order Versus Deindividuation, Impulse, and Chaos." *Nebraska Symposium on Motivation, 1969*. By David Levine and William J. Arnold. Vol. 17. Lincoln, Neb.: University of Nebraska, 1969, pp. 237–307.

## 14. Deindividuation

Britten, Nick. "Suicide Teenager Urged to Jump by Baying Crowd." *Telegraph,* Sept. 30, 2008. Web: Feb. 2011, www.telegraph.co.uk/news/uknews/3108987/Suicide-teenager-urged-to-jump-by-baying-crowd.html.

Diener, E. "Effects of Prior Destructive Behavior, Anonymity, and Group Presence on Deindividuation and Aggression." *Journal of Personality and Social Psychology* 33, no. 5 (1976): 497.

———. "Deindividuation, Self-awareness, and Disinhibition."

*Journal of Personality and Social Psychology* 37, no. 7 (1979): 1160.

————. "Deindividuation: The Absence of Self-awareness and Self-regulation in Group Members." In *The Psychology of Group Influence*. Paul B. Paulus, ed. Hillsdale, NJ: Erlbaum, 1980: 209–42.

Ebuenga, Desiree Lei. *Deindividuation (Review of Related Literature)*. *Scribd,* Apr. 14, 2010. Web: Feb. 2011, www .scribd.com/doc/29908160/Deindividuation-Review-of-Related-Literature.

Johnson, R. D., and L. L. Downing. "Deindividuation and Valence of Cues: Effects on Prosocial and Antisocial Behavior." *Journal of Personality and Social Psychology* 37, no. 9 (1979): 1532.

Myers, D. G. *Social Psychology*. New York: McGraw-Hill, 2005.

Perry, Mike. "Sports Fans: Deindividuation." *PsyberSite,* Miami University, April 18, 2002. Web: Feb. 2011, www.units .muohio.edu/psybersite/fans/deindividuation.shtml.

Restivo, Jenette. "Why Bridge Jumper Was Taunted." *ABC News,* Aug. 28, 2001. Web: Feb. 2011, abcnews.go.com/Health/story?id=117255&page=1.

Roberts, Amy. "Halloween by the Numbers." *CNN*. October 30, 2012. Web: http://www.cnn.com/2012/10/30/living/halloween-by-the-numbers.

Spivey, Cashton B., and Steven Prentice-Dunn. "Assessing the Directionality of Deindividuated Behavior: Effects of Deindividuation, Modeling, and Private Self-consciousness on Aggressive and Prosocial Responses." *Basic and Applied Social Psychology* 11, no. 4 (1990): 387–403.

Yoo, Aileen. "A Man Jumps to His Death and People—Laugh?" *SFGate,* Feb. 2, 2010. Web: Feb. 2011, blog.sfgate.com/scavenger/2010/02/17/a-man-jumps-to-his-death-and-people-laugh/.

Zimbardo, Philip G. *The Lucifer Effect: Understanding How Good People Turn Evil*. New York: Random House, 2007.

## 15. The Sunk Cost Fallacy

Arkes, Hal R., and Peter Ayton. "The Sunk Cost and Concorde Effects: Are Humans Less Rational Than Lower Animals?" *Psychological Bulletin* 125, no. 5 (1999): 591–600.

Ariely, Dan. *Predictably Irrational, Revised and Expanded Edition: The Hidden Forces That Shape Our Decisions*. New York: Harper, 2009.

Burthold, Gloria R. *Psychology of Decision Making in Legal, Health Care and Science Settings*. East Sussex, England: Gardners Books, 2008.

Busch, Jack. "Travel Zen: How to Avoid Making Your Vacation Seem Like Work." *Primer Magazine,* Jan. 2009. Web: Mar. 2011, www.primermagazine.com/2009/learn/travel-zen-how-to-avoid-making-your-vacation-seem-like-work.

Godin, Seth. "Ignore Sunk Costs." *Seth's Blog*. Typepad, Inc., May 12, 2009. Web: Mar. 2011, sethgodin.typepad.com/seths_blog/2009/05/ignore-sunk-costs.html.

Höffler, Felix. "Why Humans Care About Sunk Costs While (Lower) Animals Don't." Max Planck Institute for Research on Collective Goods, Mar. 31, 2008. Web: Mar. 2011.

Indvik, Lauren. "'FarmVille' Interruption Cited in Baby's Murder." *Mashable,* Oct. 28, 2010. Web: Mar. 2011, mashable.com/2010/10/28/farmville-murder-mother-baby/.

Kahneman, Daniel. *Thinking, Fast and Slow*. New York: Farrar, Straus and Giroux, 2011.

Kushner, David. "Games: Why Zynga's Success Makes Game Designers Gloomy." *Wired,* Sept. 27, 2010. Web: Mar. 2011, www.wired.com/magazine/2010/09/pl_games_zynga/.

Lehrer, Jonah. "Loss Aversion." *ScienceBlogs,* Feb. 10, 2010. Web: Mar. 2011, scienceblogs.com/cortex/2010/02/10/loss-aversion/.

McGonigal, Jane. "Gaming Can Make a Better World." *TED Talks,* Feb. 2010. Web: Mar. 2011, www.ted.com/talks/jane_ mcgonigal_gaming_can_make_a_better_world.html.

Schwartz, Barry. "The Sunk-Cost Fallacy: Bush Falls Victim to a Bad New Argument for the Iraq War." *Slate,* Sept. 9, 2005. Web: Mar. 2011, www.slate.com/articles/news_and_politics/ hey_wait_a_minute/2005/09/the_sunkcost_fallacy.html.

Shambora, Jessica. "'FarmVille' Gamemaker Zynga Sees Dollar Signs." *CNN Money,* Oct. 26, 2009. Web: Mar. 2011, tech .fortune.cnn.com/2009/10/26/farmville-gamemaker-zynga- sees-dollar-signs/.

Takahashi, Dean. "FarmVille 2 Has 17 Players in the Vatican and Other 'Big Data' Trivia." VentureBeat. Comments. N.p., 4 Jan. 2013. Web. 11 Feb. 2013, http://venturebeat .com/2013/01/04/farmville-2-has-17-players-in-the-vatican- and-other-big-data-trivia/.

Vidyarthi, Neil. "City Council Member Booted for Playing FarmVille." *SocialTimes,* Mar. 30, 2010. Web: Mar. 2011, socialtimes.com/fired-playing-farmville_b4754.

Walker, Tim. "Welcome to FarmVille: Population 80 Million." *Independent,* Feb. 22, 2010. Web: Mar. 2011, www. independent.co.uk/life-style/gadgets-and-tech/features/ welcome-to-farmville-population-80-million-1906260.html.

"Why Zynga's Success Makes Game Designers Gloomy: Discussion at Hacker News."*Hacker News*. Y Combinator, Oct. 7, 2010. Web: Mar. 2011, news.ycombinator.net/ item?id=1767549.

Wittmershaus, Eric. "Facebook Game's Cautionary Tale." *GameWit,* Aug. 4, 2010. Web: Mar. 2011, gamewit.blogs .pressdemocrat.com/12167/facebook-games-cautionary-tale/.

Yang, Sizhao Zao. "How Did FarmVille Takeover FarmTown, When It Was Just an Exact Duplicate of FarmTown and FarmTown Was Released Much Earlier?" *Quora,* Jan. 1, 2011.

Web: Mar. 2011, www.quora.com/How-did-FarmVille-take-over-FarmTown-when-it-was-just-a-exact-duplicate-of-FarmTown-and-FarmTown-was-released-much-earlier.

## 16. The Overjustification Effect

Ariely, Dan. *Predictably Irrational: The Hidden Forces That Shape Our Decisions*. New York: Harper, 2008.

"Behavior: Skinner's Utopia: Panacea or Path to Hell?" *Time,* Sept. 20, 1971. Web: Dec. 2011, www.time.com/time/magazine/article/0,9171,909994,00.html.

Benabou, Roland, and Jean Tirole. "Intrinsic and Extrinsic Motivation." *Review of Economic Studies* 70, no. 3 (2003): 489–520.

Benjamin, Daniel J., Ori Heffetz, Miles S. Kimball, and Alex Rees-Jones. *Do People Seek to Maximize Happiness? Evidence from New Surveys*. National Bureau of Economic Research, Oct. 24, 2010. Web: Dec. 2011, www.nber.org/papers/w16489.pdf.

Boggiano, Ann K., and Diane N. Ruble. "Children's Responses to Evaluative Feedback." In *Self-Related Cognitions in Anxiety and Motivation*. Ed. by Ralf Schwarzer. Hillsdale, NJ: L. Erlbaum Associates, 1986, pp. 195–227.

Boggiano, Ann K., Judith M. Harackiewicz, Janella M. Bessette, and Deborah S. Main. "Increasing Children's Interest Through Performance-Contingent Reward." *Social Cognition* 3, no. 4 (1985): 400–11.

Boggiano, Ann K., Marty Barrett, Anne W. Weiher, Gary H. McClelland, et al. "Use of the Maximal-Operant Principle to Motivate Children's Intrinsic Interest." *Journal of Personality and Social Psychology* 53, no. 5 (1987): 866–79.

Bradley, W., and R. C. Mannell. "Sensitivity of Intrinsic Motivation to Reward Procedure Instructions." *Personality and Social Psychology Bulletin* 10, no. 3 (1984): 426–31.

*Building Mega-objects in Minecraft*. Dir. Hal Nicholas. YouTube,

Sept. 27, 2010. Web: Dec. 2011, www.youtube.com/
watch?v=kn2-d5a3r94.

Deaton, Angus. "Income, Health, and Well-being around the
World: Evidence from the Gallup World Poll." *Journal of
Economic Perspectives* 22, no. 2 (2008): 53–72.

Deci, Edward L. "Intrinsic Motivation, Extrinsic Reinforcement,
and Inequity." *Journal of Personality and Social Psychology* 22,
no. 1 (1972): 113–20.

Deci, Edward L., Richard Koestner, and Richard M. Ryan. "A
Meta-analytic Review of Experiments Examining the Effects
of Extrinsic Rewards on Intrinsic Motivation." *Psychological
Bulletin* 125, no. 6 (1999): 627–68.

Frank, Robert. "The Perfect Salary for Happiness: $75,000." *The
Wall Street Journal, The Wealth Report* (blog),Sept. 7, 2010.
Web: Dec. 2011, blogs.wsj.com/wealth/2010/09/07/the
-perfect-salary-for-happiness-75000-a-year/.

Kahneman, D., and A. Deaton. "High Income Improves
Evaluation of Life but Not Emotional Well-being." *Proceedings
of the National Academy of Sciences* 107, no. 38 (2010): 16489–93.

Lepper, Mark R., and David Greene. *The Hidden Costs of Reward:
New Perspectives on the Psychology of Human Motivation*.
Hillsdale, NJ: L. Erlbaum Associates, 1978.

Lepper, Mark R., David Greene, and Richard E. Nisbett.
"Undermining Children's Intrinsic Interest with Extrinsic
Reward: A Test of the 'Overjustification' Hypothesis." *Journal
of Personality and Social Psychology* 28, no. 1 (1973): 129–37.

Ordóñez, Lisa D., Maurice E. Schweitzer, Adam D. Galinsky,
and Max H. Braverman. *Goals Gone Wild: The Systematic Side
Effects of Over-Prescribing Goal Setting. HBS Working
Knowledge*. Harvard Business School, Feb. 11, 2009. Web:
Dec. 2011, hbswk.hbs.edu/item/6114.html.

Pink, Daniel H. *Drive: The Surprising Truth About What Motivates
Us*. New York, NY: Riverhead, 2009.

Rosenfield, David, Robert Folger, and Harold F. Adelman. "When Rewards Reflect Competence: A Qualification of the Overjustification Effect." *Journal of Personality and Social Psychology* 39, no. 3 (1980): 368–76.

Sansone, Carol. "A Question of Competence: The Effects of Competence and Task Feedback on Intrinsic Interest." *Journal of Personality and Social Psychology* 51, no. 5 (1986): 918–31.

Tang, Shu-Hua, and Vernon C. Hall. "The Overjustification Effect: A Meta-analysis." *Applied Cognitive Psychology* 9, no. 5 (1995): 365–404.

Vargas, Julie S. "A Brief Biography of B. F. Skinner."B. F. Skinner Foundation, 2005. Web: Dec. 2011, www.bfskinner .org/BFSkinner/AboutSkinner.html.

Workman, Edward A., and Robert L. Williams. "Effects of Extrinsic Rewards on Intrinsic Motivation in the Classroom." *Journal of School Psychology*18, no. 2 (Summer 1980): 141–47.

## 17. The Self-Enhancement Bias

Alicke, Mark D. "Global Self-evaluation as Determined by the Desirability and Controllability of Trait Adjectives." *Journal of Personality and Social Psychology* 49, no. 6 (1985): 1621–630.

Alicke, Mark D., and Olesya Govorun. "The Better-Than-Average Effect." In *The Self in Social Judgment*. Ed. by Mark D. Alicke, David Dunning, and Joachim I. Krueger. New York: Psychology Press, 2005, pp. 85–108.

Bushman, Brad J., Scott J. Moeller, and Jennifer Crocker. "Sweets, Sex, or Self-esteem? Comparing the Value of Self-Esteem Boosts with Other Pleasant Rewards." *Journal of Personality* 79, no. 5 (2011): 993–1012.

Bushman, Brad J., Scott J. Moeller, Sara Konrath, and Jennifer Crocker. "Investigating the Link Between Liking Versus Wanting Self-Esteem and Depression in a Nationally

Representative Sample of American Adults." *Journal of Personality* (2012).Web: July 2012.

Campbell, W. Keith, and Constantine Sedikides. "Self-threat Magnifies the Self-serving Bias: A Meta-analytic Integration." *Review of General Psychology* 3, no. 1 (1999): 23–43.

Colvin, C. Randall, Jack Block, and David C. Funder. "Overly Positive Self-evaluations and Personality: Negative Implications for Mental Health." *Journal of Personality and Social Psychology* 68, no. 6 (1995): 1152–62.

Cummins, Robert A., and Helen Nistico. "Maintaining Life Satisfaction: The Role of Positive Cognitive Bias." *Journal of Happiness Studies* 3, no. 1 (2002): 37–69.

Dahl, Melissa. "Most of Us Think We're Hotter Than Average, Survey Says 60 Percent Satisfied with Appearance in a New Survey from Msnbc.com, *ELLE*." MSNBC, Sept. 8, 2010. Web: July 2012, www.msnbc.msn.com/id/39044399/ns/health-skin_and_beauty/t/most-us-think-were-hotter-average-survey-says/.

Dell'Amore, Christine. "Evolution of Narcissism: Why We're Overconfident, and Why It Works Overestimating Our Abilities Can Be a Strategy for Success, Model Shows." *National Geographic News,* Sept. 14, 2011. Web: July 2012, news.nationalgeographic.com/.

Diekmann, Kristina A., Steven M. Samuels, Lee Ross, and Max H. Bazerman. "Self-interest and Fairness in Problems of Resource Allocation: Allocators Versus Recipients." *Journal of Personality and Social Psychology* 72, no. 5 (1997): 1061–74.

Dobson, Keith, and Renée-Louise Franche. "A Conceptual and Empirical Review of the Depressive Realism Hypothesis." *Canadian Journal of Behavioural Science* 21, no. 4 (1989): 419–33.

Dunning, David, Judith A. Meyerowitz, and Amy D. Holzberg. "Ambiguity and Self-evaluation: The Role of Idiosyncratic

Trait Definitions in Self-serving Assessments of Ability." *Journal of Personality and Social Psychology* 57, no. 6 (1989): 1082–90.

Gray, Janice D., and Roxane C. Silver. "Opposite Sides of the Same Coin: Former Spouses' Divergent Perspectives in Coping with Their Divorce." *Journal of Personality and Social Psychology* 59, no. 6 (1990): 1180–91.

Grove, J. R., S. J. Hanrahan, and A. McInman. "Success/Failure Bias in Attributions Across Involvement Categories in Sport." *Personality and Social Psychology Bulletin* 17, no. 1 (1991): 93–97.

Headey, Bruce, and Alex Wearing. "The Sense of Relative Superiority: Central to Well-being." *Social Indicators Research* 20, no. 5 (1988): 497–516.

Hoorens, Vera. "Self-enhancement and Superiority Biases in Social Comparison." *European Review of Social Psychology* 4, no. 1 (1993): 113–39.

Jalonick, Mary Clare. "Americans Are Still Getting Fatter: Obesity Rates Increased in 28 States, Report Finds." MSNBC, June 29, 2010. Web: July 2012, www.msnbc.msn.com/id/37996593/ns/health-diet_and_nutrition/t/americans-are-still-getting-fatter/#.UP7bkCfBdBE.

Johnson, Dominic. "Overconfidence in Tanks and Banks." Blog post, *Dominic DP Johnson,* Aug. 14, 2009. Web: July 2012, www.dominicdpjohnson.com/blog/?p=17.

Johnson, Dominic D. P., and James H. Fowler. "The Evolution of Overconfidence." *Nature* 477, no. 7364 (2011): 317–20.

Jones, Edward E., and Richard E. Nisbett. "The Actor and the Observer: Divergent Perceptions of the Causes of Behavior." In *Attribution: Perceiving the Causes of Behavior*. Ed. by Edward Ellsworth Jones. Morristown, NJ: General Learning, 1972, pp. 79–94.

Kruger, Justin, and Thomas Gilovich. "'Naive Cynicism' in

Everyday Theories of Responsibility Assessment: On Biased Assumptions of Bias." *Journal of Personality and Social Psychology* 76, no. 5 (1999): 743–53.

Langer, Ellen J. "The Illusion of Control." *Journal of Personality and Social Psychology* 32, no. 2 (1975): 311–28.

Lassiter, G. Daniel, and Patrick J. Munhall. "The Genius Effect: Evidence for a Nonmotivational Interpretation." *Journal of Experimental Social Psychology* 37, no. 4 (2001): 349–55.

Loughnan, Steve, Bernhard Leidner, Guy Doron, Nick Haslam, Yoshihisa Kashima, Jennifer Tong, and Victoria Yeung. "Universal Biases in Self-perception: Better and More Human Than Average." *British Journal of Social Psychology* 49, no. 3 (2010): 627–36.

McKenna, Frank P., and Lynn B. Myers. "Illusory Self-assessments: Can They Be Reduced?" *British Journal of Psychology* 88, no. 1 (1997): 39–51.

Major, Brenda, Cheryl R. Kaiser, and Shannon K. McCoy. "It's Not My Fault: When and Why Attributions to Prejudice Protect Self-esteem." *Personality and Social Psychology Bulletin* 29, no. 6 (2003): 772–81.

Markus, Hazel R., and Shinobu Kitayama. "Culture and the Self: Implications for Cognition, Emotion, and Motivation." *Psychological Review* 98, no. 2 (1991): 224–53.

Moore, Michael T., and David M. Fresco. "Depressive Realism: A Meta-analytic Review." *Clinical Psychology Review* 32, no. 6 (2012): 496–509.

Pronin, E., D. Y. Lin, and L. Ross. "The Bias Blind Spot: Perceptions of Bias in Self Versus Others." *Personality and Social Psychology Bulletin* 28, no. 3 (2002): 369–81.

Rabin, Roni Caryn. "Choosing Self-esteem over Sex or Pizza." *The New York Times, Well* (blog), Jan. 11, 2011. Web: July 2012, well.blogs.nytimes.com/2011/01/11/choosing-self-esteem-over-sex-or-pizza/.

Ross, Michael, and Fiore Sicoly. "Egocentric Biases in Availability and Attribution." *Journal of Personality and Social Psychology* 37, no. 3 (1979): 322–36.

Sharot, Tali. "The Optimism Bias." *TED Talks*. May 2012. Web: July 2012, www.ted.com/talks/tali_sharot_the_optimism_bias.html.

Shea, Christopher. "The Power of Positive Illusions." *The Boston Globe,* Boston.com, Sept. 26, 2004. Web: July 2012, www.boston.com/news/globe/ideas/articles/2004/09/26/the_power_of_positive_illusions/?page=full.

Taylor, Shelley E. *Positive Illusions: Creative Self-deception and the Healthy Mind*. New York: Basic, 1989.

Taylor, Shelley E., and Jonathon D. Brown. "Positive Illusions and Well-being Revisited: Separating Fact from Fiction." *Psychological Bulletin* 116, no.1 (1994): 21–27.

Twenge, Jean M. *Generation Me: Why Today's Young Americans Are More Confident, Assertive, Entitled—and More Miserable Than Ever Before*. New York: Free Press, 2006.

Twenge, Jean M., and W. Keith Campbell. *The Narcissism Epidemic: Living in the Age of Entitlement*. New York: Free Press, 2009.

Twenge, Jean M., Sara Konrath, Joshua D. Foster, W. Keith Campbell, and Brad J. Bushman. "Egos Inflating over Time: A Cross-temporal Meta-analysis of the Narcissistic Personality Inventory." *Journal of Personality* 76, no. 4 (2008): 875–901.